MW00608788

CONSIDERING THE CROSS

CONSIDERING THE CROSS

How Calvary Connects Us with Christ

JOHN HILTON III

DESERET
BOOK

SALT LAKE CITY, UTAH

Library of Congress Cataloging-in-Publication Data

Names: Hilton, John, III, author.
Title: Considering the cross : how Calvary connects us with Christ / John Hilton III.
Description: Salt Lake City, Utah : Deseret Book, [2021] | Includes bibliographical references
    and index. | Summary: "A detailed look at Christ's Crucifixion and how it intersects with His
    Atonement by best-selling Latter-day Saint author John Hilton III"—Provided by publisher.
Identifiers: LCCN 2020043858 | ISBN 9781629728711 (hardback)
Subjects: LCSH: Jesus Christ—Crucifixion. | Jesus Christ—Mormon interpretations. | Atonement—
    The Church of Jesus Christ of Latter-day Saints. | The Church of Jesus Christ of Latter-day
    Saints—Doctrines. | Mormon Church—Doctrines.
Classification: LCC BX8643.A85 H55 2021 | DDC 232.96/3—dc23
LC record available at https://lccn.loc.gov/2020043858

Printed in the United States of America
LSC Communications, North Chelmsford, MA

10 9 8 7 6 5 4 3

Contents

Acknowledgments

I am indebted to many people who assisted me in writing this book. Lani Hilton provided helpful insights and was my best sounding board. My parents, Lee and Shawna Hilton, also gave important suggestions. Lisa Roper's sincere interest in this manuscript and guidance in its development were extremely valuable. Many others at Deseret Book contributed to this project in significant ways, including Laurel Christensen Day, Kara Nordstrom, Kristen Evans, Dave Kimball, Shara Meredith, Alison Palmer, Shauna Gibby, and Breanna Anderl. I also express gratitude to members of the Deseret Book editorial review board; their feedback helped shape this book.

Conversations with Matthew Grey prompted my studies on this topic, and many other colleagues shared their expertise by reading chapters and offering valuable insights. These include Daniel Becerra, Christopher Blythe, Carter Charles, Jason Combs, Rachel Cope, Amy Easton-Flake, Mark Ellison, Nick Frederick, Alonzo Gaskill, Fiona Givens, Carl Griffin, Casey Griffiths, Jared Jepson, Frank Judd, Henry Kosak, Shad Martin, Josh Matson, Robert Millet, Kerry Muhlestein, George Pierce, Noel Reynolds, Joshua Sears, Avram Shannon, Joseph Spencer, Katie Steed, Gaye Strathearn, Anthony Sweat, Christopher Thomas, Richard Turley, and Jordan Watkins. I'm also grateful to Felicity Harley-McGowan and David Chapman, both world-renowned experts in crucifixion research, for reading and commenting on specific sections of this book.

Several research assistants, including Joshua Barringer, Sarah Cox, Megan Cutler, Emily Hyde, Colby Sinclair, Joshua Stratford, and McKenna Trussel made important contributions to this work. Their efforts were made possible by funding from BYU's Department of Ancient Scripture, Religious Education, and Religious Studies Center. Monte Shelley, Scott Esplin, Steven Harper, Beverly Yellowhorse, the Faculty Support Center staff at BYU Religious Education, and the editors, staff, and reviewers at both *The Religious Educator* and *BYU Studies Quarterly* also provided valuable assistance.

Special gratitude is due to Brad Wilcox and Michelle Wilson, each of whom read drafts of the entire book and offered many valuable suggestions. I also appreciate the following individuals, who offered feedback on one or more chapters: Jackson Abhau, Ryan Baker, Rafael Bello, T.J. Bliss, Amanda Buessecker, Ann Chumbley-Snider, Maddison Dillon, Robert Eaton, Katie Gibson, Gifford Gillette, Catherine Fratianni Guevara, Annemarie Hilton, A.J. Hortin, Michael House, Marlow Hunter, Roberta Johnson, Dave LeFevre, David Macfarlane, Cameron McEwen, Michael McKinley, Abby Mitton, Whitney Permann, Eric Perry, Scott Rasmussen, Angelica Rauenzahn, Mike Ricks, Lisa Spice, Cameron Taylor, Dallas Teshima, Lisa Texeira, Rebecca Thompson, Dennis Walker, Michelle Westcott, and Tim Wilson.

I acknowledge the power of the Holy Spirit, which has consistently prompted me to study the Crucifixion of Jesus Christ and blessed me with flashes of insight I would have otherwise never received. Ultimately, I give thanks to Heavenly Father and Jesus Christ; I hope this book in some small way glorifies them and their sacred work.

WHY LEARN MORE ABOUT THE SAVIOR'S CRUCIFIXION?

You might be wondering why you should read a book that is primarily about the Crucifixion of Jesus Christ. After all, as Latter-day Saints, we focus on the *living* Christ! Among members of the restored Church, Calvary doesn't have the reputation for being the glorious or feel-good part of the Savior's Atonement. You might be worried this book will be depressing. I promise you, it's not.

This book is about finding increased peace and happiness by coming closer to Jesus Christ. President Russell M. Nelson has promised, "The more we know about the Savior's ministry and mission—the more we understand His doctrine and what He did for us—the more we know that He can provide the power that we need for our lives."[1] This book is meant to help us deepen our understanding of what Jesus did for us and therefore more fully feel of his love and strength.

I love these words from Elder Ronald A. Rasband: "Jesus Christ is always the answer."[2] Because "our focus must be riveted on the Savior," we should seek to study all we can about him.[3] President James E. Faust taught, "Any increase in our understanding of [Christ's] atoning

---

1. Russell M. Nelson, "Drawing the Power of Jesus Christ into Our Lives," *Ensign*, May 2017.
2. Ronald A. Rasband, "Jesus Christ Is the Answer," Evening with a General Authority, Salt Lake City, February 8, 2019.
3. Nelson, "Drawing the Power of Jesus Christ into Our Lives."

sacrifice draws us closer to Him."[4] Better understanding *any* aspect of Christ's Atonement—including his Crucifixion—can deepen our relationship with the Savior.[5] And the stronger our relationship with the Savior, the more we can feel his mercy and grace. As President Nelson taught, "When the focus of our lives is on . . . Jesus Christ and His gospel, we can feel joy regardless of what is happening—or not happening—in our lives. . . . For Latter-day Saints, Jesus Christ is joy!"[6] My hope is that these pages will help you deepen your connection with Christ and therefore your joy.

This book is divided into four parts. In the first, we will discuss the symbol of the cross and then see how the Savior's Crucifixion can help us feel more of his love. In the second part, we will explore what scriptures and Church leaders have taught about Christ's sacrifice on Calvary. Next, we'll take an intimate look at the Savior's final day in mortality, including his six hours on the cross. Finally, we will learn how appreciating the Crucifixion can enhance the personal connection we feel with Christ and his Atonement. On our journey together, we will answer many important questions including the following:

- Is the tendency many Church members have of avoiding the cross based on an official Church doctrine, or is it more of a cultural practice? (Chapter 1)
- How can studying Christ's Crucifixion increase our appreciation for his Atonement? (Chapter 2)
- What can we learn from the "nail . . . in the sure place" (Isa. 22:25) and other Old Testament scriptures that foreshadow Christ's atoning sacrifice? (Chapter 3)

---

4. James E. Faust, "The Atonement: Our Greatest Hope," *Ensign*, November 2001.
5. A careful study of the Savior's Atonement is vital; as Elder Joseph B. Wirthlin explained, "No other doctrine will bring greater results in improving behavior and strengthening character than the doctrine of the Atonement of Jesus Christ." "You'll Grow into It," *New Era*, November 2000, 40.
6. Russell M. Nelson, "Joy and Spiritual Survival," *Ensign*, November 2016.

- What life-changing lessons does the New Testament teach about Christ's triumph on the cross? (Chapter 4)
- How can the Savior's experience on Calvary help us when we suffer? (Chapter 5)
- How do the teachings of modern Church leaders enhance our understanding of the personal nature of Christ's Crucifixion? (Chapter 6)
- What do history and archeology teach us about Roman crucifixion? (Chapter 7)
- What insights can we learn from minor characters involved in Christ's trial, such as Barabbas? (Chapter 8)
- What lessons can we learn from the crown of thorns, an inscription written in three languages, and Christ's walk to Golgotha? (Chapter 9)
- How do the Savior's final words on the cross testify of a human Savior who experiences our emotions, a healing Savior who forgives, and a divine Savior who saves? (Chapter 10)
- How can Mary Magdalene and the other female witnesses at the empty tomb increase our hope in Jesus Christ? (Chapter 11)
- What relationships exist between temple ordinances and Christ's Crucifixion? (Chapter 12)
- How can we continue to expand our knowledge of and gratitude for Christ's Atonement? (Chapter 13)

In the Doctrine and Covenants, the Lord lists several spiritual gifts. The *very first gift listed* is to know through the Holy Ghost "that Jesus Christ is the Son of God, and that *he was crucified for the sins of the world*" (D&C 46:13).[7] This testimony is a spiritual gift that each of us can receive and continually develop at increasingly deeper levels.

I know that through the Savior's perfect Atonement, including his sufferings in Gethsemane, his death on the cross, and his glorious

---

7. Throughout this book, when words in scripture or quotations are italicized, the italics represent my own emphasis, unless otherwise specified in a footnote.

Resurrection, each of us can be strengthened in our struggles. We can be forgiven of sins, find comfort amid catastrophe, and return to live in God's presence with perfect, immortal bodies.

My heart is filled with gratitude for the Savior. I know he is "Christ crucified," "the Lamb slain from the foundation of the world" (1 Cor. 1:23; Rev. 13:8). He is the one who "liveth, and was dead; and . . . [is] alive for evermore" (Rev. 1:18). He is "our peace," "our Passover," "our life," and "our Lord Jesus Christ" (Eph. 2:14; 1 Cor. 5:7; Col. 3:3; Philip. 4:23). My personal journey to better understand the "redemption . . . wrought through the sacrifice of the Son of God upon the cross" has connected me more closely with him (D&C 138:35). I believe the same thing will happen for you.

PART I

I Feel My Savior's Love

Chapter 1

THE MEANINGS
OF THE CROSS

Jesus Christ was, in his own words, "crucified for the sins of the world" (D&C 35:2). We believe that as part of Christ's Atonement, he died for us; President Gordon B. Hinckley taught, "Jesus . . . gave His life on Calvary's cross in His wondrous Atonement because He loved us."[1] This is a doctrinal reality that will not change. But how we communicate, teach, or visualize the importance of the Savior's Crucifixion has varied over time. For example, consider the cross. In the first three centuries after the Savior's birth, it was rarely used to symbolize Jesus Christ. Yet today the cross is one of the most influential and frequently displayed symbols in the world; for many Christians, it represents the Savior's atoning mission.

Traditionally, members of The Church of Jesus Christ of Latter-day Saints (herein referred to as "the Church") have, relative to other Christians, de-emphasized symbols relating to the cross and Crucifixion. For example, Latter-day Saint church buildings do not display crosses, and a sampling of over 150 Latter-day Saint chapels found that while all of them have pictures of Jesus Christ, fewer than 3 percent display a picture of the Crucifixion. In one survey, more than one thousand Latter-day Saint adults were shown three images of the

---

1. Gordon B. Hinckley, "Testimony," *Ensign*, May 1998.

Crucifixion and three images of Gethsemane and asked which one they would choose to display in their home. Ninety-seven percent chose to display a picture of Gethsemane. When asked why they chose the painting they did, nearly half specifically mentioned an aversion to images of Christ's Crucifixion.[2]

While the saving significance of Christ's Crucifixion is a separate issue from the meaning of the cross as a symbol, because of the ubiquity of the cross in Christianity and its relative absence among Latter-day Saints, it may be helpful to begin a discussion of the Savior's sacrifice on Calvary by talking about the image of the cross.

In contrast to the unchanging doctrinal importance of Christ's Crucifixion, how Christians generally, and Latter-day Saints specifically, have viewed the image of the cross has varied over time. In other words, the meaning of the visual symbol of the cross is more cultural than doctrinal. Historically, some have viewed the cross as a symbol of death to be avoided. Others have seen it as a representation of Christ's triumph over death, a symbol of love, or an image of suffering that comforts us in pain.

Let's explore some of the various interpretations of the cross as a visual image over the centuries, beginning with the time of the early Apostles through the Emperor Constantine (~AD 35–335). Next, we will discover what happened with the cross from the time of Constantine through the Middle Ages (~335–1500) and during the Catholic-Protestant clashes over its use (~1500–1800). Then we will discuss the image of the cross in the restored Church, beginning with Joseph Smith (1820) through the 1940s, and finally from the 1950s to the present day.[3]

---

2. See John Hilton III, Anthony Sweat, Joshua Stratford, "Latter-day Saints and Crucifixion Artwork," *BYU Studies Quarterly*, forthcoming, available at http://johnhiltoniii .com/crucifixion.

3. Multiple books have been written on these topics. The three books that most heavily shaped this chapter are Robin Margaret Jensen, *The Cross: History, Art, and Controversy* (Cambridge, MA: Harvard University Press, 2017); Michael G. Reed, *Banishing the Cross: The Emergence of a Mormon Taboo* (Independence, MO: John Whitmer Books, 2012); and Ryan K. Smith, *Gothic Arches, Latin Crosses: Anti-Catholicism and American*

EARLY CHRISTIANITY, ~AD 35–335

In the first three centuries following Christ's Resurrection, the cross was rarely used as a symbol for Christianity.[4] Only two images of Christ's Crucifixion created prior to the fourth century still exist today.[5] One of these, the Palatine graffito, contains an image of a young man looking up toward a crucified figure with the head of a donkey, thought to represent Christ.[6] The accompanying inscription reads, "Alexamenos worships [his] God."[7]

This image appears to have been etched in order to ridicule Christian religious beliefs by mocking those who worshipped a god who was crucified.[8] The Roman gods were powerful—why would somebody worship a god who died a shameful death? The Palatine graffito suggests that though it was mocked, people understood the importance of the Crucifixion to Christians.

A major shift in how Christians used the image of the cross occurred during the time of Emperor Constantine. The fourth-century author Eusebius wrote that shortly before a key battle to conquer Rome

---

Church Designs in the Nineteenth Century (Chapel Hill: University of North Carolina Press, 2006). Given space constraints, I gloss over many important details, so I encourage readers to explore these three books in depth. These books also helped me identify additional relevant sources, some of which are cited in this chapter.

4. For a more in-depth discussion on the image of the cross prior to Constantine, see Bruce W. Longnecker, *The Cross before Constantine* (Minneapolis: Fortress Press, 2015), 106–10.

5. Felicity Harley-McGowan, "The Passion," in *Routledge Handbook of Early Christian Art*, ed. Robin M. Jensen and Mark D. Ellison (London: Routledge, 2018), 290–93.

6. Confusion over early Christian practices led some nonbelievers to think that Christians worshipped "the head of an ass," which may be why Christ is depicted on the cross with a head shaped like a donkey's. Tertullian, *The Apology of Tertullian*, trans. T. Herbert Bindley (Oxford: Clarendon Press, 1889), 58; see also *The Octavius of Marcus Minucius Felix*, trans. Rev. Robert Ernest Wallis, *The Ante-Nicene Fathers*, vol. 4 (Grand Rapids, MI: Wm. B. Eerdmans, n.d.), 173–98, https://www.ccel.org/fathers2.

7. Alternate translations sometimes render the text as "Alexamenos worships god" or, in the imperative form, "Alexamenos—worship god!" See Ben Witherington III, "Biblical Views: Images of Crucifixion: Fresh Evidence," *Biblical Archaeology Review* 39, no. 2 (March/April 2013): 28.

8. Witherington, "Biblical Views," 28.

(in approximately AD 312), Constantine was praying earnestly in the middle of the day: "While he was thus praying with fervent entreaty, a most marvelous sign appeared to him from heaven. . . . He saw with his own eyes the trophy of a cross of light in the heavens, above the sun, and bearing the inscription, CONQUER BY THIS."[9]

Later that night, while Constantine was pondering the meaning of this vision, Christ appeared to him "with the same sign which he had seen in the heavens, and commanded him to make a likeness of that sign which he had seen in the heavens, and to use it as a safeguard in all engagements with his enemies."[10]

Constantine made a kind of cross using the superimposed Greek letters *chi* (X) and *rho* (P), the first two letters in the Greek *Christos* ("Christ"), forming the Christogram (☧). He "commanded that others similar to it should be carried at the head of all his armies."[11] He approached Rome, "invoking His Christ to be his preserver and aid, and setting the victorious trophy, the salutary symbol [the Christogram], in front of his soldiers."[12] Constantine defeated his enemy and eventually became known as the first Christian Emperor. His use of this crosslike symbol significantly influenced the future of the image of the cross.

FROM CONSTANTINE TO THE REFORMATION, ~AD 335–1500

In the decades and centuries that followed, Christians began to display the cross in various forms and used the symbol on their monuments.

---

9. Eusebius Pamphilus of Caesarea, *The Life of the Blessed Emperor Constantine*, Bagster translation, rev. Ernest Cushing Richardson, Nicene and Post-Nicene Fathers, 2nd series, vol. 1, ed. P. Schaff and H. Wace (Grand Rapids, MI: Wm. B. Eerdmans, 1955), https://sourcebooks.fordham.edu/basis/vita-constantine.asp, capitalization in original. Early versions of Constantine's vision of a cross have significant differences; for simplicity, I only present one account. Regardless of the differences in the accounts, from the time of Constantine, the cross became a much more prominent Christian symbol. See Jensen, *Cross*, 49–56.
10. Eusebius, *Life of the Blessed Emperor Constantine*.
11. Eusebius, *Life of the Blessed Emperor Constantine*.
12. Eusebius, *Life of the Blessed Emperor Constantine*.

At first, these images were almost always of the Christogram (☧), and later they were of an empty cross. Actual depictions of Christ being crucified continued to be rare in the decades following Constantine.[13] As the centuries passed, however, crucifixes—which are crosses with a depiction of the crucified Jesus attached to them—became increasingly common. Political and religious leaders debated the virtue of crucifixes, with some arguing that a plain cross was "an adequate memorial of the crucifixion" since the cross "was the instrument of salvation and the long-established and venerable emblem of Christ."[14] Others thought a cross alone was an insufficient symbol, believing that the crucifix "presented corporeal reality, showing both Christ's likeness and human suffering."[15]

An early-ninth-century episode illustrates these differing perspectives. A man named Claudius of Turin (AD 780–827) was appointed the Catholic bishop of a city in Italy. Scholar Robin Margaret Jensen recounts:

> Soon after he arrived, Claudius noticed that members of his flock were offering some sort of veneration to images displayed in the church. Outraged at what he perceived to be idolatry, Claudius began to remove and destroy the artworks. When King Louis heard about Claudius's campaign, he sent two of his court theologians, Jonas . . . and the monk Dungalus . . . to investigate. The image that caused the most serious contention was the crucifix. Claudius argued that while showing reverence to a crucifix was intended to honor and venerate the Savior, it was actually a false and superstitious act: referring only to Jesus's degradation and death, it denied his resurrection and ascension. Essentially, because Christ no longer suffers in the flesh, venerating such an image was tantamount to recrucifying him. He apparently also

---

13. See Jensen, *Cross*, 68–76.
14. Jensen, *Cross*, 93.
15. Jensen, *Cross*, 94.

included plain crosses in his invective, as he added that adoration of ordinary wood fashioned into a cross would be like adoring any other object associated with Jesus's earthly life: a manger, a boat, or a donkey.

Both Jonas and Dungalus refuted Claudius's position, pointing out that the cross, a memorial of Christ's Passion, had been found worthy of honor from antiquity. Furthermore, they argued that rather than symbolizing death, the cross signified Jesus's triumph over death. Moreover, the wood was not venerated per se but only because it was the locus of Christ's crucifixion. Dungalus went on to recount the Old Testament passages that prefigure the cross, as well as the places in the New Testament epistles that affirm the significance of the cross apart from the resurrection.[16]

This incident, representative of many others, shows that much like today, devoted followers of Christ saw diverse meanings in the visual symbol of the cross. To some people, the cross was a symbol of Christ's victory. For example, a crucifix from a medieval church in Spain shows a muscular Jesus wearing a royal crown on the cross, indicating his ultimate triumph.

By the eleventh century, depictions of Christ on the cross were often more graphic in their portrayal of Christ's anguish.[17] With increasing frequency, Christian theologians emphasized the importance of Christ's suffering on the cross and encouraged faithful followers of Jesus to deeply reflect on Christ's wounds. In the years leading up to the Reformation, it became common for Christians to consider "Jesus's suffering, vividly imagining it, feeling sorrow and pity, and even physically experiencing pain."[18] As Jensen describes, "Artists increasingly depicted Christ's bodily torments, the cruel mockery of his persecutors,

---

16. Jensen, *Cross*, 154–55.
17. See Jensen, *Cross*, 151.
18. Jensen, *Cross*, 165.

the crown of thorns, the wounds on his body, and other evidence of his physical and mental anguish as he hung upon the cross."[19]

One famous example of this type of artwork is the Isenheim Altarpiece, created in the early sixteenth century. It was located in a monastery that functioned as a hospital for people suffering from serious skin disease. The Savior on the cross was portrayed as having sores like those of the patients, thus powerfully representing a God who understands the pains of his people. For patients in this hospital, this image was a message of hope and strength from a Jesus who empathized with their desperate situation.[20]

CATHOLIC-PROTESTANT CLASHES, ~AD 1500–1800

During the Reformation of the sixteenth century, Catholics and Protestants became sharply divided over the meaning and significance of visual representations of the cross and Christ's Crucifixion. Some reformers, such as Martin Luther, believed the image of the cross was appropriate in Christian worship. "When I hear the word Christ, there delineates itself in my heart the picture of a man who hangs on the cross," wrote Luther. "If it is not a sin, but a good thing, that I have Christ's image in my heart, why then should it be sinful to have it before my eyes?"[21]

Luther's associate, Andreas Karlstadt, disagreed, arguing "that the crucifix depicted only Christ's human suffering and neglected to display his resurrection and redemptive power." According to Jensen,

---

19. Jensen, *Cross*, 165.
20. Latter-day Saint scholar Jennifer Lane wrote, "Working on my dissertation, . . . I looked at hundreds of images of Christ bleeding profusely. The wounds in his side, hands, and feet were all a source of great attention and love. . . . There may have been a time when this devotional art was startling to me, but through my study, I could see the love that people felt for Christ reflected in these images." Jennifer C. Lane, *Finding Christ in the Covenant Path: Ancient Insights for Modern Life* (Provo, UT: Religious Studies Center, Brigham Young University, 2020), 87.
21. Joseph Leo Koerner, *The Reformation of the Image* (Chicago: University of Chicago Press, 2004), 160.

Karlstadt "urged his followers to abandon their superstitious attachment to crucifixes, even in their sickrooms and deathbeds. He asserted that nothing could be learned and no benefits gained from gazing at a crucifix, which focused only on Christ's suffering in the body."[22]

In many instances, Protestants destroyed images of the cross, believing they were smashing idols, whereas Catholics saw this destruction as a violation of their sacred images. Consider one of many conflicts that occurred: "Klaus Hottinger, having obtained a wooden wayside crucifix from its owner, broke it into pieces, which he gave to the poor as firewood. . . . First exiled, then tried for blasphemy in the Catholic city of Lucerne, Hottinger refused to honour a crucifix brought before him. He confessed that 'the passion of Christ must be received in true faith in the heart. . . .' Burnt at the stake, . . . Hottinger became [an early] Protestant martyr."[23]

Although some Protestants, such as Lutherans, retained an empty cross as a key symbol of their faith, others, such as Puritan Robert Parker, completely eschewed the image of the cross. Parker wrote of "the idolatrie of the Crosse," "the Superstition of the Crosse," "the Hipocrisie of the Crosse," and "the impietie of the Crosse."[24] Puritans did not use the symbol of the cross, and by the late 1600s, the Anglican Church, the dominant church in England, "had essentially abandoned the Latin cross and the crucifix as church fixtures."[25]

Many Pilgrims brought this perspective with them to North America, creating an environment in which the cross was largely unused as a Christian symbol. Most Christian denominations in

---

22. Jensen, *Cross*, 185.
23. Koerner, *Reformation of the Image*, 129, 131.
24. Robert Parker, *A Scholasticall Discourse against Symbolizing with Antichrist in Ceremonies: Especially in the Signe of the Crosse* (Middelburg: printed by Richard Schilders, 1607), 3, 58, 134, 166; see also Terryl Givens, *People of Paradox: A History of Mormon Culture* (New York: Oxford University Press, 2007), 114; and Margaret Aston, *Broken Idols of the English Reformation* (Cambridge: Cambridge University Press, 2016), 707–882.
25. Smith, *Gothic Arches, Latin Crosses*, 58.

early-nineteenth-century America, including Episcopalians, Methodists, Presbyterians, and Baptists, treated the cross "as a foreign symbol."[26] Thus the vast majority of church buildings in the newly formed United States did not display crosses, with the Catholic Church being a notable exception.[27] In early- to mid-nineteenth-century America, some Protestants tore down crosses from Catholic buildings and rejected efforts to place crosses in Protestant houses of worship.[28]

THE RESTORED CHURCH, 1820s–1940s

In 1820, only 124 Catholic church buildings existed in the United States, with just five in the entire state of New York.[29] In contrast, during that same year there were about 5,400 Methodist and Baptist meetinghouses in the United States, to say nothing of church buildings from other Protestant denominations.[30] Thus it seems relatively little Catholic influence existed in the area where Joseph Smith grew up. When Joseph envisioned church buildings, he would have likely pictured Protestant ones without crosses.

Because the cross is so ubiquitous in Christianity today, this idea bears repeating: In America, during the 1820s, the Baptists, Methodists, Presbyterians, and many other Protestant churches *did not* typically display the image of the cross on or in their buildings. That was a Catholic practice, and at that time Catholics comprised a very small minority of Christians in America. Historian Richard Bushman has pointed out that Joseph Smith did not consciously reject the symbol of the cross since such a choice would have "required no decision on Joseph's part. No one around him used the cross."[31]

---

26. Smith, *Gothic Arches, Latin Crosses*, 58.
27. Smith, *Gothic Arches, Latin Crosses*, 52–53.
28. Smith, *Gothic Arches, Latin Crosses*, 1–2.
29. Smith, *Gothic Arches, Latin Crosses*, 19.
30. Smith, *Gothic Arches, Latin Crosses*, 19.
31. Richard Bushman, email to Seth Payne, November 17, 2006, cited in Reed, *Banishing the Cross*, 2.

Some early Church leaders metaphorically spoke of the cross as a symbol of Jesus Christ. For example, Elders Heber C. Kimball and Orson Hyde, reporting on their mission to England, wrote to Joseph Smith, "We have fought in the name of the Lord Jesus, and under the shadow of the cross we have conquered."[32] On another occasion, Orson Hyde described his plea to the Lord: "Let the enemies of the cross be confounded and put to shame before the sublimity and power of [my] arguments. Let [me] raise the standard of the cross in every land and nation where [I] shall go; and let the simple and broken hearted flock unto it and rejoice beneath its heavenly banner."[33] In 1835, when Sidney Rigdon and Oliver Cowdery ordained an individual to the Seventy, they promised him that he would be "a swift herald of the cross."[34]

Notwithstanding this positive rhetoric regarding a figurative cross, some viewed the physical symbol with suspicion. Although Joseph Smith spoke favorably about the Catholic Church in his last recorded sermon,[35] typical Protestant discourse at the time referred to Catholicism as the "Whore of Babylon" or the "Mother of harlots." It is therefore not surprising that early Latter-day Saints, many of whom converted from Protestant churches, brought this bias with them.[36] Since the physical symbol of the cross was largely associated with the

---

32. "Letter from Heber C. Kimball and Orson Hyde, between 22 and 28 May 1838," 48, The Joseph Smith Papers, accessed July 15, 2020, https://www.josephsmithpapers .org/paper-summary/letter-from-heber-c-kimball-and-orson-hyde-between-22-and -28-may-1838/1.

33. "Elders' Journal, November 1837," 21, The Joseph Smith Papers, accessed August 25, 2020, https://www.josephsmithpapers.org/paper-summary/elders-journal-november -1837/5.

34. "Minutes, 17 August 1835," 100, The Joseph Smith Papers, accessed August 25, 2020, https://www.josephsmithpapers.org/paper-summary/minutes-17-august-1835/3.

35. Joseph Smith said that the "old Catholic Church is worth more than all," with "all" apparently referring to Protestant churches. "Discourse, 16 June 1844–A, as Reported by Thomas Bullock," [5], The Joseph Smith Papers, accessed October 25, 2019, https:// www.josephsmithpapers.org/paper-summary/discourse-16-june-1844-a-as-reported-by -thomas-bullock/5.

36. See Matthew J. Grow, "The Whore of Babylon and the Abomination of Abominations: Nineteenth-Century Catholic and Mormon Mutual Perceptions and Religious Identity," Church History 73, no. 1 (2004): 139–67.

Catholic Church, the anti-Catholic sentiment of many early Latter-day Saints led some to perceive the cross negatively.[37]

During the period when the Church was relocating to Utah, the Catholic Church grew more prominent in the United States. Between 1820 and 1860, the number of Catholic churches in the United States jumped from 124 to 2,550 as hundreds of thousands of Catholic immigrants arrived in America.[38] As the number of Catholics dramatically increased, American Protestants began to accept the cross as a Christian symbol. Between 1840 and 1870, Methodists, Episcopalians, Baptists, and Presbyterians—all of whom had fought against using crosses in church architecture in the early nineteenth century—began to welcome the image, and their members found spiritual significance in the symbol.

One individual, writing in 1877, stated that the cross was a common Christian symbol: "The use of the cross, on spires, in churches, and worn as a jewel . . . is not now [that is, "is no longer"] denominational."[39] Indeed, a book on architecture, published in the 1870s, referred to the cross as "the usual symbol of the Christian religion."[40] Significantly, the symbol of the cross helped unify different denominations and allowed them to "identify their particular faith with a broader Christian religion."[41] At the same time, the importance of Christ's Crucifixion was elevated within congregations.

As Christians throughout America embraced the cross as a symbol of Christianity, the restored Church was largely isolated in the Intermountain West and did not participate in this near-universal adoption of the cross. However, the image of the cross was not forbidden among early Latter-day Saints. Although not as common as in other Christian traditions, Latter-day Saint marriage certificates, quilts,

---

37. Reed, *Banishing the Cross*, 90.
38. Smith, *Gothic Arches, Latin Crosses*, 20.
39. Smith, *Gothic Arches, Latin Crosses*, 77.
40. Smith, *Gothic Arches, Latin Crosses*, 77.
41. Smith, *Gothic Arches, Latin Crosses*, 79.

and funeral programs sometimes featured crosses, as did the 1852 European edition of the Doctrine and Covenants.[42]

Crosses were displayed at the funerals of prominent Church members such as Eliza R. Snow (Relief Society General President, died 1887), John Taylor (Church President, died 1887), and Daniel H. Wells (counselor in the First Presidency, died 1891).[43] Although atypical, crosses appeared on some Latter-day Saint church buildings in Salt Lake City and Ogden.[44]

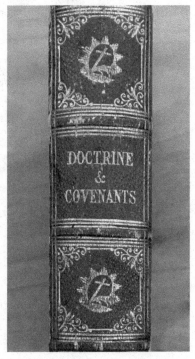

1852 European edition of the Doctrine and Covenants

Photographs indicate that Latter-day Saint men and women of prominence wore cross jewelry. Multiple relatives of Brigham Young and other Church leaders had portrait photographs taken of them wearing cross jewelry, as illustrated in the photos of Amelia Folsom Young, wife of Brigham Young, and Nabby Young Clawson, daughter of Brigham Young.[45]

Males, including Benjamin F. Johnson, a former secretary to Joseph Smith and member of the Council of Fifty, also wore crosses on watch chains or ties.[46] The fact that they and many others wore such accessories when posing for formal photographs indicates that cross jewelry was fairly common. At that time there was nothing particularly unusual and certainly nothing untoward about wearing a cross.

One of the best indicators of the Church's openness to the

---

42. Reed, *Banishing the Cross*, 70, 76–78.
43. Reed, *Banishing the Cross*, 76–78.
44. Reed, *Banishing the Cross*, 73–74.
45. These images, along with several others, are found in Reed, *Banishing the Cross*.
46. Reed, *Banishing the Cross*, 80–83.

Amelia Folsom Young, wife of   *Nabby Young Clawson, daughter of*
Brigham Young, wearing cross jewelry   *Brigham Young, wearing cross earrings*

image of the cross in the early twentieth century is the proposal to build a monument featuring a cross on Ensign Peak in Salt Lake City. In 1916, Charles W. Nibley, then the Presiding Bishop of the Church, wrote a letter to the Salt Lake City Council requesting that the Church have "the privilege of erecting on Ensign peak a suitable cross, the symbol of Christianity, as a memorial to the 'Mormon' pioneers who first established here that which the cross implies."[47] Nibley had discussed the proposal with President Joseph F. Smith and one of his counselors in the First Presidency, both of whom concurred that putting a cross on Ensign Peak was a good idea. An article published in the *Deseret Evening News* stated, "The monument is intended as an insignia of Christian belief on the part of the Church which has been accused of not believing in Christianity."[48]

However, some people in the Salt Lake Valley opposed placing the

---

47. Reed, *Banishing the Cross*, 87.
48. *Deseret Evening News,* May 5, 1916, 2, cited in Ronald W. Walker, "A Gauge of the Times: Ensign Peak in the Twentieth Century," *Utah Historical Quarterly* 62, no. 1 (1994): 14.

cross as a monument. Local rabbis argued that a cross would be an inappropriate representation of the multiple faiths in Utah, and some Church members claimed it was a Catholic symbol.[49] Although the proposal to erect a cross on Ensign Peak was eventually shelved, the fact that it was approved by the President of the Church clearly indicates that during this time the cross was not universally viewed as an inappropriate symbol for Church members. Moreover, shortly after the controversy over the Ensign Peak monument, some Latter-day Saint Boy Scouts, accompanied by General Authorities (including future Church President George Albert Smith), erected a cross as a monument in Emigration Canyon.[50]

Another indication the cross was not taboo among Latter-day Saints is the headstone of Elder B. H. Roberts of the Seventy (who died in 1933), which was inscribed with a large cross.[51]

In addition, during the 1940s, a large stone cross was erected in Provo, Utah, near Y Mountain. Several stakes, together with Brigham Young University, spon-

Gravestone of B. H. Roberts

sored interdenominational Easter services held at the cross.[52] In this same decade, Spencer W. Kimball shared experiences indicating he perceived the cross as a positive religious symbol. When called to the Quorum of the Twelve in 1943, Elder Kimball felt uneasy about receiving such an important responsibility. One evening, he went on a private walk, wrestling with the Lord in prayer, asking for a confirmation that he was acceptable to the Lord. He wrote, "As I rounded a

49. Reed, *Banishing the Cross*, 88–92.
50. Reed, *Banishing the Cross*, 99–101.
51. Reed, *Banishing the Cross*, 110–11.
52. D. Robert Carter, "Worshiping at the Easter Cross," *Daily Herald* (Provo, UT), March 27, 2005.

promontory I saw immediately above me the peak of the mountain and on the peak a huge cross with its arms silhouetted against the blue sky beyond. It was just an ordinary cross made of two large heavy limbs of a tree, but in my frame of mind, and coming on it so unexpectedly, it seemed a sacred omen."[53]

In 1945, Elder Kimball returned to the location at the top of the hill where he had seen the cross, and he noticed that it was broken. He said, "I found a cross beam and carried it up the hill (remembering the Savior as he carried his cross up Calvary) and fixed it the best I could."[54] For this new apostle, the cross was apparently a symbol of divine communication, a "sacred omen," not something to be shunned or regarded with distaste.

THE RESTORED CHURCH, 1950s–PRESENT

A key change in how Church members viewed the cross occurred during the administration of President David O. McKay. So far as can be ascertained, President McKay never publicly spoke against the symbol of the cross; however, he recorded the following in his journal in 1957:

> [Presiding] Bishop Joseph L. Wirthlin called me by telephone and asked me the Church's position on the following question: He stated that he had been asked today if it would be proper for L.D.S. girls to purchase crosses to wear. It is Bishop Wirthlin's understanding that there is a company downtown which is pushing the selling of these crosses to girls. I told Bishop Wirthlin that this is purely Catholic and Latter-day Saint girls should not purchase and wear them. I stated further that this was a Catholic form of worship. They use images, crosses, etc. Our worship should be in our hearts.[55]

---

53. Edward L. Kimball and Andrew E. Kimball, *Spencer W. Kimball: Twelfth President of the Church of Jesus Christ of Latter-day Saints* (Salt Lake City: Bookcraft, 1977), 194, cited in Reed, *Banishing the Cross,* 112.
54. In Reed, *Banishing the Cross,* 112.
55. David O. McKay, diary, April 29, 1957, cited in Reed, *Banishing the Cross,* 115–16.

Given that the cross was by this time a generally accepted symbol of Christianity, it is not clear what shaped President McKay's view that wearing a cross "was a *Catholic* form of worship." It does appear that President McKay had a negative perception of the Catholic Church (which softened over time);[56] this perspective may have led to his negative view of the cross.

While the impact of President McKay's private journal entry and conversation with Bishop Wirthlin regarding the wearing of crosses is unclear, additional factors seem to have created a growing cultural aversion to the cross in the following decades. In some instances, the Church subtly de-emphasized the cross in its curriculum materials,[57] perhaps as a result of a few General Authorities who made negative statements about the image of the cross.[58]

---

56. During the late 1940s and early 1950s, the relationship between the restored Church and the Catholic Church in Utah was strained. In later years, President McKay developed a close relationship with the leader of the Catholic Church in Utah. Interestingly, the same year President McKay made his negative statement about Latter-day Saint girls wearing crosses, he was given a charm that combined a cross and the Star of David, meant to symbolize unity in world religions. President McKay noted in his journal that he added a pin to the charm so that he could wear it on his lapel as desired. See Gregory A. Prince and Wm. Robert Wright, *David O. McKay and the Rise of Modern Mormonism* (Salt Lake City: University of Utah, 2005), 113–23.

57. For example, a 1960 painting by Keith Eddington included crosses on the horizon and was published on the cover of a Church magazine; a version of this painting was created in 1994 for a theater in the Joseph Smith Memorial Building and did not include the crosses. The 1973 handbook for missionaries includes a quote from Brigham Young that emphasizes having "your minds riveted on the cross of Christ." *Preach My Gospel* (first published by the Church in 2004) includes the quote from Brigham Young but eliminates its reference to the cross. See Noel A. Carmack, "Images of Christ in Latter-day Saint Visual Culture, 1900–1999," *BYU Studies Quarterly* 39, no. 3 (2000): 18–76; and Reed, *Banishing the Cross*, 5.

58. In addition to the examples cited in the body of the text, in a 1980 devotional at Brigham Young University, Elder Mark E. Petersen taught, "The world at large has the idea that the symbol of Christianity is the cross, but it's no such thing. . . . Christ did not give us the cross as the symbol of his great Atonement." Some Church leaders made statements regarding *worshipping* the cross (as opposed to merely displaying or wearing it). For example, Joseph Fielding Smith stated that to him, "the adoration of the cross . . . is repugnant and contrary to the true worship of our Redeemer," and President J. Reuben Clark wrote, "There is no scripture justifying the worship of the cross." Mark E. Petersen, "The Covenant People of God" (devotional, Brigham Young

When searching general conference talks and additional published writings of General Authorities,[59] I have located only three statements that speak negatively about individuals wearing or displaying crosses. In 1961, employing the same logic as Protestants from an earlier century, President Joseph Fielding Smith wrote, "If our Lord had been killed with a dagger or with a sword, it would have been very strange if religious people this day would have graced such a weapon by wearing and adoring it because it was by such a means that our Lord was put to death."[60]

In this same article, President Smith wrote that "the wearing of crosses is to most Latter-day Saints in very poor taste and inconsistent to our worship."[61] Elder Bruce R. McConkie expressed similar sentiments,[62] and Elder Marvin J. Ashton more softly wrote, "We in The Church of Jesus Christ of Latter-day Saints . . . try to teach our people to carry their crosses rather than display or wear them."[63]

Although these statements discourage wearing or displaying crosses, they do not forbid the practice. In fact, President Joseph Fielding Smith acknowledged that for some people the symbol of the cross could be helpful: "We have never questioned the sincerity of Catholics and Protestants for wearing the cross, or felt that they were doing something

University, Provo, UT, September 28, 1980); Joseph Fielding Smith, "The Wearing of the Cross," *Improvement Era*, March 1961, 144; J. Reuben Clark Jr., *The Way to Immortality and Eternal Life* (Salt Lake City: Deseret Book, 1949), 297.

59. I searched the GospeLink database (http://gospelink.com/), which contains thousands of Church-related publications.

60. Smith, "Wearing of the Cross," 144. President Smith's remarks were republished in Joseph Fielding Smith, *Answers to Gospel Questions*, vol. 4 (Salt Lake City: Deseret Book, 1963), 17–18. This viewpoint echoes a similar statement from C. H. Spurgeon, an influential nineteenth-century Baptist preacher. See *The Complete Works of C. H. Spurgeon*, vol. 14, *Sermons 788 to 847* (Woodstock, Ontario: Devoted Publishing, 2017), 326.

61. Smith, "Wearing of the Cross," 144.

62. Elder McConkie wrote, "In apostate days the . . . Christian Church developed the practice of using symbolic crosses in the architecture of their buildings and jewelry attached to the robes of their priests. . . . All this is inharmonious with the quiet worship and reverence that should attend a true Christian's remembrance of our Lord's sufferings and death." Bruce R. McConkie, *Mormon Doctrine* (Salt Lake City: Bookcraft, 1958), 160. This statement also appeared in subsequent editions of *Mormon Doctrine*.

63. Marvin J. Ashton, *Be of Good Cheer* (Salt Lake City: Deseret Book, 1990), 31.

which was wrong." President Smith continued, "The motive for such a custom by those who are of other churches, we must conclude, is a most sincere and sacred gesture. To them the cross does not represent an emblem of torture but evidently carried the impression of sacrifice and suffering endured by the Son of God."[64] This statement illustrates that how one views an image of a cross can vary. For some, a cross necklace was "in very poor taste," while for others, it represented the sacred "sacrifice and suffering endured by the Son of God."

When Latter-day Saints are asked why our church buildings do not display crosses, they often paraphrase words stated by President Gordon B. Hinckley in 1975. Although President Hinckley did not directly discourage individuals from wearing or displaying crosses, he explained the Church's institutional practice of not having crosses in our buildings by relating an experience he had while giving a tour of the Mesa Arizona temple. A Protestant minister pointed out the absence of the cross throughout the temple and, noting that it was the symbol of Christianity, asked how Latter-day Saints could claim to be Christians without the image of the cross. President Hinckley responded, "I do not wish to give offense to any of my Christian brethren who use the cross on the steeples of their cathedrals and at the altars of their chapels, who wear it on their vestments, and imprint it on their books and other literature. *But for us, the cross is the symbol of the dying Christ, while our message is a declaration of the living Christ.* . . . The lives of our people must become the only meaningful expression of our faith and, in fact, therefore, the symbol of our worship."[65]

Some may have misinterpreted President Hinckley's statement as

64. Smith, "Wearing of the Cross," 144.
65. Gordon B. Hinckley, "The Symbol of Christ," *Ensign*, May 1975. This talk was slightly modified to become a First Presidency message in the April 2005 *Ensign* and also appears in the March 1989, April 1990, and April 1994 editions of the *Liahona*. This phrase has been quoted more than twenty times in Church magazines, manuals, and other writings of Church leaders. Elders M. Russell Ballard and Bruce D. Porter have also made statements similar to President Hinckley's regarding why the Church does not use the cross as a symbol. M. Russell Ballard, *Our Search for Happiness: An Invitation to Understand The*

a de-emphasis of the atoning importance of Christ's death,[66] glossing over President Hinckley's later statement in the same talk:

> No member of this Church must ever forget the terrible price paid by our Redeemer, who gave His life that all men might live—the agony of Gethsemane, the bitter mockery of his trial, the vicious crown of thorns tearing at his flesh, the blood cry of the mob before Pilate, the lonely burden of his heavy walk along the way to Calvary, the terrifying pain as great nails pierced his hands and feet. . . . This was the cross, the instrument of His torture, the terrible device designed to destroy the Man of Peace. . . . We cannot forget that.[67]

A MULTIFACETED SYMBOL

The importance of worshipping the *living* Christ cannot be overstated. I love these words from Elder David A. Bednar: "With all the energy of my soul, I witness the resurrected and living Christ directs the affairs of His restored and living Church."[68] Jesus Christ lives, and I testify of that reality. At the same time, if we focus on the cross exclusively as a representation of a dying Christ, we ignore the fact that symbols are multifaceted: they permit, even invite, layers of meaning. Indeed, were a Church member to say to a fellow Christian, "Why do you focus on Christ's death by wearing a cross?" the result would likely be misunderstanding and hurt feelings. Eric Huntsman, professor of ancient scripture at Brigham Young University, recounted the following:

Church of Jesus Christ of Latter-day Saints (Salt Lake City: Deseret Book, 1993), 13–14; Bruce D. Porter, *The King of Kings* (Salt Lake City: Deseret Book, 2000), 91.

66. In a Q&A article in the *New Era* about displaying the cross, a reader wrote, "Our church believes that Christ's crucifixion was an important part of the atonement, but we believe that a more important part was when he suffered for our sins in the Garden of Gethsemane." This statement demonstrates how the importance of Christ's sacrifice on Calvary, in connection with the symbol of the cross, was misunderstood by one young reader. "Q&A: Questions and Answers," *New Era*, September 1996.

67. Hinckley, "Symbol of Christ."

68. David A. Bednar, "Chosen to Bear Testimony of My Name," *Ensign*, November 2015.

I remember being surprised once when a . . . Presbyterian friend corrected me when I told her that we preferred to worship a living rather than a dead Christ; she responded that she did too. The cross reminded Protestants that Jesus died for their sins, but it was empty because he was risen and was no longer there on it. I was chastened by her response, realizing that just as we do not appreciate others mischaracterizing our beliefs, neither should we presume to understand or misrepresent the beliefs and practices of others.[69]

Although this instance focuses on the empty cross, additional examples could be provided to show how crucifixes remind some people of Christ's love and devotion, rather than torture and death. Elliott Wise, an assistant professor of art history and curatorial studies at Brigham Young University, shared his perspective on Crucifixion symbolism: "Far from being bothered or uncomfortable by images of Christ on the cross, I am profoundly moved and inspired by those depictions. The representation of his agony and blood is not disrespectful—there is no better way of communicating his descent below all things. The crucifixion proclaims that he was broken and lifted up for his people. For me, looking upon the crucified Christ focuses on much more than just his death. The cross manifests the depths of his eternal, living love, love that we are to emulate."[70] Thus while the cross can be a symbol of the dying Christ, it also has many other meanings.

One of the "defining moments" in the life of Elder Edward Dube of the Seventy occurred when he was pondering images of Jesus Christ, including an image of the Crucifixion.[71] At the age of ten, he visited a Catholic church in his native country of Zimbabwe. Elder Dube said, "I saw paintings with scenes from the Savior's life pasted on the wall:

---

69. Eric D. Huntsman, "Preaching Jesus, and Him Crucified," in *His Majesty and Mission*, ed. Nicholas J. Frederick and Keith J. Wilson (Provo, UT: Religious Studies Center, Brigham Young University; Salt Lake City: Deseret Book, 2017), 73.

70. Elliott Wise, interview by John Hilton III, December 17, 2019.

71. Edward Dube, "Gaining My Faith One Step at a Time," *New Era*, April 2020.

scenes of Jesus Christ's birth, teaching in the temple, praying in the Garden of Gethsemane, carrying the cross to Calvary, being crucified at Golgotha, and His Resurrection. It really made me feel sad to see those nails and thorns. By the time I got to the painting of the Crucifixion, my eyes were filled with tears. And each time I would cry and say, 'Hey, He really went through a lot, just for me.'"[72] For Elder Dube, viewing the image of Christ on the cross was a moving, spiritual experience.

To many people, the cross is a sacred reminder of their belief in Jesus Christ. For example, Alonzo Gaskill, professor of Church history and doctrine at Brigham Young University, was born to Greek Orthodox parents. At his infant baptism, his godparents gave him a 24-karat-gold cross with his Greek name inscribed on it. He always wore it as a treasured token of his faith in Christ. Gaskill recounts,

> After my baptism in The Church of Jesus Christ of Latter-day Saints, I continued to wear my cross, under my shirt, as I always had. On a couple of occasions, while at church, the cross peeked out from between two buttons on my shirt, and a member saw it. In each case, I was chided and told that it was a "pagan" symbol and—as a member of the Church—I should not be wearing it any longer.
>
> Embarrassed that I had been wearing this "pagan" symbol, I took the cross off and sold it for its gold. Thirty-five years later, I have such regrets that I did that. What I was told was not true. The cross had always been a reminder to me of the tremendous price Jesus had paid on my behalf. It continues to be a reminder of that to me today—even though I no longer have that cross that I received at my baptism, and which I had worn and cherished for nearly two decades.[73]

---

72. Dube, "Gaining My Faith One Step at a Time."
73. Alonzo Gaskill, email to John Hilton III, November 20, 2019. I share the experiences of other people with their permission. In order to protect anonymity (if it is desired), I sometimes do not disclose names and slightly alter details of the story.

Unfortunately, some Latter-day Saints today continue to criticize others who choose to wear a cross. A woman recently shared with me that she had been struggling with her faith and decided to double her efforts to cling to Jesus. She wrote, "I made a cross necklace out of jewelry pieces and wore it frequently. I felt I needed that constant reminder of what I could hold to." For her, this cross was a sacred emblem that helped sustain her through a difficult time. She felt hurt when a loved one criticized her for (in the words of her relative) "celebrating and promoting the murder of Christ." Her fragile feelings were wounded by the unkind remarks of one who didn't appreciate the varied meanings of the cross.

Regrettably, such experiences still occur in today's Latter-day Saint culture. In many instances, new converts or those learning about the Church are treated inappropriately when they wear or display a cross. A woman named Kendall shared the following story with me:

> I was raised attending a Lutheran church. As with most Protestant churches, the cross was a central and revered symbol. When I was introduced to the Church of Jesus Christ of Latter-day Saints, I learned about the suffering Christ experienced in Gethsemane, which greatly added to my understanding of the Atonement of Jesus Christ.
>
> I moved to Utah to attend BYU one week after being baptized. I regularly wore a necklace with a small cross pendant that my grandmother had given me. On campus, I had a few experiences where students would start talking to me in a really kind way and I would realize they thought I was not a member, probably because of my necklace. One of my friends even asked me to stop wearing the necklace.
>
> I know the Savior suffered for my sins in Gethsemane and on the cross. I have hesitated to share my thoughts and experiences about this, always wondering if my testimony of the Atonement

of Jesus Christ is not enough because I have a different balance between both Gethsemane and his Crucifixion.[74]

How tragic Kendall questions if her testimony of the Atonement of Jesus Christ is enough because she cherishes both the Garden of Gethsemane and Christ's Crucifixion. I'm grateful she has remained firm in her commitment to the Church of Jesus Christ but wonder how many newcomers have left because of unnecessary comments about the cross.

Some people may feel justified in criticizing those who, like Kendall, choose to wear a cross. They might say, "Latter-day Saints today shouldn't wear crosses—it was discouraged in previous decades." We certainly *should* follow the counsel of living prophets, seers, and revelators. At the same time, we know that specific practices and applications can shift over time.[75]

Some people choose *not* to wear or display an image of a cross for legitimate reasons. One popular Latter-day Saint speaker told me, "I do not wear a cross, not because of cultural reasons, but because so many people wear it for an accessory that it then becomes meaningless. For me, it's not what's around my neck, but what's in my heart that is most important. I show my discipleship not by what I wear, but how I treat others." Other Latter-day Saints might feel that while a cross is a general symbol of Christianity, they are not "general Christians" but rather members of The Church of Jesus Christ of Latter-day Saints, and they would prefer to have a symbol that reflects their unique beliefs.

At the same time, some people choose to wear or display an image

---

74. Personal communication to John Hilton III, August 19, 2019.

75. For example, there are at least sixteen public statements from Church leaders in previous decades that discourage drinking caffeinated soda. The statements cautioning against caffeinated soft drinks are more severe and vastly outnumber the statements discouraging wearing or displaying crosses. Caffeinated soda no longer carries a stigma in Latter-day Saint culture—should displaying or wearing a cross? See, for example, John A. Widtsoe, "Caffeine in Cola Drinks," *Improvement Era*, October 1939.

of the cross—also for legitimate reasons, such as publicly communicating their belief in Christ. Latter-day Saint Tamu Smith, of "Sistas in Zion," wrote, "I don't wear a cross for God. I wear a cross for YOU, and my other brothers & sisters! Jesus & God know who I am. Those I meet on the street don't. My wearing of the cross lets other followers know that they can hold me accountable to the laws of Christianity & discipleship."[76] One Latter-day Saint woman living in Montana felt inspired to start wearing cross earrings. Shortly thereafter, an acquaintance approached her and said, "I didn't realize you were Christian until I saw your earrings!" This opened the door for a wonderful gospel discussion.

For other people, wearing or displaying a cross could help them follow Mormon's counsel to let Christ's death rest in our minds "forever" (Moro. 9:25). A Latter-day Saint musician sent me the following message: "The cross is a meaningful symbol that reminds me to take up my cross daily and follow Christ. I wear a cross under my shirt—it's just for me and the Lord. When I go throughout the day, I often feel it moving against my chest—right over my heart—which does something powerful to my spirit. I don't suggest anyone else should do what I do, and I hope no one will criticize my choice, but I felt called to it, and it has been incredibly meaningful to me." These perspectives are all valid. Whatever position people hold regarding wearing or displaying a cross, we can be supportive and not critical of their approach to worship.

As we look at the history of the image of the cross, we see that over the centuries of Christianity, and even across the decades in the Church, the image of the cross has meant different things to different people. Let's conclude our discussion of this symbol with a parable from Elder Boyd K. Packer: "A merchant man . . . found at last the perfect pearl. He had the finest craftsman carve a superb jewel box and line it with blue velvet. He put his pearl of great price on display so others could share his treasure. He watched as people came to see it. Soon

---

76. Sistas in Zion (@SISTASinZION), "I don't wear a cross for God," Twitter, October 2, 2019, https://twitter.com/SISTASinZION/status/1179425482439380992.

he turned away in sorrow. It was the box they admired, not the pearl."[77] Perhaps we can see the pearl in this parable as representing the Savior's Crucifixion—it is precious, and vital for our salvation. We might think of the box as the visual symbol of the cross; if we focus excessively on the cross (either by adoring or denigrating it), we may miss the beauty of the pearl. Our feelings about the cross as a symbol should not distract us from the saving importance of Christ's gift from Golgotha.

We've begun this book by discussing the box; in the following chapters we will turn our focus to the pearl, seeking to understand why Jesus Christ said, "My Father sent me that I might be lifted up upon the cross" (3 Ne. 27:14).

———————— ◄►━━━ ————————

Throughout the history of Christianity, faithful believers have had differing perspectives on how the cross should be used to represent Christ's atoning sacrifice. Varying meanings of the image of the cross have been found among many denominations and geographic regions and even within the history of the restored Church. Today, some may choose to wear or display images of the cross or Crucifixion to remind themselves or teach their children of Christ's love, shown through his atoning sacrifice. Others prefer to avoid images related to Christ's death and instead focus on other symbols that remind them of the Savior's Atonement. Either way, instead of judging the actions of others, we can all treasure the doctrine that Jesus Christ was "crucified for the sins of the world" (D&C 53:2).

---

77. Boyd K. Packer, "The Cloven Tongues of Fire," *Ensign*, May 2000. A sad example of focusing on the box instead of the pearl occurred among the Israelites in approximately 700 BC. The people had begun to worship the brazen serpent that Moses had created as a symbol of Jesus Christ, treating it as an idol. This story demonstrates the danger of focusing on the symbol rather than on what it symbolizes. See 2 Kings 18:4.

Chapter 2

THE LOVING CHRIST

My journey to better understanding the Savior's sacrifice on Calvary began on a hot summer afternoon. I was on a hill overlooking the border between Syria and Israel; my family had recently moved to Jerusalem, where I would be teaching for a year at the Brigham Young University Jerusalem Center. I had traveled with some colleagues to northern Israel to prepare for a series of future field trips.

As I walked down the hill with my friend and fellow religion professor Matt Grey, he asked me, "Where do you think the emphasis Church members place on Gethsemane comes from?" We had been discussing Christ's Atonement, and his question made me realize that whenever I gave a lesson on this topic, I focused on Gethsemane and said little about Christ's Crucifixion. In fact, I tended to avoid thinking a lot about the Savior's death when pondering his atoning sacrifice. I didn't know it then, but Matt's question would launch me on a process of discovery that would forever change how I think—and feel—about Christ's Atonement.

The reality is Gethsemane and Calvary are both important parts of the Savior's Atonement.[1] Each is significant for our salvation. However, several scholars have pointed out that Church members seem to place

1. The Bible Dictionary, under "Atonement," states that Christ's work in the premortal realm, his sinless life, and his Resurrection are also part of his Atonement.

more significance on Gethsemane. For example, John G. Turner, a Protestant scholar, explained that for Latter-day Saints, "the principal scene of Christ's suffering and, thus, his atonement, was at Gethsemane rather than on the cross."[2] Anglican theologian Douglas J. Davies wrote that "Mormonism relocates the centre of gravity of Christ's passion in Gethsemane rather than upon the cross and Calvary."[3]

Scholars within the Church have made similar observations; Robert Millet wrote, "It is probably the case that if one hundred Protestants were asked where the atonement of Christ took place, those one hundred persons would answer: At Golgotha, on the cross. It is also no doubt true that if one hundred Latter-day Saints were asked the same question, a large percentage would respond: In Gethsemane, in the garden."[4]

While I am not aware of any scientific studies that address Millet's hypothesis, a series of online surveys indicate that students at Brigham Young University and other Latter-day Saint adults tend to heavily emphasize Gethsemane when discussing Christ's Atonement. Professor Anthony Sweat and I asked 752 BYU students in an online class survey, "Where would you say Christ's Atonement mostly took place? A. In the Garden of Gethsemane, or B. On the Cross at Calvary." Eighty-eight percent responded, "In the Garden of Gethsemane," and only 12 percent said, "On the Cross at Calvary." When I shared this result with Scott Esplin, a BYU religion professor, he observed, "You forced people into a false choice. You should have given people a third option of "Christ atoned for our sins equally in Gethsemane and Calvary." Anthony and I acted on this suggestion by surveying an additional 792 BYU students on where Christ mostly atoned for our sins, asking the same question we had previously. Even with a third option of "Equally in Gethsemane and Calvary," a majority (58 percent) chose

---

2. John G. Turner, *The Mormon Jesus* (Cambridge, MA: Harvard University Press, 2016), 284.
3. Douglas J. Davies, *The Mormon Culture of Salvation* (Burlington, VT: Ashgate, 2000), 49.
4. Robert L. Millet, "This Is My Gospel," in *A Book of Mormon Treasury: Gospel Insights from General Authorities and Religious Educators* (Provo, UT: Religious Studies Center, Brigham Young University, 2003), 401.

"Gethsemane only." Additional, less-formal surveys of Latter-day Saint adults inside and outside of the United States yielded similar results.[5]

Although the specific location where the Atonement occurred may seem trivial to some, more than a few antagonists have written critically about the Church, claiming our beliefs about Gethsemane mean that we de-emphasize Christ's Crucifixion and are therefore not true Christians. Indeed, in a conversation with Robert Millet, who has spent thirty years in interfaith work, he lamented the fact that because we teach of the redemptive nature of the Savior's suffering in Gethsemane, many Christians have concluded that Latter-day Saints do not actually believe that Jesus suffered and died on the cross for our sins.[6] It is possible some Latter-day Saints focus so much on the saving power of Gethsemane, they fail to sufficiently recognize Calvary as a place where Christ also atoned for our sins.

In some cases, misunderstandings about Calvary as part of Christ's Atonement have led to incorrect beliefs. According to Elder Gerald N. Lund, some Church members have thought that Christ atoned for our sins and overcame spiritual death in Gethsemane and then, separately, conquered physical death on the cross. Elder Lund called this a "doctrinal error" and wrote, "Nowhere in the scriptures do we find indications that the cross alone overcame physical death or that the Garden alone overcame spiritual death."[7]

A related doctrinal error comes if we minimize Christ's experience on the cross by saying, "What Christ experienced on the cross was no different than the suffering experienced by thousands of others who were crucified." That statement is false. The Savior's experience on the

---

5. See John Hilton III, "Teaching the Scriptural Emphasis on the Crucifixion," *The Religious Educator* 20, no. 3 (2019): 132–53; and John Hilton III, Anthony Sweat, and Joshua Stratford, "Latter-day Saints and Crucifixion Artwork," *BYU Studies Quarterly*, forthcoming. Both articles are available at http://johnhiltoniii.com/crucifixion.

6. Personal communication to John Hilton III, March 8, 2019.

7. Gerald N. Lund, "The Fall of Man and His Redemption," in *Second Nephi, The Doctrinal Structure*, ed. Monte S. Nyman and Charles D. Tate Jr. (Provo, UT: Religious Studies Center, Brigham Young University, 1989), 94.

cross was completely different from other victims of crucifixion. Jesus did not just die—he "died *for our sins*" (1 Cor. 15:3); his Crucifixion had atoning efficacy. President Russell M. Nelson taught that the suffering Christ experienced in Gethsemane was "intensified as He was cruelly crucified on Calvary's cross."[8] Gethsemane and Calvary work together, not in opposition to each other.

The scriptures and our Church leaders describe the atoning importance of *both* Gethsemane and Calvary. Surprisingly, though, while some members focus more on Gethsemane, Christ's Crucifixion is more frequently emphasized in both the scriptures and the words of our prophets. While at least two powerful passages of scripture explicitly teach Christ suffered for our sins in Gethsemane,[9] more than fifty verses specifically link Christ's death with our salvation.[10]

In his speeches and writings, Joseph Smith mentioned Gethsemane one time, using it as an example of Christ submitting his will to his Father's.[11] On more than thirty occasions, Joseph Smith referenced

---

8. Russell M. Nelson, "The Correct Name of the Church," *Ensign*, November 2018.

9. See Mosiah 3:7; D&C 19:16–19. Other verses, such as Isaiah 53:4 and Alma 7:11–13, may connect to the Garden of Gethsemane, but the verses themselves do not directly reference Christ's sufferings there. In addition, some passages speak of Christ's suffering in association with his Atonement without specifically locating that suffering in Gethsemane, on the cross, or elsewhere (see Mosiah 18:2; Alma 16:9; 21:9; 22:14; 33:22). Although in the Book of Mormon, Christ's suffering is sometimes linked with Gethsemane (see Mosiah 3:7), it is also linked with his death (see 1 Ne. 19:10–12; Jacob 1:8; Hel. 14:20; see also Heb. 9:26; 1 Pet. 3:18). Thus we cannot textually establish that passages about the sufferings of Christ refer solely to events in Gethsemane. See also Luke 22:44.

10. See John 3:14–15; 12:32; Rom. 5:6, 8, 10; 1 Cor. 5:7; 15:3; 2 Cor. 5:15; Gal. 3:13; Eph. 2:16; Col. 1:20, 21–22; 2:14; 1 Thes. 5:10; Heb. 9:15, 26; 10:10, 12; 1 Pet. 2:24; 3:18; Rev. 5:8–9; 1 Ne. 11:33; 2 Ne. 2:7–8; 9:5; 26:24; Mosiah 14:12; 15:7–9, 12; 18:2; Alma 21:9; 22:14; 30:26; 33:22; 34:15; Hel. 14:15–16; 3 Ne. 9:21–22; 11:14; 27:14; Ether 12:33; D&C 18:11; 20:23–25; 21:9; 35:2; 45:2–5; 46:13; 53:2; 54:1; 76:41; 138:2, 35, 57; Moses 7:45–47, 55. For a discussion of these passages, see Hilton, "Teaching the Scriptural Emphasis on the Crucifixion," 132–53.

11. For a comprehensive discussion of Joseph Smith's teachings regarding these topics, see John Hilton III, "The Teachings of Joseph Smith on Gethsemane and Jesus Christ's Crucifixion," in *How and What You Worship*, ed. Rachel Cope, Carter Charles, and Jordan Watkins (Provo, UT: Religious Studies Center, Brigham Young University, 2020), 303–29, available at http://johnhiltoniii.com/crucifixion.

Christ's Crucifixion. For example, he said, "The fundamental principles of our religion are the testimony of the Apostles and Prophets, concerning Jesus Christ, *that he died*, was buried, and rose again the third day, and ascended into heaven; and all other things which pertain to our religion are only appendages to it."[12] Other Church leaders, from Brigham Young to the present day, have taught more frequently about the saving importance of Christ's death than about his sufferings in Gethsemane. Across thousands of talks by Church leaders recorded in the *Journal of Discourses* and given in general conferences through 2020, for each one reference to the atoning power of Gethsemane, there are more than five references to the atoning power of Christ's death.[13] An emphasis on Calvary is also evident in the document "The Living Christ: The Testimony of the Apostles."[14]

Because many Latter-day Saints locate Christ's Atonement primarily in Gethsemane, some, like my friend Matt, mentioned earlier in the chapter, might wonder where this focus on Gethsemane over Calvary comes from. It likely stems from a combination of the following: our lack of cross iconography (see chapter 1); doctrinal errors, such as those discussed earlier in this chapter; a desire to differentiate ourselves by focusing on unique teachings regarding Gethsemane;[15] and a few statements from Church leaders (see chapter 6).

---

12. *"Elders' Journal*, July 1838," [44], The Joseph Smith Papers, accessed August 13, 2019, https://www.josephsmithpapers.org/paper-summary/elders-journal-july-1838/12.

13. For an analysis of these references, see John Hilton III, Emily Hyde, and McKenna Trussel, "The Use of 'Crucifixion' by Church Leaders: 1852–2018," *BYU Studies Quarterly* 59, no. 1, 49–80, available at http://johnhiltoniii.com/crucifixion.

14. "The Living Christ: The Testimony of the Apostles," The Church of Jesus Christ of Latter-day Saints, https://www.churchofjesuschrist.org/bc/content/shared/content/english/pdf/36035_000_25_livingchrist.pdf.

15. Robert Millet wrote, "It is inevitable that over time individuals and whole faith communities begin to define themselves, at least to some extent, over against what others believe and thus to emphasize most strongly those doctrinal distinctives that make them who they are. And so it was with the hours of atonement. Because we had come to know, through the Book of Mormon and Doctrine and Covenants, concerning the purposes for the Master's pains in the Garden, we seem to have begun to place

Before continuing, let me be very clear—the events that took place in Gethsemane are a significant part of the Savior's Atonement; I am certainly *not* recommending we de-emphasize them. In the past, I focused primarily on Christ's sufferings in Gethsemane and did not often think of his death on the cross. I'm not suggesting that any of us should reverse this error by exclusively prioritizing Golgotha and ignoring Gethsemane. This book is centered on Calvary, but that doesn't mean we should talk less about Gethsemane, Christ's Resurrection, or other aspects of the Savior's Atonement. Indeed, we should pay more attention to every facet of Christ's life, ministry, and sacrifice.

Given that this book focuses on Christ's Crucifixion, a person might wonder, "How will learning about the Savior's death help me?" Speaking from personal experience, studying Christ's death is changing my life. I can't describe every way this change is happening, but I'm a little more loving, a little kinder, and a little more patient than I used to be. I'm a better husband and father. I think about Jesus more than I did before, and I feel a closer connection with him. I find greater meaning in the sacrament and temple ordinances. Pondering the Savior's suffering on the cross has solidified my witness that he is the living Christ who leads and guides the Church today.

You can receive numerous blessings from learning more about the Savior's sacrifice on Calvary. At a minimum it will increase the love you feel for and from Jesus. You will also better appreciate an aspect of Christ's Atonement that is personally meaningful to him, as shown by how much he speaks of it in scripture. Learning more about Christ's Crucifixion will also help you feel the Holy Ghost more abundantly and more effectively teach others about the Savior's sacrifice. Knowledge of the Crucifixion can also help each of us build important bridges with other Christians.

---

a greater stress upon Gethsemane than upon the cross." *What Happened to the Cross? Distinctive LDS Teachings* (Salt Lake City: Deseret Book, 2007), 107.

FEELING A DEEPENING LOVE

A faithful Church member once expressed to me, "I understand Christ died for my sins, but I don't really like to think about his death. I prefer to remember the *living* Christ." Church leaders have focused on the living Christ, and it is certainly the living Christ who we worship. We cannot emphasize enough the importance that Jesus Christ lives today! As Elder M. Russell Ballard explained, "Without the *living Christ*, our fondest expectations will be unfulfilled."[16]

We also worship a *loving* Christ, and the scriptures repeatedly teach that both Heavenly Father and Jesus Christ manifested their love for us through the Savior's death. In fact, the Apostle John wrote that we understand what love means "*because* [Christ] laid down his life for us" (1 John 3:16).

Christ taught that his death was a central part of his Father's love: "Therefore doth my Father love me, *because* I lay down my life" (John 10:17). On another occasion, Jesus again connected his Crucifixion with his Father's love: "As Moses *lifted up* the serpent in the wilderness, even so must the Son of man be *lifted up*: That whosoever believeth in him should not perish, but have eternal life. *For God so loved the world*, that *he gave* his only begotten Son, that whosoever believeth in him should not perish, but have everlasting life" (John 3:14–16).[17]

Christ's ancient apostles also taught that Heavenly Father showed his love through the death of his Son. Paul declared, "*God commendeth his love toward us*, in that, while we were yet sinners, *Christ died for us*" (Rom. 5:8; see also 1 John 4:9–10).

In addition to manifesting Heavenly Father's love, the Crucifixion demonstrates Christ's personal love for us. Jesus taught, "Greater love

---

16. M. Russell Ballard, "Return and Receive," *Ensign*, May 2017.
17. Note the parallel statements in John 3:15 and 3:16. Both verses say, "That whosoever believeth in him should not perish, but have eternal [everlasting] life." This parallel suggests that "lifted up" in verse 14 and "gave" in verse 16 share a similar meaning— that of being lifted up on the cross.

hath no man than this, that a man lay down his life for his friends" (John 15:13). Christ's showing his love for us through his death is also taught in the Book of Mormon. Nephi testified that Christ "*loveth the world, even that he layeth down his own life* that he may draw all men unto him" (2 Ne. 26:24; see also Ether 12:33).

We can feel more love for Jesus and more deeply feel his love for us as we study the Crucifixion—the event Christ personally defined as his greatest act of love. By better understanding the Savior's death, we will feel his love in greater abundance and be increasingly able to share that love with others.

While we believe in the living Christ, we can also be strengthened by learning more about his sacrifice and death. Jennifer Lane, dean of Religious Education at BYU–Hawaii, wrote, "As we think about the Lamb slain from the foundation of the world, we can also know that he is the life and the light of the world: Christ as the sacrifice and Christ as the living Word. We don't have to pick which one to focus on because we can't have one without the other."[18] Jesus is both the living *and* the loving Christ.

CREATING A STRONGER CONNECTION WITH CHRIST

When we care about others, we want to strengthen our relationship with them. One way we do that is by paying attention to what is important to them. I once presented at a conference with several other speakers on the day of a highly anticipated college football game. Throughout the afternoon, I observed one speaker asking others for updates on the game. I said to him, "Why are you asking everyone about the game? I thought you didn't care about football."

"I don't," he replied. "But I care about them, and they care about it. And when I focus on what is important to others, I develop better relationships with them."

---

18. Jennifer C. Lane, *Finding Christ in the Covenant Path: Ancient Insights for Modern Life* (Provo, UT: Religious Studies Center, Brigham Young University, 2020), 148.

Likewise, if we want to build a stronger connection with the Savior, we need to focus on the things he considers important. Jesus's own words show us that his Crucifixion is central; as we study and feel of its significance, we will build a stronger relationship with him. In scripture, Christ personally refers to his death more than twenty times.[19] For example, when he spoke to those in the Western Hemisphere during the three days of darkness accompanying his death, some of his first words were, "I have come . . . to save the world from sin. . . . For such *I have laid down my life*" (3 Ne. 9:21–22; see also 11:14).

Christ's focus on his Crucifixion continues into the modern day. In Joseph Smith's earliest recorded account of his First Vision, Christ introduces himself by saying, "I am the Lord of glory. *I was crucified for the world,* that all those who believe on my name may have eternal life."[20] Our Redeemer's repeated references to his death suggest it is significant, personal, and meaningful to him. Studying Christ's Crucifixion thus demonstrates that we care about the Savior. On multiple occasions Jesus has given each of us this invitation: "Learn of me" (Matt. 11:29; D&C 19:23; 32:1; 58:1). Jesus Christ wants us to learn as much as we can about him—including his sacrifice and death. Doing so will deepen our relationship with him.

I first experienced drawing closer to Christ by studying his Crucifixion when I lived in Jerusalem. I regularly visited the Garden of Gethsemane and sites related to Christ's Crucifixion and Resurrection to read and reflect on the scriptures about his Atonement. During this time, I recorded the following in my journal:

> [I go to] a sacred place each week and study about the Savior.

---

19. In mortality, Christ referred to his death at least ten times: Matt. 16:21; 17:22; 20:18; 26:2; John 3:14; 8:28; 10:15, 17; 12:32; 15:13 (this list does not include references in Mark and Luke that parallel those given by Matthew). In addition, after his Crucifixion, he referred to his death at least eleven times: 3 Ne. 9:21–22; 11:14; 27:14; 28:6; D&C 6:37; 27:2; 35:2; 45:4–5, 52; 53:2; 110:4.

20. "Circa Summer 1832 History," [1], The Joseph Smith Papers, accessed August 13, 2019, https://www.josephsmithpapers.org/articles/primary-accounts-of-first-vision.

Part of this time [has been] spent reading all of the references to Christ in the Topical Guide as suggested by President Nelson.[21] Part has been simply pondering, and I've also done focused synoptic readings [carefully studying similarities and differences in the Gospel accounts][22] on the last 24 hours of Christ's life. . . . This has been a real treasure for me.[23]

My growing understanding of the importance of the Savior's sacrifice did not require a trip to Jerusalem, but it did require increased study and pondering. If we have not yet carefully studied Christ's Crucifixion, we have a valuable opportunity to learn more about it now. In my experience, many Latter-day Saints have not examined the events of Calvary in-depth, creating opportunities for us to, as President James E. Faust said, "increase in our understanding of His atoning sacrifice" and therefore come "closer to Him."[24]

FEELING THE SPIRIT AND TEACHING OTHERS

A beautiful blessing from studying any aspect of the Savior's life and Atonement is that it concentrates our attention on Christ. Can we think and speak too much of him? A heightened focus on the Savior leads us to increasingly feel the Holy Ghost because, as Jesus taught, "The Spirit of truth . . . testif[ies] of me" (John 15:26). Indeed, the bond between Jesus and the Spirit is so strong that nobody "can say that Jesus is the Lord, but by the Holy Ghost" (1 Cor. 12:3).

Modern revelation specifically teaches that one of the Spirit's roles is to testify of the Savior's death. The Lord revealed to Joseph Smith that "*the Comforter . . . manifesteth that Jesus was crucified . . . for the*

---

21. See President Russell M. Nelson, "I Studied More Than 2,200 Scriptures about the Savior in Six Weeks: Here Is a Little of What I Learned," The Church of Jesus Christ of Latter-day Saints, https://www.churchofjesuschrist.org/blog/i-studied-more-than-2200-scriptures-about-the-savior-in-six-weeks-here-is-a-little-of-what-i-learned?
22. See chapter 13 herein.
23. John Hilton III, journal, May 11, 2018.
24. James E. Faust, "The Atonement: Our Greatest Hope," *Ensign*, November 2001.

sins of the world" (D&C 21:9; see also 46:13). Each of us has opportunities with friends, family members, or in church classrooms to speak of the atoning efficacy of Christ's Crucifixion. We can find spiritual power, feel the Holy Ghost, and help others do the same by frequently testifying of what occurred on Calvary. We will have many opportunities to do so since nearly every gospel principle connects to the cross. Giving a talk or a lesson on agency? Covenants? Faith? Forgiveness? Humility? Obedience? Repentance? Sacrifice? Service? Zion? All of these topics and many more directly relate to the Savior's Crucifixion.

The only thing the Apostle Paul wanted to know was "Jesus Christ . . . him crucified" (1 Cor. 2:2). As one influential Christian thinker has observed, "All [Paul] does and teaches is tied to the cross. He cannot long talk about Christian joy, or Christian ethics, or Christian fellowship, . . . or anything else, without finally tying it to the cross."[25] As we follow Paul's example by testifying more about the atoning power of the Savior's death for us, the Spirit's influence in our lives will increase and we will find a greater ability to teach others about Christ's Atonement.

BUILDING BRIDGES

2,300,000,000—that is a big number. Two billion, three hundred million: that's about how many Christians there are in the world, and members of the Church compose less than one percent of them. Nearly all Christians believe Christ died for our sins, providing Latter-day Saints with a perfect opportunity to build on common beliefs. Unfortunately, we sometimes instead focus on our differences.

Robert Eaton, associate academic vice president for Learning and Teaching at BYU–Idaho, shared how, when teaching missionary-preparation classes, he would role-play with students. When students pretending to be missionaries would ask him (acting as somebody

---

25. D. A. Carson, *The Cross and Christian Ministry* (Grand Rapids, MI: Baker Books, 2006), 38.

learning about the Church) if he knew about Christ's Atonement, he would say, "Yes, I saw a movie about Christ dying for our sins on the cross." At least half of his students would correct him, stating that Christ atoned for our sins in Gethsemane, not on the cross. He felt it was unfortunate that these missionaries didn't use this opportunity to focus on what we have in common with Christians—our understanding of the saving importance of Christ's Crucifixion—in addition to teaching about Gethsemane.[26]

It's natural for us to focus on what is different or unique. When Robert Millet was about to leave on his mission, he asked his father, "What does it mean to be saved by grace?" His dad responded, "We don't believe in that." When further asked why we didn't believe that, Millet's father said, "Because the Baptists do!"[27] Of course, we *do* believe in the saving grace of Christ, but this humorous incident illustrates our propensity to differentiate our religious beliefs from those of others. In some cases, however, this inclination can lead to unfortunate challenges and misunderstandings.

For example, a pastor at a Christian church in Provo, Utah, said, "We can always tell when one of your wards has a lesson about the cross because on Monday our kids pay the price for it on the playground." He described some Latter-day Saint boys who at recess told a girl from his congregation that wearing a cross necklace was of the devil. She had to see the school nurse after the boys violently ripped off her necklace.[28]

Coming to a deeper knowledge of the Savior's Crucifixion will give us more love and awareness as we interact with hundreds of millions of Christians for whom the cross is the primary symbol of their belief that Christ was both crucified and resurrected. As we talk with other

---

26. Personal communication to John Hilton III, March 7, 2019.
27. Robert L. Millet, *Grace Works* (Salt Lake City: Deseret Book, 2003), 6–7.
28. This story was told to Richard Holzapfel as he was gathering information about Utah County for the Utah Centennial County History Series (published by the Utah State Historical Society and county commissions).

Christians about our shared faith in Jesus Christ, we can highlight that the Book of Mormon itself testifies Christ died on the cross to atone for our sins (see 1 Ne. 11:33).

The Prophet Joseph Smith taught that Latter-day Saints have much in common with other Christians and should be unified with them. He said, "The enquiry is frequently made of me, 'Wherein do you differ from others in your religions views?' In reality and essence we do not differ so far in our religious views. . . . *Christians should cease wrangling and contention with each other and cultivate the principles of union and friendship in their midst*; and they will do it before the Millennium can be ushered in, and Christ takes possession of his kingdom."[29]

Perhaps in an earlier generation there was a need to focus on the differences between Church members and other Christians.[30] But just as people in the Book of Mormon who had historically been at odds united to face serious threats in their time (see 3 Ne. 2:10–14), we too can link arms with other believers. Elder Ronald A. Rasband said, "We have to invite our members to be part of a chorus of believers and not just soloists. We do much better if we join with our friends of other faiths. . . . We are putting the things that we disagree on aside right now, and we're lining up on the things we can agree on."[31]

The importance of Christ's Crucifixion is something Latter-day

---

29. "History, 1838–1856, volume E-1 [1 July 1843–30 April 1844]," 1666, The Joseph Smith Papers, accessed October 1, 2019, https://www.josephsmithpapers.org/paper -summary/history-1838-1856-volume-e-1-1-july-1843-30-april-1844/36.

30. See Armand L. Mauss, *The Angel and the Beehive* (Chicago: University of Illinois Press, 1994).

31. Scott Taylor, "Church Leaders Discuss Faith and Religious Freedom with U.S. Vice President Pence," *Church News*, August 24, 2019. In addition, the Gospel Topics Essay on "Are Mormon Christian?" states, "While members of The Church of Jesus Christ of Latter-day Saints have no desire to compromise the distinctiveness of the restored Church of Jesus Christ, they wish to work together with other Christians—and people of all faiths—to recognize and remedy many of the moral and family issues faced by society. . . . There is no good reason for Christian faiths to ostracize each other when there has never been more urgent need for unity in proclaiming the divinity and teachings of Jesus Christ." https://www.churchofjesuschrist.org/study/manual/gospel-topics -essays/christians?

Saints and other Christians can agree on. In an era where religious liberties are frequently attacked, working with others of faith is increasingly important. Learning more about Christ's Crucifixion can help us build bridges, both individually and as a Church collectively, with other Christians.

Although many Latter-day Saints focus primarily on Gethsemane when discussing the Savior's Atonement, the scriptures and modern Church leaders more frequently mention Calvary. The living Christ himself often emphasizes his Crucifixion. Studying Christ's death can change our lives. It can increase the love we feel for and from Jesus. We will fortify our relationship with the Savior by focusing on an event he often uses to identify himself. We will feel a greater abundance of the Spirit as we study and speak more about the Savior's atoning sacrifice and become more united with other Christians.

As we ponder and study both the living and the loving Christ, our hearts will echo more fully these words from our beloved hymn:

> *I think of his hands pierced and bleeding to pay the debt!*
> *Such mercy, such love and devotion can I forget?*
> *No, no, I will praise and adore at the mercy seat,*
> *Until at the glorified throne I kneel at his feet.*
>
> *Oh, it is wonderful that he should care for me*
> *Enough to die for me!*
> *Oh, it is wonderful, wonderful to me!*[32]

We must never forget the mercy, love, and devotion Jesus so fully proffers us through his Atonement. Rather, we must strive to learn all we can about him—including the sacrifice he made on Calvary.

---

32. "I Stand All Amazed," *Hymns* (Salt Lake City: The Church of Jesus Christ of Latter-day Saints, 1985), no. 193.

PART II

Teachings about the Crucifixion of Jesus Christ

Chapter 3

"A NAIL IN A SURE PLACE"

FORESHADOWING IN THE OLD TESTAMENT

Were you interested in your shadow when you were a child? I remember being eight years old, looking at my shadow in the evening and thinking I had magical powers because I seemed to have grown so much taller. Even though shadows don't reveal the complete perspective, they can provide a glimpse of a thing's true nature. This is true of shapes, and it's true of the gospel as well. Abinadi taught that the law of Moses was "a shadow" of Jesus Christ and his Atonement, a principle reiterated in the New Testament (Mosiah 16:14; see also Heb. 10:1; 2 Ne. 11:4).

Indeed, when bathed in the light of New Testament and Restoration scripture, the Old Testament is rich with passages that foreshadow Christ's death.[1] Abraham offered up his son Isaac in "similitude of God and his Only Begotten Son" (Jacob 4:5),[2] and Jonah was sacrificed to save

---

1. In some cases, ancient prophets explicitly testified of Christ's Crucifixion. In other instances, Old Testament authors may not have intended a specific event or detail to refer to Christ's death, but the Spirit inspired New Testament and Book of Mormon authors to identify connections that help us better appreciate the Crucifixion. Often prophecies can have multiple meanings (see Dallin H. Oaks, "Scripture Reading and Revelation," *Ensign*, January 1995). These Old Testament prophecies were not obvious to Christ's first apostles. When Christ told the Twelve that he would die, Peter's response was not, "Great, this is just like the prophecies I've heard," but instead, "Be it far from thee, Lord: this shall not be unto thee" (Matt. 16:22).
2. Additional parallels are found between Jesus and Ishmael, Abraham's son through Hagar. Scholar Julie M. Smith notes, "Both Jesus and Ishmael are positioned as the rejected son. . . . The same word for the women watching [Christ on the cross] from

his shipmates just as the Savior was sacrificed to save all humanity (see Jonah 1:1–17; Matt. 12:40).[3] Isaiah wrote of one who "was wounded for our transgressions" and who "poured out his soul unto death" (Isa. 53:5, 12); this was a prophecy about Jesus Christ.[4] The Savior himself explained that "Moses and all the prophets" had taught about Christ and his death (Luke 24:27; see also Luke 24:20; John 5:46).[5]

Looking at these shadows in the light of New Testament and Restoration scripture brings the Savior's sacrifice into clearer view. Let's explore five Old Testament passages and learn how salvation through Christ's Crucifixion was anticipated and revered centuries before he came to earth. Seeing the importance ancient prophets placed on Christ's sacrifice can help us better appreciate its significance. We will also see how these Old Testament practices apply to our lives and point us to the Savior.

SACRIFICE BY THE SHEDDING OF BLOOD

Shortly after Adam and Eve were expelled from the Garden of Eden, they were commanded to sacrifice "the firstlings of their flocks,

---

'afar off' . . . is used for Hagar watching Ishmael from far off (LXX Gen. 21:16). Jesus describes himself as feeling abandoned on the cross; Ishmael is similarly abandoned by his mother because she cannot bear to see the death of her child. . . . In light of the intertext, it is clear that God's abandonment of Jesus is not an actual abandonment (inasmuch as Hagar is still there), but rather that God has, like Hagar, withdrawn from the scene out of anguish. . . . Hagar . . . neither chooses Ishmael's death nor consents to it. This parallel would then nuance the view of God's role in Jesus' death." *The Gospel According to Mark*, Brigham Young University New Testament Commentary (Provo, UT: BYU Studies, 2019), 804.

3. There are also interesting contrasts between Jonah and Christ. For instance, Jonah became frustrated when those he taught repented (see Jonah 4), while Christ's "merciful . . . arm is lengthened out all the day long" (2 Ne. 28:32).

4. See Mosiah 13:33–35; 15:1–7; Acts 8:31–35.

5. For example, Zechariah prophesied, "They shall look upon me whom they have pierced" (Zech. 12:10; compare John 19:37). His writings also include the passage "What are these wounds in thine hands? Then he shall answer, Those with which I was wounded in the house of my friends" (Zech. 13:6). The Doctrine and Covenants reveals that this is an allusion to the Savior's Crucifixion wounds; he will reference them at his Second Coming (see D&C 45:51–52).

for an offering unto the Lord" (Moses 5:5). Though they obediently followed this counsel, they did not understand why the Lord required them to kill their firstborn animals. This sacrifice was undoubtedly difficult since those animals may have been needed to provide food or clothing for Adam and Eve's family; nevertheless, they obeyed without understanding why. After many days, an angel appeared to them and explained the purpose of these offerings: "This thing is a similitude of the sacrifice of the Only Begotten of the Father" (Moses 5:7).

Animal sacrifice eventually became a key aspect of the law of Moses and represented atoning for sins. The Lord said, "The life of the flesh is in the blood: and I have given it to you upon the altar to make an atonement for your souls: for *it is the blood that maketh an atonement for the soul*" (Lev. 17:11). These animal sacrifices, offered for thousands of years, specifically pointed to the death of Christ (see Alma 34:10–15).[6]

When we hear a phrase like "For us the blood of Christ was shed,"[7] some of us think of the Savior suffering only in Gethsemane, though he clearly bled for us both in Gethsemane and on Calvary. Multiple scriptural passages, however, equate making a sacrificial offering or shedding blood with death.[8] For example, as Nephi debated whether or

---

6. Wilford Woodruff taught, "The blood of . . . lambs [was] spilt upon the altar as a type of the great and last sacrifice . . . [which was Christ] lay[ing] down his life for the redemption of man." Joseph Smith also explained that these ancient animal sacrifices pointed to Christ: "It must be the *shedding of the blood of the Only Begotten* to atone for man; for this was the plan of redemption; and without the *shedding of blood* was no remission; and as the sacrifice was instituted for a type, by which man was to discern the great Sacrifice which God had prepared." Wilford Woodruff, in *Journal of Discourses*, 26 vols. (Liverpool: F. D. Richards, 1855–86), 23:127 (May 14, 1882); "Letter to the Church, circa March 1834," 143, The Joseph Smith Papers, accessed August 13, 2019, https://www.josephsmithpapers.org/paper-summary/letter-to-the-church-circa-march-1834/2.

7. "While of These Emblems We Partake," *Hymns* (Salt Lake City: The Church of Jesus Christ of Latter-day Saints, 1985), no. 173. The following line states, "For us on Calvary's cross he bled," indicating that the author of the hymn was thinking of Christ's Crucifixion when describing the Savior's blood being shed.

8. See Gen. 37:20–22; Deut. 21:6–7; Matt. 23:35; Acts 22:20; Mosiah 17:10; Alma 1:13; 20:19; 39:5; D&C 132:19, 26; 136:36; Moses 7:45, 47.

not to kill Laban, Nephi said, "Never at any time have I *shed the blood of man*. And I shrunk and would that I might not *slay him*" (1 Ne. 4:10). Joseph Smith also clearly equated the phrase "shedding blood" with death. While traveling with Zion's Camp, he recorded, "I told them I felt much depressed in Spirit, and lonesome, and that there had been a great deal of blood shed in that place, and whenever a man of God is in a place, where many have been killed; he will feel lonesome and unpleasant."[9]

Understanding that ancient animal sacrifices foreshadowed Christ's death helps us more clearly see the importance of the Savior's sacrifice for us. If we previously associated the shedding of blood only with Gethsemane, we can now realize that these practices primarily foreshadow the Savior's death. Seeing how Christ's Crucifixion has been typified for millennia can deepen the reverence we feel for his atoning sacrifice.

In addition, although we no longer kill our firstborn animals as a shadow, or type, of Christ's death,[10] the Savior has invited us to make a different sacrifice to him. Speaking after his Crucifixion, Jesus said, "Ye shall offer for a sacrifice unto me a broken heart and a contrite spirit" (3 Ne. 9:20). Sister Neill F. Marriott referred to this as "sacrificing our heart, or our will, to the Lord."[11] These modern sacrifices could be as simple as following a prompting from the Spirit or staying faithful even

---

9. "History, 1838–1856, volume A-1 [23 December 1805–30 August 1834]," 7 [addenda], The Joseph Smith Papers, accessed September 1, 2020, https://josephsmithpapers .org/paper-summary/history-1838-1856-volume-a-1-23-december-1805-30 -august-1834/566. On another occasion, Joseph wrote, "A man that accepts a challenge or fights a duel, is nothing more nor less than a *murderer*, for holy writ declares that 'whoso *sheds man's blood*, by man shall his blood be shed." In recent years, Church leaders have spoken of Christ's blood that was shed in Gethsemane and on Calvary. For example, Elder Boyd K. Packer taught, "At Gethsemane and Golgotha the Savior's blood was shed." "Letter to Henry Clay, 13 May 1844," [2], The Joseph Smith Papers, https:// josephsmithpapers.org/paper-summary/letter-to-henry-clay-13-may-1844/1; Boyd K. Packer, "Atonement, Agency, Accountability," *Ensign*, May 1988.

10. Christ ended this practice with his Crucifixion. See 3 Ne. 9:19.

11. Neill F. Marriott, "Yielding Our Hearts to God," *Ensign*, November 2015.

when we don't fully comprehend some things. By sacrificing our wills, even when we don't understand why, we emulate Adam and Eve's first sacrifices in similitude of the Savior.[12]

One woman shared an example of what this might look like in everyday life: "I wanted to minister to a sister I was assigned to visit, but I also wanted to do the other pressing things on my to-do list. The person I minister to didn't have any dire needs—she just loves company, which meant a visit would require quite a bit of time. I knew going to her home meant less time doing what I wanted to do, but I went anyways. As I visited her, my thoughts turned to the Savior's sacrifice for me, and I felt his love and approval."

THE DAILY SACRIFICE

One of the challenges with *daily* living is that we have to do it *every day*. I could perhaps do something heroic for a day or two, but daily discipleship can be a struggle. In my efforts to live a more consecrated life *each day*, I've found meaning in the connections between the Savior's death and the daily sacrifice described in Exodus: "This is that which thou shalt offer upon the altar; two lambs of the first year *day by day continually*. The one lamb thou shalt offer in the morning; and the other lamb thou shalt offer at even" (Ex. 29:38–39; see also Num. 28:1–8). Some ancient Israelites considered this daily sacrifice as "a means for atoning for sin."[13]

Elements of the daily sacrifice have parallels to Christ's Crucifixion.

---

12. Neal A. Maxwell taught, "Real, personal sacrifice never was placing an animal on the altar. Instead, it is a willingness to put the animal in us upon the altar and letting it be consumed! Such is the 'sacrifice unto the Lord . . . of a broken heart and a contrite spirit.'" "Deny Yourselves of All Ungodliness," *Ensign*, May 1995.

13. Mary L. Coloe, "'Behold the Lamb of God': John 1:29 and the Tamid Service," *Rediscovering John: Essays on the Fourth Gospel in Honour of Frédéric Manns*, ed. L. Daniel Chrupcala (Milan: Edizioni Terra Santa, 2013), 340. All other sacrifices, including sin and guilt offerings, were sandwiched between the two daily offerings, except in the case of the Passover sacrifice. See Peter L. Trudginer, *The Psalms of the Tamid Service: A Liturgical Text from the Second Temple* (Boston: Brill, 2003), 20.

In the daily animal sacrifices, which were still taking place during the time of Christ, temple priests would cast lots to see who would perform specific acts of the sacrificial ritual, including dividing up portions of the animal. This process foreshadows what happened on Calvary, where soldiers cast lots for and divided up Christ's clothing (see John 19:24).

Specific prayers were offered at the temple during the daily sacrifice. Imagine the significance of these words, which may have been uttered by worshippers at the temple during the afternoon sacrifice, at the very hour Christ was on the cross:[14] "Forgive us, our Father, for we have sinned against you. Blot out and remove our transgressions from before your eyes. . . . Redeem us for the sake of your name. . . . You are powerful; . . . Alive forever, raising the dead."[15] These prayers were answered that day—not in the daily animal sacrifice, but in the eternal sacrifice made on Calvary.

Even though the Savior fulfilled the daily sacrifice with his death on the cross, he still beckons us: "If any man will come after me, let him deny himself, and take up his cross *daily*, and follow me" (Luke 9:23). We can all make daily sacrifices and think of the Savior as we do so. For example, a caregiver might say, "Serving my ailing parent day after day is a privilege and a joy, but it's also very challenging. I am comforted when I remind myself that I'm following the Savior as I offer my own form of daily sacrifice." Whatever our offerings may be,

14. In the timing presented by John, the morning sacrifice may have occurred at the same time Christ was on trial before Pilate and the afternoon sacrifice at the approximate hour Christ was nailed to the cross. See Coloe, "Behold the Lamb of God," 343. For Jesus as the Passover Lamb, see chapter 10 herein.

15. David Instone-Brewer, "The Eighteen Benedictions and the MINIM before 70 CE," *The Journal of Theological Studies* 54, no. 1 (2003): 29–30. It appears that community prayers were said at the temple in conjunction with the daily sacrifice (see Acts 3:1). The words of the prayers offered with the daily sacrifice are not found in scripture; for a discussion of the specific words that were used in daily prayers (which may have accompanied the daily sacrifice), see Instone-Brewer, "Eighteen Benedictions," 25–44. It is not certain if these prayers were said at the time of Christ or if they were a later development.

the daily sacrifices of the law of Moses remind us to take up our crosses *daily* and follow Jesus.

A FREEWILL OFFERING

Another Israelite sacrifice that prefigures the Savior's death is the "freewill offering" (Lev. 22:18). The scriptures don't provide many details regarding these offerings, but, as their name implies, they were completely voluntary.[16] This offering is a type of Christ's sacrifice—his life wasn't taken from him; he freely gave it for us. He said, "I lay down my life for the sheep. . . . No man taketh it from me, but I lay it down of myself. I have power to lay it down, and I have power to take it again" (John 10:15, 18; see also 19:10–11).[17]

Although we don't have formal freewill offerings today, thinking about them, along with Christ's willing sacrifice, can alter our feelings about the sacrifices we make. How we view our offerings can completely change when we transform our perspective from doing things because we *have* to into doing things because we *willingly choose* to do them. One mother shared:

> Raising three little children is exhausting! I was feeling frustrated with my lack of time and energy and resenting the fact that I had to give up so much of my time to make another meal, wipe another nose, and change another diaper. But one day, I thought about Jesus—nobody *made* him sacrifice for me—he did it because he wanted to. And I realized that I had always wanted to be a mom. It was my choice. This realization changed everything. Well, most things—it's still exhausting to do the required

---

16. Freewill offerings were often given during religious festivals. Although the offering was typically an animal sacrifice, the Hebrew word used to describe the freewill sacrifices made by the Israelites also refers to donations of precious materials used to build and decorate the tabernacle. See Deut. 16:10; Ex. 25:29.

17. I appreciate Dave Hadlock for sharing with me the connection between this scripture and the freewill offerings.

motherly tasks, but now I feel so much happier as I serve my children, knowing that it's something I've chosen to do.

When we choose to see our sacrifices as *voluntary* or *freewill* offerings, our hearts soften and our service becomes more joyful. We also become more like the Savior as we emulate the one who "freely give[s] us all things" (Rom. 8:32).

THE GREAT HIGH PRIEST
AND THE DAY OF ATONEMENT

The Day of Atonement, the holiest day of the Jewish calendar, was the only day in which the high priest could enter the most sacred part of the temple.[18] This location, called the "Holy of Holies," represented God's dwelling place. On this momentous occasion, the high priest would sacrifice a goat to make "an atonement for . . . all the congregation of Israel" (Lev. 16:17).

Of course, neither the high priest nor the goat could truly atone for the sins of the people. The sacrifice was a shadow of the Savior, the "high priest of good things to come" (Heb. 9:11). Rather than offering the blood of an animal, Christ used his own blood to atone for our sins. Instead of figuratively entering the presence of God by going into the Holy of Holies, he literally returned to God's presence, where he remains, interceding for us (see Heb. 9:11; 10:10–14).

What lesson might we draw from Jesus and the sacrifice on the Day of Atonement? The high priest's sacrifice atoned for "the congregation of Israel." In contrast, the Savior was "slain and hast redeemed . . . [people from] *every* kindred, and tongue, and people, and nation" (Rev. 5:9). Unlike the original Day of Atonement ceremony, Christ's sacrifice knows no boundaries.

In light of Christ's universal gift, the gospel has no room for racism, sexism, or any type of exclusionary practice. Christ invites "*all* to come

---

18. The Day of Atonement is also known as Yom Kippur.

unto him . . . black and white, bond and free, male and female; . . . *all are alike unto God*" (2 Ne. 26:33; see also John 12:32). Jesus told the Nephites, "Ye see that I have commanded that none of you should go away, but rather have commanded that ye should come unto me, that ye might feel and see [the marks of my Crucifixion]" (3 Ne. 18:25).

Joseph and Emma Smith are examples of people who warmly welcomed others, regardless of their race or circumstances. When Jane Manning, a Black woman, arrived in Nauvoo with no place to stay and few resources because her luggage had been lost, Joseph and Emma invited Jane to stay with them.[19] As we follow their example by loving and including everyone, we emulate Christ on the cross. His sacrifice welcomes all who come unto him to enter the presence of God.

SHEBNA AND ELIAKIM

In what Elder Jeffrey R. Holland called a "moving Messianic tribute,"[20] the prophet Isaiah foreshadowed the Crucifixion through an obscure story about Shebna and Eliakim. Shebna, who held a high position as an official in King Hezekiah's court, apparently abused his power, perhaps siphoning off royal funds for his own purposes (see Isa. 22:15).

Isaiah said a man named Eliakim would replace Shebna in the king's court. Eliakim would be given many important responsibilities, including receiving "the key of the house of David," which would give Eliakim authority, for "he shall open, and none shall shut; and he shall shut, and none shall open" (Isa. 22:22). Eliakim is a type of the Savior, who identified himself as having "the key of David" and being the person "that openeth, and no man shutteth; and shutteth, and

---

19. See Jane Manning James, autobiography, in "Autobiography of Jane Elizabeth Manning James," ed. James Goldberg and Veronica Anderson, *BYU Studies Quarterly* 57, no. 4 (2018): 153–54.
20. Jeffrey R. Holland, *Witness for His Names* (Salt Lake City: Deseret Book, 2019), 113.

no man openeth" (Rev. 3:7).[21] The similarity between these phrases connects Eliakim and the Savior. Eliakim had the power to open and close palace doors, and Christ can unlock the gate to immortality and eternal life.

Speaking of Eliakim, the Lord said, "I will fasten him as a nail in a sure place; and he shall be for a glorious throne to his father's house. And they shall hang upon him all the glory of his father's house. . . . In that day, saith the Lord of hosts, shall the nail that is fastened in the sure place be removed, and be cut down, and fall; and the burden that was upon it shall be cut off" (Isa. 22:23–25). Elder Holland commented on these verses as follows:

> When the Roman soldiers drove their four-and-one-half-inch crucifixion spikes into their victim's flesh, they did so first in the open palm. But because the weight of the body might tear that flesh and not sustain the burden to be carried, they also drove nails into the wrist, down in the nexus of bones and sinews that would not tear no matter what the weight. Thus, the nail in the wrist was the "nail in a sure place."
>
> Once it was removed and the Savior was "cut down," the burden of the crucified body (more literally, the burden of the Atonement) was brought to an end. In terms of our salvation, Christ is the Nail in a Sure Place—never failing, never faltering.[22]

Although faithful Eliakim was granted temporary authority, Jesus has "all power . . . given unto [him] in heaven and in earth" (Matt. 28:18).

---

21. Isaiah 22:22 and Revelation 3:7 are the only two instances in scripture that speak of the key of David.
22. Holland, *Witness for His Names*, 113. The Hebrew word for "nail" in this passage can also refer to a sturdy peg that one could hang items on for storage. In this reading, Isaiah could be saying that all different types of vessels will hang on this peg, symbolic of Eliakim's great importance in Hezekiah's palace (see Isa. 22:24). If the phrase "fasten him as a nail in a sure place" refers to a sturdy object of support, Eliakim is still a type of Christ. Just as Eliakim was the strongest steward in Hezekiah's palace, with all things resting on him, so can all our sins, sorrows, and struggles be supported by the Savior, because of his atoning sacrifice.

Our deepest hopes and desires safely rest in his hands, nailed in the sure place. We can have total confidence in Christ, even during trouble and despair.

Such was the case for a woman I'll call Megan. One day, Megan's husband told her he was gay and no longer wanted to be married to her. Recalling a Sunday when she was sitting in sacrament meeting, Megan said, "I hadn't anticipated how awkward and painful it would be to sit there in church, pretending that everything was okay when inside my heart was breaking and my stomach was churning. The thoughts in my mind seemed to be on a continual loop of pleadings with the Lord: 'What am I going to do? What is going to happen to my family? How can I be a single parent and provide the kind of life I want for my kids? Will I be strong enough?'"

On that occasion Megan's answer came in the closing hymn: "How Firm a Foundation." As she heard the lyrics "As thy days may demand, so thy succor shall be," her heart felt peace.[23] "To succor" literally means "to run to,"[24] and Megan powerfully felt Christ's comfort. She was safe in his hands.

No matter how deep our demands, Christ runs to us. If we allow him to, he will catch us when we stumble, encourage us when we feel weak, hope for us when we can't hope for ourselves, and give us all the grace we need. He *is* the nail in the sure place.

———— ·•· ————

We have explored only a few Old Testament passages containing shadows of the Savior's Crucifixion. The relationship between Jesus Christ and animal sacrifice, including the daily and freewill offerings, reminds us of the atoning power of his death and encourages us to make daily, voluntary sacrifices by submitting our will to his. The

---

23. "How Firm a Foundation," *Hymns*, no. 85.
24. *American Dictionary of the English Language* (1828), ed. Noah Webster, s.v. "succor," accessed February 11, 2020, http://webstersdictionary1828.com/Dictionary/succor.

representations of Jesus Christ as our high priest and Eliakim, emphasizes the Savior's constant and sure outreach to all of God's children.

Identifying and reflecting on these prophecies and types can heighten our awareness that "the whole meaning of the law" of Moses was to point ancient Israelites and us "to that great and last sacrifice; and that great and last sacrifice will be the Son of God" (Alma 34:14). Calvary is a connecting point between ancient religious practices and our knowledge of the Savior today, drawing our eyes and hearts toward Jesus Christ.

Interestingly, in order to have a shadow, you must have light. Jesus Christ *is* the light of the world. Seeing the beauty and meaning of shadows in the scriptures can motivate us to make studying this aspect of the Savior's Atonement a more important part of our lives. As we do so, we will see not only the light behind the shadows but also his light in our lives today.

Chapter 4

"I GLORY IN THE CROSS"
TESTIMONIES FROM THE NEW TESTAMENT

I magine a fast and testimony meeting in which an unfamiliar person in the congregation approaches the pulpit and shares the following testimony: "Dear brothers and sisters, Christ died for our sins. Even though people boast about many things, as for me, I never boast about anything except the cross of Christ! The Savior's death is swallowed up in victory. I know Jesus gave up his divine privileges, humbled himself in obedience to God, and died on a cross. When I am at church with you, I forget everything except Jesus Christ, the one who was crucified."

What would be your reaction to this testimony? Does any part of it sound out of the ordinary to you? Although it's unlikely the ancient apostle Paul will come and share his testimony over the pulpit next Sunday, nearly every word of the testimony above comes directly from his letters.[1] For Latter-day Saints, his testimony might seem a little un-usual with its emphasis on the cross and Crucifixion, but it would not

---

1. Here is an annotated version of the testimony, with all quotations taken from the New Living Translation (NLT): "Dear brothers and sisters" (1 Cor. 15:1), "Christ died for our sins" (1 Cor. 15:3). Even though people boast about many things, "as for me, may I never boast about anything except the cross of our Lord Jesus Christ" (Gal. 6:14). The Savior's "death is swallowed up in victory" (1 Cor. 15:54). I know Jesus "gave up his divine privileges; . . . he humbled himself in obedience to God and died . . . on a cross" (Philip. 2:7–8). When I am at church "with you I . . . forget everything except Jesus Christ, the one who was crucified" (1 Cor. 2:2).

have sounded strange to the early Saints because these principles were frequently taught in the New Testament church.

Paul wrote, "The preaching of the cross . . . is the power of God" and "I determined not to know any thing among you, save Jesus Christ, and him crucified" (1 Cor. 1:18; 2:1–2). Paul specifically adopted a style of teaching that avoided detracting from "the cross of Christ" (1 Cor. 1:17). Similar messages were given by other apostles, such as Peter and John (see Acts 4:8–12; 1 Pet. 2:24; 1 John 3:16).

The Savior's Crucifixion is a key focus of the New Testament. In it we find the narrative of Christ on Calvary (see chapters 8–10), as well as other truths regarding his sacrifice. Let us examine a few key New Testament teachings that can connect us with the Savior.

DIED ON THE CROSS FOR OUR SINS

Recently I received a message from the wife of Jeff, one of my former mission companions. She told me Jeff had been arrested, and she asked me to reach out to him. When I visited Jeff, he shared a long list of his serious mistakes. As he spoke, I could see the weight bearing down on his sloped shoulders and hear the regret in his voice. He had received legal penalties and lost his Church membership. Although he took responsibility for his actions and wanted to become a better person, the question still hung in the air—"Could somebody who has done this much bad ever truly be forgiven?"

We all *know* that the answer is "Of course, nobody is past the point of forgiveness." But sometimes, when we are in the depths of sorrow, standing on the beginning side of repentance, we might wonder if that is really true. Paul repeatedly affirmed that we can have hope, even in our sinful state, reminding us "Christ *died for the ungodly*" and "while we were yet sinners, *Christ died for us*" (Rom. 5:6, 8). In fact, in speaking to the Corinthians, Paul taught the things of "*first importance*" are "that Christ *died for our sins* . . . , and that he was buried, and that he was raised on the third day" (1 Cor. 15:3–4, NRSV).[2] That Christ atoned for our sins through his death was part of Paul's core message— it is of *first* importance.

Jesus "forgave us all our trespasses, erasing the record that stood against us with its legal demands. He set this aside, nailing it to the cross" (Col. 2:14, NRSV). This beautiful doctrine is repeatedly emphasized throughout the New Testament (see 1 Pet. 3:18; Heb. 9:26; Rev. 5:9). Knowing and *really feeling* Christ died for sinners helps us believe his atoning sacrifice can heal everyone, including ourselves, those we love, and those who have hurt us.

It's important for us to admit that *we* are sinners, for "*all* have sinned and come short of the glory of God" (Rom. 3:23; see also 1 Ne. 10:6). No matter how many times we go to the temple, no matter how many chairs we stack after church, no matter how many baked goods we make for others, our actions will never be enough to save us (see Mosiah 2:21). Our own goodness and grit, our diligence and determination, will *not* redeem us from our wrongdoings. Writing at a time when he was diligently serving the Lord, Paul unashamedly admitted he was *chief among sinners* (see 1 Tim. 1:15). If Paul, such a dedicated disciple, is a chief sinner, what does that make you and me?

Although for some people this thought may seem discouraging, I find it hopeful. We cannot *earn* Jesus's mercy, but that's okay because we don't have to! He has already extended it to everyone! Elder Dieter F. Uchtdorf taught, "It is not repentance per se that saves man. It is the blood of Jesus Christ that saves us. It is not by our sincere and honest change of behavior alone that we are saved, but 'by grace that we are saved, after all we can do' (2 Nephi 25:23)."[3]

Being a sinner does not disqualify us from the Savior's love, grace,

---

2. Although I often quote the King James Version of the Bible (KJV), I sometimes use an alternate translation, like the New Revised Standard Version (NRSV), to clarify the meaning of a verse. When I do so, it will be noted.

3. Dieter F. Uchtdorf, "Point of Safe Return," *Ensign*, May 2007.

or access to his Atonement. This message is especially important for those who are overly hard on themselves. We can say to ourselves, "I'm not perfect. I'm repenting, and Jesus atoned for my sins and shortcomings. His grace is enough; I don't need to keep beating myself up. It's not all up to me—I am working together with him."

Our beloved hymn "Reverently and Meekly Now" portrays the Savior singing to us. Imagine Jesus saying these words to you:

> *Oh, remember what was done*
> *That the sinner might be won.*
> *On the cross of Calvary*
> *I have suffered death for thee. . . .*
> *At the throne I intercede;*
> *For thee ever do I plead.*
> *I have loved thee as thy friend,*
> *With a love that cannot end.*[4]

In addition to knowing Christ atoned for *our* sins, we can rejoice knowing he has atoned for the sins of *those we love*. Like my mission companion's wife, many Latter-day Saints feel their greatest sorrow when others choose to deviate from the covenant path. Some of us may look at our loved ones and sorrowfully think, "There's no hope for them." That might seem true, but each of us—and our loved ones—can receive "redemption through his blood, the forgiveness of sins, according to *the riches of his grace*" (Eph. 1:7). No matter how serious the sin, we *and our loved ones* can repent and return into Christ's loving embrace (see D&C 29:1–2; Matt. 23:37). Jesus hasn't given up on those we love, and we shouldn't either (see 3 Ne. 18:32).

Christ died not only for us and those we love but also for those who sin *against* us. This fact may remind us of the Savior's statement "I, the Lord, will forgive whom I will forgive, but of you it is required to

---

4. "Reverently and Meekly Now," *Hymns* (Salt Lake City: The Church of Jesus Christ of Latter-day Saints, 1985), no. 185.

forgive all men" (D&C 64:10). Here is a wonderful part of the gift of grace: though it's not always easy, as we deeply integrate into our hearts the mercy Christ extends to us, we will be increasingly able to extend forgiveness to others. Christian authors Timothy and Kathy Keller expressed this idea by stating, "If you see Jesus dying on the cross for others, forgiving the people who killed him, that can be just a crushing example of forgiving love that you will never be able to live up to. But if instead you see Jesus dying on the cross for *you*, forgiving you, putting away your sin, that changes everything. . . . The joy and freedom that comes from knowing that the Son of God did that for you enables you to do the same for [others.]"[5]

Can my former mission companion receive full forgiveness through Jesus? Can his wife find solace and even come to forgive him? Absolutely, as can you and I for every sin we commit and are wronged by. We can be confident that Christ's "arm is lengthened out all the day long" toward us, those we love, and even those who have hurt or offended us (2 Ne. 28:32). All who repent and come unto the Savior "can receive the eternal inheritance God has promised [us]. For Christ died to set [us] free from the penalty of the sins [we have] committed" (Heb. 9:15, NLT).

TRIUMPHED ON THE CROSS

Imagine watching a sporting event in which you care deeply about the outcome. What if you knew from the outset that no matter how far behind your team was, no matter how many mistakes your favorite player made, no matter how bleak things looked, your team would win? You would probably feel less anxiety during the game. Although you still might experience an array of emotions, you could watch the event with happy anticipation, feeling safe in the known outcome.

We can relate this analogy to the plan of redemption. Some of us

---

5. Timothy and Kathy Keller, *The Meaning of Marriage* (New York: Penguin Books, 2016), 185–86, emphasis in original.

live in a constant state of worry, troubled that we are too far behind, making too many mistakes, and we can't see how things are going to work out. We lose sight of the ultimate victory when we are stuck in one of life's frequent battles. But we don't need to be worried—if we are on Christ's side, our team will win. Jesus Christ has already overcome Satan, in part through what Eliza R. Snow termed "the triumphs of the cross."[6] The Savior prophesied shortly before his death, "Now shall the prince of this world [Satan] be cast out" (John 12:31). We can have confidence in "the triumph and the glory of the Lamb, who was slain" (D&C 76:39).[7]

In Paul's epistle to the Colossians, he wrote that on "the cross [Christ] disarmed the powers and authorities, he made a public spectacle of them, triumphing over them by the cross" (Col. 2:14–15, New International Version). This claim must have seemed audacious at the time—did Christ really "disarm" authorities and "triumph" over them? After all, when Paul wrote to the Colossians, a Roman emperor "was still on the throne."[8] As one New Testament scholar explains, "[The emperor's] local officials around the world were still running the show with brutal efficiency. The chief priests were still in charge of the Temple in Jerusalem. Paul himself was in prison!"[9] How then was Christ's death a triumph?

His death didn't overthrow a worldly kingdom, but rather he accomplished a cosmic victory by overcoming "the rulers of the darkness of this world" and "spiritual wickedness in high places" (Eph. 6:12). Paul explained that the satanic forces at work in the world were not aware Christ's Crucifixion would lead to exaltation, "for had they

---

6. Eliza R. Snow, cited in "Lucy Mack Smith, History, 1845," 334, The Joseph Smith Papers, accessed August 25, 2020, https://www.josephsmithpapers.org/paper-summary/lucy-mack-smith-history-1845/343.

7. For an expanded perspective on Christ's victory over Satan, see Gregory A. Boyd, "Christus Victor View," in *The Nature of the Atonement: Four Views*, ed. James Beilby and Paul R. Eddy (Downers Grove, IL: Intervarsity Press, 2006): 23–49.

8. N. T. Wright, *The Day the Revolution Began* (New York: HarperCollins, 2016), 259.

9. Wright, *Day the Revolution Began*, 259–60.

known it, they would not have crucified the Lord of glory" (1 Cor. 2:8).[10]

Knowing of the Savior's victory on Calvary can sustain us when life becomes crushingly burdensome. One friend shared this story with me:

> I experienced a time when many things went wrong. There was growing contention at my workplace, to the point where I sometimes didn't even want to show up. This increased the nervousness I felt about how upcoming management changes would affect me. At the same time, a side job I had been counting on fell through, costing me a great deal of money that I had already allocated to the family budget. Moreover, I made some poor investment decisions that led to anxiety about my family's financial future. All of this led me to feel increasingly discouraged.
>
> Amid these challenges, I spent some time thinking about Jesus Christ. I realized that because of his Atonement, I can return to live with him and Heavenly Father. Everything I was worried about was temporal and probably would resolve itself within a few months or years. And even if these things did *not* work out, from the viewpoint of eternity, everything was going to be just fine. Having this perspective completely changed the way I felt about my circumstances.

Knowing that Christ *has been* and *will always be* victorious gives us a priceless perspective. It worked for my friend, and it worked for Paul, who while imprisoned, wrote of Christ's triumph. It can also work for each of us. We will face serious difficulties in the coming days. Mistakes and missed opportunities, sorrows and sickness, disappointments and death will come to each of us. But we can face our challenges with an optimistic perspective when we know that Jesus has already triumphed over sin and death.

---

10. Perhaps this is why an early hymn sung by the Latter-day Saints states, "Satan rages at his loss, and hates the doctrine of the cross." *A Collection of Sacred Hymns for the Church of Jesus Christ of Latter Day Saints* (Nauvoo, IL: E. Robinson, 1841), no. 65.

The day will come when "God shall wipe away all tears from their eyes; and there shall be no more death, neither sorrow, nor crying, neither shall there be any more pain" (Rev. 21:4). This day is coming because of "Christ that died, yea rather, that is risen again, who . . . maketh intercession for us" (Rom. 8:34). When we are connected with Christ, we can not only look ahead to future peace but also feel peace in our lives today. Right now. We can trust in a triumphant Savior who is working on our behalf in this very moment and forever.

DRAWS US TO HIM THROUGH THE CROSS

Consider the following parable: A mother loved her daughter. When the daughter was young, the mother would pull her close and read stories to her each night. Sadly, the daughter rebelled in her teenage years despite the mother's efforts to keep her close. After graduating from high school, the daughter left home and cut off all communication with her mother. The mother constantly longed to draw her daughter close to her again. One day, the mother received an unexpected phone call from her daughter. Through tears, her daughter explained that she had kidney failure. To live, she needed a new kidney. Before her daughter could apologize for her past behavior, the mother volunteered to donate her own kidney to save her. The mother's kidney was compatible, and the daughter returned home to receive the transplant. The mother's willing sacrifice drew her daughter back to her.

In the New Testament, Jesus Christ said that when he would be "lifted up from the earth" (that is, crucified), he would "draw all men unto [him]" (John 12:31–32). The Greek word *pros*, translated as "unto" in this verse, also means "toward," as in pulling somebody closer *toward* you.[11] Just as the mother's sacrifice in the parable brought her daughter home, Christ's sacrifice draws us nearer to him.

Some people think to themselves, "Why did the Savior have to die

---

11. See Blue Letter Bible Lexicon, s.v. "*pros*," accessed August 1, 2020, https://www .blueletterbible.org/lang/lexicon/lexicon.cfm?Strongs=G4314&t=KJV.

such a terrible death?" Jesus answered that question—to bring us closer to him. Paul explained that Christ "*died for us*, that . . . we should *live together with him*" (1 Thes. 5:10). The purpose of Christ's Crucifixion is to bring us to where he is. He laid down his life *for* us so he could have a life *with* us.

THE SCANDAL OF THE CROSS

What if you were called to preach the gospel to a group of people who believed that anybody who saw God was cursed? It would be pretty difficult to teach people about Joseph Smith and the First Vision! The Apostle Paul faced a similar situation when telling people about the Savior's Atonement. He wrote that preaching of "Christ crucified" was "a *stumblingblock*" to the Jews (1 Cor. 1:23). The Greek word translated as "stumblingblock" in this passage is *skandalon*. You don't need to understand Greek to recognize this as the root of the English word *scandal*. Christ's Crucifixion was scandalous to many Jewish people. Why?

Devout Jews were familiar with Deuteronomy 21:22–23, which states that those who were hung on a tree (including those being crucified) were "accursed of God." Imagine being an early Christian missionary, telling Jewish people about the Savior. "Have you heard about Jesus Christ?" you might ask. "He worked miracles, taught with power, and died for our sins on the cross."

"What?" your listeners respond. "He was hung on a tree? He must be cursed!" It is easy to see how the message that Christ bore "our sins in his own body on the tree" would be scandalous to Jewish listeners (1 Pet. 2:24). Paul reversed the scandal by teaching that everybody is cursed because nobody perfectly keeps all the commandments (see Gal. 3:10; compare Deut. 28:15). Paul in essence taught, "Yes, Christ was cursed—but he was cursed for us, and by doing so, he redeemed us from being unable to fully comply with God's laws. His curse overcomes our curse" (see Gal. 3:13).

Christ's Crucifixion was also a stumbling block for the Greeks. Paul wrote, "We preach Christ crucified . . . [which is] unto the Greeks foolishness" (1 Cor. 1:22–23). Greeks contemplating converting to Christianity would need to trade in their powerful gods for one who died a disgraceful death of the sort that was not even discussed in polite society. The idea of worshipping a being who shamefully died was ludicrous to the Greeks. As Martin Hengel, an eminent Christian scholar, wrote:

> [For Greeks] to believe that the . . . son of the one true God, the mediator at creation and the redeemer of the world, had appeared in very recent times in out-of-the-way Galilee as a member of the obscure people of the Jews, and even worse, had died the death of a common criminal on the cross, could only be regarded as a sign of madness. The real gods of Greece and Rome could be distinguished from mortal men by the very fact that they were immortal—they had absolutely nothing in common with the cross as a sign of shame.[12]

Even though the Jews thought the message of the cross was scandalous and the Greeks believed it was foolishness, Paul relentlessly proclaimed "Christ crucified" (1 Cor. 1:23). The message of Christianity is more acceptable in our day than it was in Paul's, but all of us will have opportunities to stand up for the Savior in situations where his teachings seem foolish to some. In future days the message of the life, death, and Resurrection of Jesus Christ may become increasingly scandalous. Elder Robert D. Hales of the Quorum of the Twelve taught, "'The Family: A Proclamation to the World' was given long before we experienced the challenges now facing the family. 'The Living Christ: The Testimony of the Apostles' was prepared in advance of when we will need it most."[13] Now, as well as in the days ahead, Paul's example

---

12. Martin Hengel, *Crucifixion: In the Ancient World and the Folly of the Message of the Cross* (Philadelphia: Fortress Press, 1977), 6–7.
13. Robert D. Hales, "Strengthening Faith and Testimony," *Ensign,* November 2013.

of boldly proclaiming the Savior encourages us to be "not ashamed of the gospel of Jesus Christ" (Rom. 1:16). Christ's Crucifixion is not scandalous—it is Jesus showing us his love.

HUMBLED AND EXALTED ON THE CROSS

Imagine you were present when Jesus prophesied, "Behold, we go up to Jerusalem; and the Son of man shall be delivered unto the chief priests, and unto the scribes; and they shall condemn him to death, and shall deliver him to the Gentiles: And they shall mock him, and shall scourge him, and shall spit upon him, and shall kill him" (Mark 10:33–34).

What would you think? How would you feel? What kind of response would be appropriate?

I'm not sure what I would think or feel, but I'll tell you what an *inappropriate* response would be. Right after this declaration from the Savior, James and John said to Jesus, "We want you to do for us whatever we ask of you" (Mark 10:35, NRSV).

What? Why would they say such a selfish thing at this tender moment?

But Jesus listened to their request, which was for each of them to get to sit next to him in heaven (see Mark 10:37). Think of it! The Savior was telling them about his impending death, and they were focused on who would get the best seats in heavenly mansions.

In response, the Savior taught James and John the importance of serving others. He said, "Whosoever of you will be the chiefest, shall be servant of all. For even the Son of man came not to be ministered unto, but to minister, and to give his life a ransom for many" (Mark 10:44–45). For Jesus, the goal was to give, not to get.

Throughout his life, rather than exalting himself, the Savior chose the path of humility. The Apostle Paul focused on this theme in a poetic passage found in Philippians 2:6–11.[14] Anglican scholar N. T. Wright

---

14. Some scholars believe this passage is an early Christian hymn or poem, with which the Philippians would have been familiar.

notes that "the poem consists of three three-line stanzas, and the line in the middle, as it were, holds its arms out in both directions. . . . The poem is clearly telling the story of Jesus with the cross at its center."[15] Here is the text in the New Revised Standard Version, reformatted into potential poetic stanzas as identified by Wright:

Who, though he was in the form of God, did not
regard equality with God
as something to be exploited,

> but emptied himself,
> taking the form of a slave,
> being born in human likeness.

>> And being found in human form,
>> he humbled himself and became
>> obedient to the point of death—

>>> even death on a cross.

>> Therefore God also highly exalted him
>> and gave him the name
>> that is above every name,

> so that at the name of Jesus
> every knee should bend,
> in heaven and on earth and under the earth,

and every tongue should confess
that Jesus Christ is Lord,
to the glory of God the Father.

The Savior had more power than anybody else on earth, but rather than exploit his unique capabilities, he "emptied himself, taking the form of a slave." Christ disregarded the shame of the cross and instead

---

15. Wright, *Day the Revolution Began*, 254–55.

focused on the joy of helping us (see Heb. 12:2). Christ has left us this legacy of self-giving sacrifice as "an example, that [we] should follow his steps" (1 Pet. 2:21). Following Christ's example may sound hard, but remember, Jesus is looking for intention, not perfection.

One example of Christlike self-sacrifice was shown by a friend who recently made an extra effort to spend a few hours with her niece who was going through a difficult time. Her efforts to help somebody who wasn't going to return the favor reminded me of the Savior's sacrifice for us. Throughout our lives we can follow the Savior's example of self-abasing love in many simple ways. For example:

- A parent on a tight budget could forgo a personal purchase so that a child can get a snack with friends on a school field trip.
- Ministering sisters or brothers could go the extra mile for somebody who isn't easy to serve.
- People can cheerfully spend time doing an activity their spouse or friend considers important, even if it is not something they would otherwise choose to do.

The ways we can emulate Jesus Christ are endless. The specifics of how we follow Jesus's example of humble service will vary—but each of us will have the opportunity to prioritize the needs of others above our own.[16]

Paradoxically, as we lower ourselves for others, God lifts us up. It was because of Christ's humiliating "death on a cross" that God "highly exalted him" (Philip. 2:8–9). Similarly, "lifted up," a phrase John uses to describe Christ's Crucifixion, comes from the Greek word *hypsoo* and means "to exalt."[17] Ultimately, his Crucifixion was not a shameful

---

16. Of course, following Christ's example of humble service does not mean we should allow ourselves to be mistreated or taken advantage of.

17. Blue Letter Bible Lexicon, s.v. "*hypsoo*," accessed August 1, 2020, https://www.blueletterbible.org/lang/lexicon/lexicon.cfm?Strongs=G5312&t=KJV. This same Greek word is translated as "exalt" in Acts 2:33 and is related to the phrase translated as "hath highly exalted" in Philippians 2:9. See Blue Letter Bible Lexicon, s.v. "*hyperypsoo*," accessed September 1, 2020, https://www.blueletterbible.org/lang/lexicon/lexicon.cfm?Strongs=G5251&t=KJV.

death—far from it! Christ repeatedly taught he would be "lifted up" or "exalted" on the cross (see John 3:14–15; 8:28; 12:32–34). Humility is intertwined with exaltation; Peter wrote, "*Humble yourselves* therefore under the mighty hand of God, *that he may exalt* [*hypsoo*] *you* in due time" (1 Pet. 5:6). Christ on the cross is a testament to the importance of this eternal principle.

<hr />

Although we might not quote Paul exactly in our next fast and testimony meeting, the New Testament teaches us that Jesus died for sinners, triumphed on Calvary, and sacrificed in order to draw all of us to him. To some of Paul's listeners the Crucifixion was scandalous, but like Paul, we can "glory . . . in the cross of our Lord Jesus Christ" (Gal. 6:14). Throughout his life, and especially in his final twenty-four hours of mortality, Christ demonstrated humility, living his teaching that "he that is greatest among you shall be your servant" (Matt. 23:11).

The authors of the New Testament focused on Christ's Crucifixion and point us to its saving significance. President Harold B. Lee stressed the importance of following their examples in our day: "It would be our hope and prayer that . . . in all our activities and all our teachings, that we, like the apostle Paul, resolve to know nothing save Jesus Christ and him crucified."[18] As we treasure these teachings of the New Testament, our testimony of Jesus Christ will increase. We will be drawn to him.

---

18. Harold B. Lee, "To Know Nothing Save Jesus Christ, and Him Crucified," *Ensign*, 1973.

Chapter 5

"HE SUFFERED THE PAIN OF ALL MEN"

INSIGHTS FROM RESTORATION SCRIPTURE

A friend of mine was shopping for a new car. For the first time, he discovered the Toyota Sequoia, an eight-seater SUV—perfect for his family's needs. Once he learned about it, something interesting happened: although he had never noticed them before, he started seeing Toyota Sequoias *everywhere*. Coworkers drove them, another was right next to him on the freeway, and the parking lot was full of them at soccer games. What happened? Sequoias didn't suddenly come out of the woodwork (pun intended); rather, once my friend learned about them, he saw with new eyes how prevalent they were. He experienced what is known as the "frequency illusion."[1] This phenomenon occurs when we start more frequently seeing something we have just learned about—often in unexpected places. It's an illusion because although it seems like the thing is suddenly appearing all the time, in reality it has always been there—we are just now starting to notice it.

You have likely experienced the frequency illusion in some area of your life—including the gospel. Have you ever noticed that once you learn about a doctrinal concept, you start to see it in verses where you

---

1. This is also called the Baader-Meinhof phenomenon. See Kate Kershner, "What's the Baader-Meinhof Phenomenon?" How Stuff Works, accessed August 3, 2020, https://science.howstuffworks.com/life/inside-the-mind/human-brain/baader-meinhof-phenomenon.htm.

had overlooked it before? Speaking to the theme of this book, once we learn of the centrality of Christ's Crucifixion in conquering sin, we suddenly start seeing teachings on the saving nature of his death everywhere, including Restoration scripture—the Book of Mormon, Doctrine and Covenants, and Pearl of Great Price. With our newly noticing eyes, we discover the tender and reverent feelings ancient writers had for the cross. In fact, we see that Christ's Crucifixion takes center stage early in the Book of Mormon and is taught by almost every major speaker.[2] We also find more than twenty passages in the Doctrine and Covenants and Pearl of Great Price that refer to Christ's death.[3]

As I've reread Restoration scripture, I've discovered how it emphasizes the Savior's sacrifice on Calvary. This emphasis is not a frequency illusion—it's a doctrinal reality! Let's discover together some valuable messages from Restoration scripture that can deepen our understanding of and appreciation for one aspect of Christ's Atonement—his sacrifice on the cross.

REPEATED WITNESSES

If you had an important message to share, would you mention it only one time? Of course not! You would try to spread your news through multiple channels and ask friends to help broadcast it to others. When a message is important, you amplify it. In a similar way, the repeated mention of the redeeming power of Jesus's death in Restoration scripture helps us recognize that the Crucifixion is a core

2. There are fifteen speakers in the Book of Mormon whose individual words compose at least 1 percent of the overall text. Eleven of these individuals speak of Christ's death, including Lehi$_1$, Nephi$_1$, Jacob$_1$, King Benjamin, Abinadi, Alma$_2$, Amulek, Samuel the Lamanite, Jesus Christ, Mormon, and Moroni$_2$. The four major speakers who do not explicitly speak of Christ's death are the Lord, Isaiah, Helaman$_1$, and Moroni$_1$. For discussions on why "Jesus Christ" and "the Lord" are counted as separate speakers and on why differences in their word patterns matter, see John Hilton III and Jana Johnson, "The Word *Baptize* in the Book of Mormon," *Interpreter: A Journal of Mormon Scripture* 29 (2018): 65–80.

3. See D&C 18:11–12; 20:23; 21:9; 27:2; 35:2; 45:4–5, 52; 46:13; 53:2; 54:1; 76:35, 39, 41; 110:4; 138:5, 7, 13, 27, 35, 57; Moses 7:47, 55.

principle the Lord wants all people to deeply understand. For example, in the Book of Mormon we learn that

- Lehi taught that Jesus "*layeth down his life* . . . that he may bring to pass the resurrection of the dead," and Christ's Crucifixion was part of Nephi's vision of the tree of life (2 Ne. 2:8; 1 Ne. 11:33)

- An angel revealed to Jacob that those in Jerusalem would "scourge [Christ] and *crucify him*" (2 Ne. 6:9).

- King Benjamin prophesied of Christ's Crucifixion, and Abinadi declared that the Savior would "be led, *crucified*, and slain . . . having . . . *died, to redeem them* from their transgressions" (Mosiah 3:9; 15:7–8, 12).

- Alma the Elder taught King Noah's people that "the *redemption* of the people . . . was to be brought to pass *through the . . . death of Christ*" (Mosiah 18:2).

- Alma the Younger explained that Christ "will take upon him death, that he may loose the bands of death," and Amulek testified, "*The death of Christ shall loose the bands* of this temporal death" (Alma 7:12; 11:42).

- Aaron's powerful testimony that "the sufferings and *death of Christ atone* for [our] sins" prompted the king of the Lamanites to ask, "What shall I do that I may be born of God?" (Alma 22:14–15).

- As Christ's birth approached, Nephi, the son of Helaman, testified that Christ would be "lifted up," and Samuel the Lamanite taught, "[Christ] surely must *die, that salvation may come*" (Hel. 8:14; 14:15).

- Inspired people spoke "concerning the *redemption* which the Lord would make . . . and they did testify boldly of *his death*" (3 Ne. 6:20).

- When Christ visited people in the Western Hemisphere, he personally emphasized his Crucifixion (3 Ne. 11:14–15; 27:14–15).

- In his final words written on the plates, Mormon urged readers to "believe in Jesus Christ . . . *that he was slain* . . . and . . . brought to pass the *redemption* of the world" (Morm. 7:5–7; see also 3:21).

• Moroni taught that Christ was "lifted up upon the cross" and laid down his life "to prepare a place for the children of men" (Ether 4:1; 12:33).

The beloved Book of Mormon prophets reach through the centuries, consistently concentrating our attention on the importance of the Savior's death in our behalf. Nephi said his whole purpose was to persuade us to come unto Jesus (see 1 Ne. 6:4). Learning about Christ's Crucifixion is a key part of this process.

EVIDENCE OF OUR WORTH

Christian author Cecil A. Newell shared an insight into our worth by describing a television show in which antique specialists examined people's old possessions, looking for items of value. He wrote:

It is always of special interest to see how someone discovers through an expert valuer that some old painting or piece of pottery, which the owner thought was of no great worth, was a real treasure for which people might pay many thousands of [dollars]. It is the price that someone is willing to pay for it that reveals its great value. When people look to the cross of Calvary, where Jesus died for the salvation of mankind, they learn the true worth of a human soul. They see what God was willing to pay for them and realize that their lives must be of immense value. Anyone who looks to that cross and says, "He loved me and gave Himself for me," can never again doubt the supreme worth and importance of his life.[4]

Keep this in mind as you read Doctrine and Covenants 18:10–11: "Remember the worth of souls is great in the sight of God; for behold [meaning "fix the eyes upon"[5]] the Lord your Redeemer suffered death

---

4. Cecil Andrew Newell, *Pilgrims: On a Journey in Company, Part Three* (n.p.: Lulu.com, 2015), 32–33.
5. *American Dictionary of the English Language* (1828), ed. Noah Webster, s.v. "behold,"

in the flesh . . . that all men might repent and come unto him."[6] In this passage, the evidence Christ provides for our great worth is his death for us. Stop and think about this for a moment. *Really*—think about it. His Crucifixion is a key way Christ showed you and me how much he values us. His death on the cross was an act of love, evidence of what we mean to him.

Before Elder F. Enzio Busche of the Seventy joined the Church, he was hospitalized with a serious liver infection. Believing he was about to die, he began to panic, realizing that he had not prepared himself to meet God. He wrote, "On the wall of my [hospital] room was a cross with the crucified Christ on it. It was the only object on the wall, and as I focused upon it, I developed a tremendous hope: If it were true that there was a Son of God named Jesus, who died *for me* also, then this was the greatest news ever spread in the history of mankind. I knew that I needed someone to do something *for me* that I could not do for myself—to wash me clean."[7]

As Elder Busche focused on the cross, he began to realize that Jesus Christ was his personal Savior; this perspective changed his beliefs about his own potential and helped him powerfully witness to others of the Savior's love. As sung by the early Saints, "Happy beyond description he who knows 'The Saviour died *for me*!'"[8] When we truly know that Christ died for us personally, we can more clearly see our own worth and the worth of others. This can, in turn, increase our desire to share the gospel with those around us (see D&C 18:10–16).

---

accessed July 7, 2020, http://webstersdictionary1828.com/Dictionary/behold.

6. In this quotation, I use punctuation from the first edition of the Doctrine and Covenants (1835). See *Doctrine and Covenants of the Church of the Latter Day Saints* (Kirtland, OH: F. G. Williams and Co., 1835), 43:3, available at https://www.josephsmithpapers.org/paper-summary/doctrine-and-covenants-1835/180.

7. F. Enzio Busche and Tracie A. Lamb, *Yearning for the Living God: Reflections from the Life of F. Enzio Busche* (Salt Lake City: Deseret Book, 2004), 52.

8. *A Collection of Sacred Hymns for the Church of Jesus Christ of Latter Day Saints* (Kirtland, OH: E. Robinson, 1841), no. 17.

CHRIST'S PERSONAL EMPHASIS

In Restoration scripture, Jesus himself frequently focuses on the importance of his Crucifixion.[9] To help us understand his teachings about this sacred event, let's look at two examples of how the Savior refers to his death.

When Christ taught his disciples in the New World, he defined his gospel—notice the centrality of his Crucifixion in this description:

> This is the gospel which I have given unto you—that I came into the world to do the will of my Father, because my Father sent me. And my Father sent me that I might be *lifted up upon the cross*; and after that I had been *lifted up upon the cross*, that I might draw all men unto me, that as I have been *lifted up* by men even so should men be lifted up by the Father, to stand before me, to be judged of their works, whether they be good or whether they be evil—And for this cause have I been *lifted up.* (3 Ne. 27:13–15)[10]

As the Savior continues his definition of the gospel, he discusses faith, repentance, baptism, and enduring to the end (see 3 Ne. 27:13–21), but he mentions his Crucifixion more than anything else. The core of Christ's definition of his gospel in 3 Nephi 27 is repeated four times: *God sent Jesus to earth to be lifted up on the cross for you and me.*

Another example of Jesus Christ personally referencing his Crucifixion is recorded in the Doctrine and Covenants: "Listen to him who is *the advocate* with the Father, who is *pleading your cause* before

---

9. See 3 Ne. 9:21–22; 11:14; 27:14; 28:6; D&C 6:37; 27:2; 35:2; 45:4–5, 52; 53:2; 110:4.

10. In a modern revelation, the Savior similarly emphasizes his Crucifixion when defining his gospel: "And this is the gospel, the glad tidings, which the voice out of the heavens bore record unto us—That he came into the world, even Jesus, to be crucified for the world, and to bear the sins of the world, and to sanctify the world, and to cleanse it from all unrighteousness; That through him all might be saved whom the Father had put into his power and made by him" (D&C 76:40–42).

him—Saying: Father, *behold ["look at"*[11]*]* the sufferings and death of him who did no sin. . . . Wherefore, Father, *spare these . . .* that believe on my name" (D&C 45:2–5; see also 110:3–4). In this passage we learn that Christ uses his atoning suffering and death to advocate to the Father on our behalf. Envision yourself standing next to Christ, who is personally pleading for you: "Father, please forgive my beloved friend. I love her so much, I died for her." What would that be like? What would you feel?

In the Savior's own teachings on the Crucifixion, we learn that his death is central to his gospel and a principal piece of evidence he uses to advocate for us. These are only two themes among many that Christ repeatedly emphasizes concerning the importance of his death. Do we hear him? As we become more aware of and attentive to the Savior's personal teachings about what transpired on Calvary, we will feel increasing gratitude for his atoning sacrifice.

SYMBOLIC REFERENCES TO CHRIST'S CRUCIFIXION

Three prominent symbols used in the Book of Mormon—the tree of life, a seed, and the brazen serpent—directly relate to Christ's Crucifixion. Let's examine them together.

The Tree of Life

When Nephi asked to know the interpretation of the tree his father saw, he saw in vision a beautiful young woman, Mary, living in Nazareth. Nephi next saw Jesus lowering himself from his heavenly status by being born as a helpless baby, baptized, and then "lifted up upon the cross and slain for the sins of the world" (1 Ne. 11:13, 20–21, 27, 33).

As Nephi conversed with the angel, he came to understand that the tree Lehi saw represents "the love of God" (1 Ne. 11:21–22). Since the Savior showed us that love by laying down his life, it becomes clear the tree of life can represent Christ's Crucifixion (see John 15:13). I

---

11. *American Dictionary of the English Language,* s.v. "behold," accessed July 6, 2020, http://webstersdictionary1828.com/Dictionary/behold.

love the juxtaposition of these two trees: the tree of life and the tree, or wood, Christ hung from. The tree of life can represent the cross, and because we would all be spiritually and physically dead without the Savior's Crucifixion, perhaps the cross itself is a tree of life.[12]

The Seed

Christ's Crucifixion was also an important part of Alma's message to the Zoramites. Alma told the Zoramites, "We will compare *the word* unto a seed" (Alma 32:28; see also John 1:1, 14). This statement is sometimes misread as Alma comparing faith to a seed, but in fact, he compares *the word* to a seed. This distinction is important since the Zoramites want to know "how they should plant the seed, or *the word* of which he had spoken" (Alma 33:1). Even though "the word" could have multiple meanings, Alma implies he is referring to a *specific* word. At the end of his discourse, he teaches that Christ will "come to redeem his people and that he shall *suffer and die to atone* for their sins; and . . . he shall rise again from the dead, which shall bring to pass the resurrection" (Alma 33:22). In the very next verse, Alma states, "I desire that ye shall plant *this word* in your hearts" (Alma 33:23). Thus it appears the *word* the Zoramites were to plant is the doctrine that Christ's sufferings and death atone for our sins and that his Resurrection will bring to pass our own.[13]

How does recognizing that the *seed* and the *word* are Christ's suffering, death, and Resurrection affect our understanding of Alma's message? Consider the following phrases from Alma's discourse, with the above-stated definitions in mind:

- "Give place, that a seed may be *planted in your heart*" (Alma 32:28).

---

12. The representation of the cross as a tree of life is often found in medieval artwork. See, for example, Pacino di Bonaguida, *Tree of Life*, 1305–10, panel painting, Accademia Gallery, Florence, Italy.

13. See Jennifer C. Lane, *Finding Christ in the Covenant Path: Ancient Insights for Modern Life* (Provo, UT: Religious Studies Center, Brigham Young University, 2020), 150.

- "*Nourish* the word" (Alma 32:41). To *nourish* means "to feed and cause to grow."[14]
- "Because of your *diligence and your faith and your patience* with the word *in nourishing it,* that it may take root in you, behold, by and by . . . ye shall *feast upon this fruit*" (Alma 32:42).

We are blessed when we follow Alma's counsel to give place in our hearts for Christ's sufferings, death, and Resurrection. As we work to grow our testimonies, are we sufficiently centered on the Savior? By continuing to act on Alma's invitations, we will taste the "most precious" fruit that is "sweet above all that is sweet" (Alma 32:42).[15]

The Brazen Serpent

After Moses led his people out of Egypt, many of the Israelites complained about the food they had to eat. As a result, "the Lord sent fiery serpents among the people, and they bit the people; and much people of Israel died." When the people repented, the Lord told Moses to make a serpent and put it on a pole, promising that everyone who looked at the serpent would live (see Num. 21:6–8).

Nephi, the son of Helaman, teaches that these events parallel Christ's death: "And as [Moses] lifted up the brazen serpent in the wilderness, even so shall he be *lifted up* who should come" (Hel. 8:14). The phrase "lifted up" is frequently used to signify Christ's Crucifixion (see John 12:32–33; 3 Ne. 27:14). As the Israelites were able to look at the lifted-up serpent and be healed, we can look to the Savior, "lifted up," and find spiritual healing in all of our struggles.

---

14. *American Dictionary of the English Language,* s.v. "nourish," accessed July 6, 2020, http://webstersdictionary1828.com/Dictionary/nourish.
15. Alma describes the fruit of the tree as being "sweet above all that is sweet, and . . . white above all that is white, yea, and pure above all that is pure" (Alma 32:42). These words echo Lehi's description of the fruit of the tree he saw in 1 Nephi 8:11, tying together these Book of Mormon symbols of Christ's Crucifixion. In addition, in the New Testament Christ himself used a "seed" parable, which also alludes to his death. Just after saying to his apostles that "the hour is come," Jesus said that "except a corn of wheat fall into the ground and die, it abideth alone: but if it die, it bringeth forth much fruit" (John 12:24).

The tree of life, the seed, and the brazen serpent are key symbols in the Book of Mormon, each of which provides a powerful witness of Christ's Crucifixion. As we "plant *this word* in [our] hearts," we can experience "the love of God" and be filled with "gladness and . . . rejoice" (Alma 33:23; 1 Ne. 11:25; Hel. 8:17).

THE SAVIOR'S SUFFERING OF OUR PAINS

In recent years, Church leaders have increasingly emphasized that as part of his Atonement, Jesus Christ experienced our pains and afflictions.[16] In Restoration scripture, only three passages speak of the Savior suffering our pains, and each one has some relationship with the death of Christ.[17]

First, Nephi's brother Jacob teaches, "[Christ] suffereth the pains of all men, yea, the pains of every living creature, both men, women, and children, who belong to the family of Adam. And he suffereth this [the pains of all people] that the resurrection might pass upon all men, that all might stand before him at the great and judgment day" (2 Ne. 9:21–22). Although Jacob does not state when or where this suffering would occur, he links Christ's suffering the pains of all people to the Resurrection. This connection may allude to Lehi's teachings to Jacob that Christ "layeth down his life . . . that he may bring to pass the resurrection" (2 Ne. 2:8), suggesting that Christ's death is part of the suffering Jacob was describing.

Second, Alma the Younger provides this powerful teaching: "[Christ] shall go forth, suffering pains and afflictions and temptations of every kind" (Alma 7:11).[18] The very next verse simultaneously

---

16. For example, Elder Neal A. Maxwell taught: "We can confidently cast our cares upon the Lord because, through the agonizing events of Gethsemane and Calvary, atoning Jesus is already familiar with our sins, sicknesses, and sorrows." "Yet Thou Art There," *Ensign*, November 1987, 32.

17. The Bible makes it clear that Christ experienced our pains and frailties but does not specifically mention where this suffering took place. See, for example, Isa. 53:4; Heb. 4:15–16.

18. The phrase "go forth" suggests not a one-time event but a continual suffering throughout

speaks of the Savior's death and his experiencing our infirmities: "He will take upon him death, that he may loose the bands of death which bind his people; and he will take upon him their infirmities" (Alma 7:12). Although this passage does not directly state that Christ suffered our pains on the cross, in between the parallel statements that Christ suffered "pains and afflictions" and that "he will take upon him their infirmities" is the declaration "He will take upon him death." This construction suggests that at least part of Christ's experiencing of our pains may have occurred on the cross.

A third scriptural example of Christ suffering our pain through his death comes in the Doctrine and Covenants: "The Lord your Redeemer suffered death in the flesh; wherefore he suffered the pain of all men, that all men might repent and come unto him" (D&C 18:11). If in this verse we understand "pain" to mean our afflictions and sorrow, this scripture is yet another indicator that the Lord felt our cries of anguish as he died for us.[19]

As we face serious sorrows because of sickness, the wrong choices of others, personal failures, and a host of other hurts, we can gain strength knowing that Christ understands us. When we cry out in anguish, "It's not fair!" Christ compassionately calls back, "I truly understand. What happened to me wasn't fair either."

In the book of Moses, we see from the prophet Enoch that when we experience deep pain, we can find comfort at Calvary. Enoch labored

---

life. Matthew 8:16–17 appears to reference a similar prophecy as being fulfilled in the context of Christ healing the sick. Natural life experiences, as well as unusual experiences such as his fasting in the wilderness and being tempted by the devil, all contributed to his enormous capacity for empathy. See Matt. 4:1–11; see also Mosiah 3:7.

19. As my colleague Scott Woodward pointed out in a personal communication, the English word *pain* comes from the Latin word *poena*, meaning "penalty." One meaning of *pain* in Noah Webster's 1828 dictionary is "penalty; punishment suffered; suffering or evil inflicted as a punishment for a crime." It is possible that references to Christ's suffering our "pain" in Restoration scripture allude not to his experiencing our physical discomfort, but rather his paying the atoning penalty for our sins. *American Dictionary of the English Language*, s.v. "pain," accessed July 7, 2020, http://webstersdictionary1828 .com/Dictionary/pain.

for much of his life to bring people to Jesus Christ. Even though he had success with those in his own city, many other people rejected his message (see Moses 7:20, 24–26). In a vision, Enoch learned that the people would become so wicked that God would send a flood to destroy them. Enoch was devastated when he saw those he loved choose not to follow God (see Moses 7:41).

Enoch "had bitterness of soul" and said, "I will refuse to be comforted" (Moses 7:44). In response, the Lord showed Enoch "the Son of Man lifted up on the cross," causing Enoch's soul to rejoice (Moses 7:55; see also 7:47). Christ's Crucifixion was the answer to Enoch's heartache. It can be the answer to our heartache as well, no matter what type suffering we experience, be it mental, spiritual, emotional, or physical. One woman shared her experience of how looking to Christ on the cross helped her amid chronic back pain:

> I was lying on the bathroom floor in the middle of the night. I had been vomiting all night and was too weak even to crawl back to my bed. My back felt like it was on fire—the inflammation in each individual vertebra of my spine was the worst it had been. . . .
>
> With the eye of faith, I saw Christ on the cross . . . taking on physical pain far greater than my own. Thorns in his head, blood dripping down his face, nails in his hands and feet, love in his face. I felt his pain in my own body, the fire in my spine intensifying as I looked at him. But I also felt him holding me like a child. . . .
>
> I was completely overwhelmed with the knowledge that my God not only knows what's wrong with my body even when no human doctor does—he also knows my physical pain more intimately than anyone else ever could. The loneliness of suffering and the frustration of not having answers were taken away in an instant. . . . Until that moment, I had never understood the relevance of Christ's death on the cross to the details of my daily life,

my pains and my joys. *Only in the light of the cross could I make sense of my own suffering.*[20]

Whether our pain is physical, mental, or emotional, whether it is inflicted by ourselves or by others, Jesus understands it. Shalissa Lindsay explained that although we sometimes say Christ *felt* our pain, we can also say Christ *feels* our pain—with us, here and now:

> At some point, it dawned on me that I could speak of the Atonement in present rather than past tense. True, that victory is 100 percent complete, finalized, an absolute historical fact. Christ said, "It is finished" [John 19:30]. Yet Christ also said . . . "all things are present with me, for I know them all" (Moses 1:6). Because Jesus remembers all things as present, He can still be in the very thick of our experiences, swallowing the pain with us, here and now, whatever we are suffering. . . . He doesn't just watch our pain. It is continually before Him.[21]

I am so grateful for sacred Restoration scripture and its emphasis on the atoning efficacy of Christ's Crucifixion. Recognizing the attention that ancient prophets and symbols, as well as Christ himself, gave to our Savior's death can enhance how we feel about this sacred event. Teachings that connect Christ's death with his experiencing *our* pain and with *our* great worth can increase the love we feel for and from the Savior.

Restoration scripture does exactly what its name suggests—it restores vital truths. It also restores our knowledge of the importance of the cross. As we integrate Restoration scripture's teachings on the Savior's Crucifixion into our lives, we will more fully feel a restoration of the hope, peace, and love his Atonement brings for each of us.

---

20. Kirsten Ryken, "Why I Thank God for My Chronic Pain," The Gospel Coalition, August 22, 2018, https://www.thegospelcoalition.org/article/thank-god-chronic-pain/.
21. Shalissa Lindsay, *Answers Will Come: Trusting the Lord in the Meantime* (American Fork, UT: Covenant Communications, 2017), 23.

Chapter 6

"AN INDIVIDUAL OFFERING WITH A PERSONAL MESSAGE"

TEACHINGS FROM CHURCH LEADERS

I love general conference! As a child, one of my favorite treats was the special "conference cake" my mom would make each conference weekend. We've continued that tradition in our family[1] and also enjoy other activities that help us celebrate the opportunity to learn from living prophets. But of course, general conference is more than traditions and good food—it's an opportunity to come closer to Christ. The teachings of living prophets, along with other General Authorities and General Officers of the Church, have shaped my life on numerous occasions.

To identify what Church leaders have taught about the Savior's Crucifixion, I searched every general conference talk that references Christ's death. I discovered I had *a lot* to learn—collectively, more than 330 Church leaders have spoken of the Savior's death more than three thousand times![2] So grab some conference cake as we explore five themes discussed by Church leaders on this sacred topic.[3]

---

1. See https://johnhiltoniii.com/conference-cake/.
2. I searched a corpus of talks found on WordCruncher (http://wordcruncher.com) that includes addresses found in the *Journal of Discourses* (approx. 1850–1890) and general conference talks (approx. 1890–2020). I also searched statements from Joseph Smith as published by The Joseph Smith Papers Project (http://josephsmithpapers.org). For more details on the methodology, see the articles cited in the following note.
3. This chapter uses insights from the following three articles: John Hilton III and Joshua P. Barringer, "The Use of 'Gethsemane' by Church Leaders: 1859–2018," *BYU Studies Quarterly* 58, no. 4 (2019): 49–76; John Hilton III, Emily Hyde, and McKenna Trussel, "The Use of 'Crucifixion' by Church Leaders: 1852–2018," *BYU Studies Quarterly*

CRUCIFIED FOR THE SINS OF THE WORLD

When Church leaders speak of Christ's Crucifixion, they most frequently connect it with his atoning for our sins. In Joseph Smith's revelations, as well as his personal statements and writings, he repeatedly testified of "Jesus Christ of Nazareth, *who was crucified for the sins of the world.*"[4]

Following Joseph's death, Church leaders continued to emphasize the saving importance of Calvary. In 1860, President Brigham Young taught, "Jesus was appointed, from the beginning, *to die for our redemption,* and he suffered an excruciating *death on the cross.*"[5] Many other early Church leaders testified of Christ's redeeming death, and this emphasis continued throughout the twentieth century.

In 1920, in contrast to the more solemn tone that many speakers use when speaking of the Crucifixion, President Charles W. Penrose of the First Presidency joyfully exclaimed, "What a blessing was his crucifixion to all the world. . . . By and through him and his atonement we can be redeemed from . . . everything that is hurtful and injurious and

59, no. 1 (2020), 49–80; and John Hilton III, "Joseph Smith, Gethsemane, and the Crucifixion of Jesus Christ," in *How and What We Worship: Christology and Praxis in the Revelations of Joseph Smith*, ed. Rachel Cope, Carter Charles, and Jordan Watkins (Provo, UT: Religious Studies Center, Brigham Young University, 2020), 303–29. Special gratitude is extended to Joshua P. Barringer, Emily Hyde, and McKenna Trussel for their work on these articles, which are available at http://johnhiltoniii.com/crucifixion/.

4.   "Account of Meetings, Revelation, and Blessing, 5–6 December 1834," [19], The Joseph Smith Papers, accessed August 13, 2019, https://www.josephsmithpapers.org/paper-summary/account-of-meetings-revelation-and-blessing-5-6-december-1834/3. Joseph's peers expressed similar feelings regarding the atoning nature of Christ's Crucifixion. For example, Orson Hyde spoke of "Him who died to save me and wash me from my sins, in his own most precious blood," and Oliver Cowdrey spoke of "the blood of a Saviour, who groaned upon Calvary's summit, to expiate our sins and cleans us from all unrighteousness." "Times and Seasons, 15 July 1842," 850, The Joseph Smith Papers, accessed October 24, 2019, https://www.josephsmithpapers.org/paper-summary/times-and-seasons-15-july-1842/4?highlight=die%20sins; "History, 1834–1836," 81, The Joseph Smith Papers, accessed May 4, 2019, https://www.josephsmithpapers.org/paper-summary/history-1834-1836/85.

5.   Brigham Young, in *Journal of Discourses*, 26 vols. (Liverpool: F. D. Richards, 1855–86), 8:115 (July 8, 1860).

that brings unhappiness."[6] We too can embrace this perspective of joy and gratitude when we think of Christ's Crucifixion as a blessing!

Recent Church leaders have continued to focus on Christ's atoning for our sins on the cross. President Dallin H. Oaks testified, "I know . . . Jesus Christ died for our sins and is our Savior."[7] Sister Silvia H. Allred, then a member of the Relief Society General Presidency, stated, "Jesus Christ took upon Himself our sins, suffered, and died to satisfy the demands of justice that we might not suffer if we repent."[8]

The reality that Christ was crucified for our sins has been taught by every Church President. Every single one. This is significant. The following chart contains illustrative statements from each President of the Church regarding the saving importance of Christ's Crucifixion:

Joseph Smith	"He *died* for the sins of all men."[9]
Brigham Young	"Jesus *died* to redeem the world."[10]
John Taylor	"He *was . . . crucified . . .* to open up the way of life and salvation, that man might attain to exaltation."[11]
Wilford Woodruff	"Jesus Christ . . . *died* as a ransom for the sins of the world."[12]

6. Charles W. Penrose, in *Ninetieth Annual Conference of The Church of Jesus Christ of Latter-day Saints* (Salt Lake City: The Church of Jesus Christ of Latter-day Saints, 1920), 33. This positive perspective is also found in many hymns. For example, a hymn in the Church's 1840 hymnbook referred to Calvary as the "happiest place." *A Collection of Sacred Hymns, for the Church of Jesus Christ of Latter-day Saints, in Europe* (Manchester: W. B. Thomas, 1840), no. 26.

7. Dallin H. Oaks, "Why Do We Serve?" *Ensign*, November 1984.

8. Silvia H. Allred, "Steadfast and Immovable," *Ensign*, November 2010.

9. "History, 1838–1856, volume C-1 [2 November 1838–31 July 1842]," 1014, The Joseph Smith Papers, accessed August 3, 2020, https://www.josephsmithpapers.org/paper-summary/history-1838-1856-volume-c-1-2-november-1838-31-july-1842/186.

10. Brigham Young, in *Journal of Discourses*, 3:96 (August 8, 1852).

11. John Taylor, in *Journal of Discourses*, 16:307 (November 16, 1873).

12. Wilford Woodruff, in *Journal of Discourses*, 19:360 (June 30, 1878).

Lorenzo Snow	"[They understood that] Jesus . . . *would die* for their sins, *and be crucified* in order to complete the plan of salvation."[13]
Joseph F. Smith	"Redemption [was] wrought . . . upon the *cross*."[14]
Heber J. Grant	"Jesus . . . came to the earth with a divinely appointed mission *to die* for the redemption of mankind."[15]
George Albert Smith	"Jesus *was crucified* by sinful men for the sins of the world, yea, for the remission of sins unto the contrite heart."[16]
David O. McKay	"He was *crucified* for the sins of the world."[17]
Joseph Fielding Smith	"On the *cross* he paid the price for our sins and at the same time for Adam's transgression."[18]
Harold B. Lee	"[Jesus] suffered to *his death upon the cross* for the sins of mankind."[19]
Spencer W. Kimball	"We proclaim the divine sonship of Jesus Christ and him *crucified*, that his divine sacrifice was a ransom for all mankind."[20]

---

13. Lorenzo Snow, in *Journal of Discourses*, 14:303 (January 14, 1872).
14. D&C 138:35.
15. Heber J. Grant, in *Ninety-First Annual Conference of The Church of Jesus Christ of Latter-day Saints* (Salt Lake City: Deseret Book, 1921), 203.
16. George Albert Smith, in *One Hundredth Annual Conference of The Church of Jesus Christ of Latter-day Saints* (Salt Lake City: The Church of Jesus Christ of Latter-day Saints, 1930), 66. In this statement, President Smith is quoting Doctrine and Covenants 21:9.
17. David O. McKay, in *One Hundred Thirtieth Annual Conference of The Church of Jesus Christ of Latter-day Saints* (Salt Lake City: The Church of Jesus Christ of Latter-day Saints, 1960), 6.
18. Joseph Fielding Smith, in *The One Hundred Thirty-Seventh Annual Conference of The Church of Jesus Christ of Latter-day Saints* (Salt Lake City: The Church of Jesus Christ of Latter-day Saints, 1967), 122.
19. Harold B. Lee, "I Walked Today Where Jesus Walked," *Ensign*, April 1972.
20. Spencer W. Kimball, "The Stone Cut without Hands," *Ensign*, May 1976.

Ezra T. Benson	"On *Calvary*, [Jesus] worked out the infinite and eternal atonement."[21]
Howard W. Hunter	"I know Jesus Christ is his Son. He *gave his life* in the great atoning sacrifice whereby he became my Savior, your Savior."[22]
Gordon B. Hinckley	"[Jesus] *gave His life on Calvary's cross* to pay the debt of mortal sin."[23]
Thomas S. Monson	"Jesus the Christ . . . took upon himself the sins of the world and so *willingly died* that we might forever live."[24]
Russell M. Nelson	"[Jesus was] *slain* for the sins of the world."[25]

The quotes in this list are only a tiny fraction of statements Church leaders have made about Christ's atoning for our sins on the cross. No matter what sins we have committed, repentance and redemption are available through Jesus Christ. If our loved ones have wandered from the Good Shepherd's gentle care, we can have confidence that they can find forgiveness through returning to him. Christ's Crucifixion provides hope for us all!

THE INDIVIDUAL NATURE OF CHRIST'S CRUCIFIXION

While the knowledge that Christ atoned for the sins of all humanity is important, it may be even more powerful to know that he suffered and died for each of us personally. One of my favorite insights

---

21. *The Teachings of Ezra Taft Benson* (Salt Lake City: Bookcraft, 1988), 72.
22. Howard W. Hunter, in *One Hundred Fortieth Semi-annual Conference of The Church of Jesus Christ of Latter-day Saints* (Salt Lake City: The Church of Jesus Christ of Latter-day Saints, 1970), 132.
23. Gordon B. Hinckley, "The Victory over Death," *Ensign*, May 1985.
24. Thomas S. Monson, in *One Hundred Thirty-Fifth Annual Conference of The Church of Jesus Christ of Latter-day Saints* (Salt Lake City: The Church of Jesus Christ of Latter-day Saints, 1965), 143.
25. Russell M. Nelson, "Perfection Pending," *Ensign*, November 1995.

from Church leaders concerns the individual nature of Christ's experience on the cross. In 1929, President Heber J. Grant taught, "Not only did Jesus come as a universal gift, *He came as an individual offering with a personal message to each one of us.* For each of us He died on Calvary and His blood will conditionally save us. Not as nations, communities or groups, but *as individuals.*"[26]

I love pondering President Grant's statement: "He came as an individual offering with a personal message to each one of us." What is Christ's personal message for you? For me, the personal message from the Savior on the cross is "I love you. I see you. I know you. I will always care for you." Can you hear his personal message to you?

In 1989, Elder John H. Groberg of the Seventy testified that Christ saw us from Calvary: "I feel that as he hung upon the cross and looked out over the dark scene, he saw more than mocking soldiers and cruel taunters. . . . His huge, magnanimous, loving soul encompassed all eternity and took in all people and all times and all sins and all forgiveness and all everything. Yes, *he saw down to you and to me* and provided us an all-encompassing opportunity to escape the terrible consequences of death and sin."[27] Christ saw down to you and me in that moment. Can you picture yourself looking up at him? How would it feel to lock eyes with the one who perfectly understands us?

Elder Merrill J. Bateman of the Seventy also taught that Christ suffered for us individually:

> For many years I thought of the Savior's experience in the garden and on the cross as places where a large mass of sin was heaped upon Him. . . . However, my view has changed. Instead of an impersonal mass of sin, there was a long line of people, as Jesus felt "our infirmities" (Heb. 4:15), "[bore] our griefs, . . . carried our sorrows . . . [and] was bruised for our iniquities" (Isa. 53:4–5).

---

26. Heber J. Grant, "The Greatest Gift," *Juvenile Instructor*, December 1929, 697.
27. John H. Groberg, "The Beauty and Importance of the Sacrament," *Ensign*, May 1989.

The Atonement was an intimate, personal experience in which Jesus came to know how to help each of us.[28]

Christ sees and knows us as individuals—we have had and will have individual moments with him. He is not a distant Savior. Elder Gerrit W. Gong, then of the Seventy, taught that Christ was "lifted up upon the cross that He might draw each of us, *by name*, to Him."[29] Similarly, Bishop Gérald Caussé taught, "[Jesus] died for each one of us, *personally*, as if you or I were the only person on earth. He extends to us a personal invitation to come unto Him and draw upon the marvelous blessings of His Atonement."[30]

Others, including our loved ones, may not understand the personal struggles we are going through—but Jesus does, and knowing he understands can strengthen us in difficult moments. James Stokes wrote about his experience with serious illnesses that required him to have more than fifty surgeries before the age of thirty:

> On what felt like the darkest and most dismal night I had ever faced, . . . negativity engulfed me, and I began to doubt all I had been taught about my Heavenly Father and His Son, Jesus Christ. A loving God, I rationalized, would not have left me alone to face this nightmarish reality.
>
> Worst of all, no one knew what I was going through. My family felt a portion, but they did not fully understand how painful my experiences had been. No one did. I was about to voice these thoughts in prayer when I heard my name.
>
> Through my anguish I recognized the voice of the Spirit, carrying a message to my soul from my Savior reminding me I was not alone. Jesus Christ knew what I was going through. He had felt my pain. . . . In my self-pity, I had forgotten about Jesus

28. Merrill J. Bateman, "A Pattern for All," *Ensign*, November 2005, 75–76.
29. Gerrit W. Gong, "Always Remember Him," *Ensign*, May 2016, 110.
30. Gérald Caussé, "A Living Witness of the Living Christ," *Ensign*, May 2020.

Christ . . . that in the Garden of Gethsemane and on the cross, the Lord had . . . borne my grief and carried my pain. . . .

My disabilities and the trials that accompany them have not been easy to bear. But because I know that my Savior completely understands what I am going through, even if no one else does, I know He will always be there for me.[31]

The fact that the Savior died for me and for you brings a special intimacy to our relationship with him. When we understand the personal nature of Jesus's sacrifice, his Atonement becomes a one-on-one experience between the Savior and each of us. He knows us and wants us to know him. Christ hung on the cross—not to make us feel bad, but to make us feel good. His death is a tender and personal sacrifice for us, and our acceptance of his sacrifice can be just as tender and personal to him.

THE WITHDRAWAL OF THE FATHER'S SPIRIT

In Matthew 27:46, amid the agony of his Crucifixion, the Savior cried, "My God, my God, why hast thou forsaken me?" Some Church leaders have clarified that God did not completely *forsake* his Son but rather briefly *withdrew* so that Christ could better relate to each of us.[32] Elder Charles W. Penrose, then of the Quorum of the Twelve, explained, "God had [not] forsaken Him, but He left Him to bear the brunt, that He might feel the pain . . . that He might be touched with a feeling for our infirmities, because He bore the pains of us all."[33]

Imagine seeing your child in agony and then turning away. How would you feel? I'm a parent—I know it would be excruciating! What do you think the Father felt when he temporarily withdrew from his

---

31. James G. Stokes, "Christ Has Felt My Pain," *Ensign*, July 2015.
32. This idea was first taught by Brigham Young. See *Journal of Discourses*, 3:206 (February 17, 1856).
33. Charles W. Penrose, in *Seventy-Sixth Annual Conference of The Church of Jesus Christ of Latter-day Saints* (Salt Lake City: Deseret News, 1906), 90.

Son? Elder Melvin J. Ballard of the Quorum of the Twelve provided this insight:

> [Heavenly Father] saw that Son next stretched upon the cross, and the nails driven into His flesh. He saw the quivering flesh, wounded and bleeding. . . . He saw the life blood of His beloved Son streaming and gushing out, and He stopped it not. . . . I imagine that He had looked upon that Son until even the Father could not stand it, and He turned to some secluded spot and bowed and wept for the suffering of His Son. I am so thankful in my heart that whatever doubts may have risen in His heart as He looked upon the suffering of His Son—"Shall I save him, or shall I allow him to suffer and die for the world?" O, I thank God that He decided in your favor and in my favor, and by that He has redeemed us.[34]

As we contemplate the Father and the pain he must have felt as he watched his Son suffer, we can better feel his love for his Son and for each of us.

As with all aspects of his sacrifice, Christ's feelings of forsakenness were consecrated for our blessing. Elder Jeffrey R. Holland articulated his feelings about this significant aspect of Christ's Atonement:

> It is my personal belief that in all of Christ's mortal ministry the Father may never have been closer to His Son than in these agonizing final moments of suffering. Nevertheless, that the supreme sacrifice of His Son might be as complete as it was voluntary and solitary, the Father briefly withdrew from Jesus the comfort of His Spirit, the support of His personal presence. It was required, indeed it was central to the significance of the Atonement, that this perfect Son who had never spoken ill nor done wrong nor touched an unclean thing had to know how the

---

34. Melvin J. Ballard, in *Eighty-First Semi-annual Conference of The Church of Jesus Christ of Latter-day Saints* (Salt Lake City: Deseret News, 1910), 83.

rest of humankind—us, all of us—would feel when we did commit such sins. For His Atonement to be infinite and eternal, He had to feel what it was like to die not only physically but spiritually, to sense what it was like to have the divine Spirit withdraw, leaving one feeling totally, abjectly, hopelessly alone.[35]

We may be humbled as we ponder Christ's feelings of forsakenness, recognizing that at least one reason the Father withdrew his Spirit was so the Savior could understand us when we feel abandoned and alone. Because of the Father's withdrawal, Christ can offer us perfect compassion when we feel detached from or even deserted by God.

Many of us will feel at times like we have been abandoned by heaven. When this happens, we can follow Christ's example on Calvary and *keep on going*. Consider the case of Mother Teresa, a devoted disciple who spent her life serving the poorest of the poor. Although she had powerful spiritual experiences as a young adult, for the final fifty years of her life, Mother Teresa often felt disconnected from God. She wrote, "In my soul I feel just that terrible pain of loss—of God not wanting me—of God not being God—of God not really existing."[36]

In time, her "questions about God's existence faded, and she began to see this searing experience as an invitation to unite herself more closely with Jesus in his abandonment on the cross and with the poor, who also feel abandoned. . . . In continuing with her ministry to the poor, she made a radical act of fidelity based on a relationship she still believed in, even if she could not sense God's presence. She trusted that earlier experience. In other words, she had faith."[37] Just as Jesus did, Mother Teresa did not quit when she felt abandoned by God. Rather, she continued in the work God had sent her to do. We can follow the example set by her and by our Savior—even when heaven feels distant.

---

35. Jeffrey R. Holland, "None Were with Him," *Ensign*, May 2009.
36. Quoted in James Martin, SJ, *Seven Last Words: An Invitation to a Deeper Friendship with Jesus* (New York: Harper Collins, 2016), 67.
37. Martin, *Seven Last Words*, 68.

Elder D. Todd Christofferson taught, "Each of us, whenever [we feel isolated] must stop and think, 'Jesus Christ died for me. Jesus Christ thought me worthy of His blood. And He loves me. He has hopes for me. And He can make a difference in my life. His grace can transform me.'"[38] We may not feel God in a way we immediately recognize, but we will not be abandoned. The Savior has promised, "I will not leave you comfortless, I will come to you" (John 14:18).

THE REOCCURRENCE OF THE PAINS OF GETHSEMANE ON THE CROSS

A few Church leaders have taught that what Christ experienced in Gethsemane reoccurred on the cross. In his landmark book *Jesus the Christ*, Elder James E. Talmage tentatively wrote, "*It seems*, that in addition to the fearful suffering incident to crucifixion, the agony of Gethsemane had recurred, intensified beyond human power to endure."[39] In his final conference talk, Elder Bruce R. McConkie taught, "While [Christ] was hanging on the cross for another three hours . . . all the infinite agonies and merciless pains of Gethsemane recurred."[40]

So far as can be determined, nobody since Elder McConkie has unambiguously stated in general conference that the specific agonies of Gethsemane returned on the cross. However, other speakers have supported the general idea of a relationship between the suffering experienced in these two events. For example, Elder Joseph B. Wirthlin taught, "Jesus Christ suffered in the Garden of Gethsemane more than you can comprehend. Willingly and lovingly, He took upon Himself not only our sins but the pains, sicknesses, and sufferings of

---

38. D. Todd Christofferson, "Is There a Place for Me?" (video), Unity in Diversity, Gospel Media, The Church of Jesus Christ of Latter-day Saints, https://www.churchofjesuschrist.org/media/video/2016-03-0020-is-there-a-place-for-me?

39. James E. Talmage, *Jesus the Christ* (Salt Lake City: Deseret Book, 1986), 661.

40. Bruce R. McConkie, "The Purifying Power of Gethsemane," *Ensign*, May 1985, 10.

all mankind. He *suffered similarly* on the cross."[41] President Russell M. Nelson declared that the agony Christ experienced in Gethsemane "*was intensified* as He was cruelly crucified on Calvary's cross."[42] These teachings from Church leaders point to an important connection between Gethsemane and Calvary.

TEACHINGS ABOUT CHRIST'S CRUCIFIXION AND GETHSEMANE

Gethsemane and Calvary are *both* vital aspects of Christ's Atonement; from a historical perspective, however, Church leaders have more frequently taught of the saving importance of Christ's Crucifixion. For each one statement by Church leaders about Christ suffering for our sins in Gethsemane, there are more than five about him dying for our sins. When looking only at the words of Church Presidents, for every one statement they have made about the atoning efficacy of Gethsemane, there are twelve such statements about Calvary.[43]

Given this emphasis, let's recall the question from my friend discussed in chapter 2: why do many Church members locate Gethsemane as the primary place of Christ's atoning suffering? One possible explanation is that three different Church leaders taught that Christ's sufferings in Gethsemane were more significant than his death at Calvary. In 1944, Elder Joseph Fielding Smith, then of the Quorum of the Twelve, became the first Church leader to explicitly attribute greater saving importance to Gethsemane than to the cross. He said:

> It is understood by many that the great suffering of Jesus Christ came through the driving of nails in His hands and in His feet, and in being suspended upon a cross, until death mercifully released Him. That is not the case. As excruciating, as severe as was that punishment . . . yet still greater was the suffering which

---

41. Joseph B. Wirthlin, "Growing into the Priesthood," *Ensign*, November 1999.
42. Russell M. Nelson, "The Correct Name of the Church," *Ensign*, November 2018.
43. See Hilton, Hyde, and Trussel, "Use of 'Crucifixion' by Church Leaders."

He endured in carrying the burden of the sins of the world—my sins, and your sins, and the sins of every living creature. This suffering came before He ever got to the cross, and it caused the blood to come forth from the pores of his body.[44]

Elder Smith made similar statements on three other occasions.[45] In 1953, Elder Marion G. Romney likewise taught that Gethsemane was the location of Christ's greatest suffering, stating, "Jesus then went into the Garden of Gethsemane. There he suffered most. He suffered greatly on the cross, of course, but other men had died by crucifixion; in fact, a man hung on either side of him as he died on the cross."[46] In both the April and October general conferences in 1982, Elder Romney again compared Gethsemane and Christ's Crucifixion, emphasizing the importance of Gethsemane each time.[47]

Between 1953 and 1982 (the years of Elder Romney's remarks), Elder Bruce R. McConkie authored two books containing statements like those from Elders Smith and Romney. In one case, Elder McConkie wrote, "It is to the Cross of Christ that most Christians look when centering their attention upon the infinite and eternal atonement. And certainly the sacrifice of our Lord was completed when he was lifted up by men. . . . But in reality the pain and suffering, the triumph and grandeur, of the atonement took place primarily in Gethsemane."[48] These statements, although very rare in comparison

44. Joseph Fielding Smith, in *One Hundred Fourteenth Annual Conference of The Church of Jesus Christ of Latter-day Saints* (Salt Lake City: The Church of Jesus Christ of Latter-day Saints, 1944), 50.

45. See *Seventy-Seventh Semi-annual Conference of The Church of Jesus Christ of Latter-day Saints* (Salt Lake City: Deseret News, 1947), 147–48; *Doctrines of Salvation*, comp. Bruce R. McConkie (Salt Lake City: Bookcraft, 1954), 1:130; and *Seek Ye Earnestly* (Salt Lake City: Deseret Book, 1970), 119–21.

46. Marion G. Romney, in *One Hundred Twenty-Fourth Semi-annual Conference of The Church of Jesus Christ of Latter-day Saints* (Salt Lake City: The Church of Jesus Christ of Latter-day Saints, 1953), 35.

47. Marion G. Romney, "The Resurrection of Jesus," *Ensign*, May 1982; Marion G. Romney, "Gratitude and Thanksgiving," *Ensign*, November 1982.

48. Bruce R. McConkie, *Doctrinal New Testament Commentary*, vol. 1 (Salt Lake City:

to those about the saving importance of Calvary, became influential in Church curriculum and other materials.

For example, a 1979 institute manual as well as the 1982 and 1986 Gospel Doctrine manuals quote the above statement from Elder McConkie to suggest that what happened in Gethsemane was more significant than what occurred on the cross.[49] Similarly, a supervisor manual for home-study seminary, used during this general period, includes the statement cited above from President Marion G. Romney.[50] Although atypical, a Sunday School manual for teenagers copyrighted in both 1975 and 1980 includes an activity specifically teaching that Christ demonstrated more love in Gethsemane than he did on Calvary.[51] In addition, the influential but noncanonical *Encyclopedia of Mormonism*, published in 1992, states, "For Latter-day Saints, Gethsemane was the scene of Jesus' greatest agony, even surpassing that which he suffered on the cross."[52] While such statements had an impact on how some of us were taught, they are not in harmony with the

Bookcraft, 1973), 774; see also Bruce R. McConkie, *The Mortal Messiah: From Bethlehem to Calvary*, vol. 4 (Salt Lake City: Deseret Book, 1981), 127–28.

49. See *The Life and Teachings of Jesus & His Apostles* (Salt Lake City: The Church of Jesus Christ of Latter-day Saints, 1979), 172; *The New Testament: Gospel Doctrine Teacher's Supplement* (Salt Lake City: The Church of Jesus Christ of Latter-day Saints, 1982; 1986); 94–97.

50. *The New Testament Seminary Home Study: Supervisor Manual* (Salt Lake City: The Church of Jesus Christ of Latter-day Saints, 1979), 61. In addition, the 1979 home-study seminary manual contains statements that prioritize Gethsemane over Calvary. See *The New Testament Seminary Home Study, Unit Five/Week One: The Turning Point* (Salt Lake City: The Church of Jesus Christ of Latter-day Saints, 1979), 7, 9.

51. See *Introduction to the Scriptures, Part B* (Salt Lake City: The Church of Jesus Christ of Latter-day Saints, 1980), 56; see also Joyce N. Woodbury, "Christ's Atoning Sacrifice," *Sunstone Magazine*, November–December 1983. The 1984 edition of this manual changes the text to revise the answer to the question "What was Jesus' greatest act of love?" to include Christ's suffering on the cross in addition to his suffering at Gethsemane. Interestingly, a 1971 manual answers the question "What was [Christ's] greatest act of love for all of us?" with "His atoning sacrifice on the cross." *Introduction to the Scriptures, Part A* (Salt Lake City: The Church of Jesus Christ of Latter-day Saints, 1984), 132; *Fundamentals of the Gospel, Part 2: Living to Be a Light to the World* (Salt Lake City: The Church of Jesus Christ of Latter-day Saints, 1971), 284.

52. S. Kent Brown, "Gethsemane," in *Encyclopedia of Mormonism*, ed. Daniel H. Ludlow (New York: MacMillan, 1992), 542.

collective teachings of Church leaders past and present and do not appear in current Church manuals.

The three Church leaders who accentuated the role of Gethsemane likely had important reasons for doing so—perhaps to help members focus on an aspect of Christ's Atonement (Gethsemane) that is underappreciated by many fellow Christians. However, though these three individuals emphasized Gethsemane on occasion, they also specifically discussed the importance of Christ's Crucifixion. For example, Elder Bruce R. McConkie emphasized the Crucifixion and omitted any reference to Gethsemane when he wrote, "A testimony in our day consists of three things: . . . the knowledge that Jesus is the Lord, that he is the Son of the living God *who was crucified for the sins of the world[,]* . . . the fact that Joseph Smith was a prophet . . . [and] that The Church of Jesus Christ of Latter-day Saints is the only true and living Church."[53] At times, materials opposing the Church of Jesus Christ have used the quotations emphasizing Gethsemane, cited earlier in this chapter, to criticize the Church for not believing in the saving importance of Christ's Crucifixion. Such attacks, however, paint an incomplete picture.

Just as some statements from Church leaders highlight the importance of Gethsemane, others focus on Calvary. For example, Joseph Smith called the death of Christ one of the "fundamental principles"[54] of our religion, and General Authorities have referred to the Crucifixion

---

53. Bruce R. McConkie, "Gaining a Testimony of Christ," *Ensign*, December 1980. In 1948, Elder Marion G. Romney taught, "I believe that in Gethsemane and on the cross Jesus suffered for the sins of all men," and in 1967, Elder Joseph Fielding Smith said, "*On the cross he paid the price for our sins* and at the same time for Adam's transgression." Marion G. Romney, in *One Hundred Eighteenth Annual Conference of The Church of Jesus Christ of Latter-day Saints* (Salt Lake City: Deseret Book, 1948), 77; Joseph Fielding Smith, in *One Hundred Thirty-Seventh Annual Conference of The Church of Jesus Christ of Latter-day Saints* (Salt Lake City: The Church of Jesus Christ of Latter-day Saints, 1967), 122.

54. "*Elders' Journal*, July 1838," [44], The Joseph Smith Papers, accessed August 13, 2019, https://www.josephsmithpapers.org/paper-summary/elders-journal-july-1838/12.

as "the Rock upon which the gospel rests,"[55] "the greatest event . . . in the life of the Savior,"[56] "the most important event in all eternity,"[57] and "the greatest contribution ever made to the human race."[58]

In recent years, when discussing Christ's Atonement, Church leaders frequently talk about the importance of *both* Gethsemane and Calvary. For example, Sister Jean B. Bingham declared, "*In the Garden of Gethsemane and on the cross of Calvary*, He felt all of our pains, afflictions, temptations, sicknesses, and infirmities."[59] President Henry B. Eyring similarly stated, "Jesus Christ bore *in Gethsemane and on the cross* the weight of all our sins. He experienced all the sorrows, the pains, and the effects of our sins so that He could comfort and strengthen us through every test in life."[60] We can rejoice in the Savior's Atonement that took place both in Gethsemane and on the cross.

We have seen how the teachings of Church leaders expand our understanding of Christ's atoning sacrifice. They testify that Jesus Christ was crucified for our sins and that he suffered for each of us individually on the cross. His Atonement is infinite *and* intimate, perfect *and* personal. He knows *you*.

These truths about the Savior's Crucifixion, taught by modern prophets, expand our intellectual knowledge, but more importantly, they give us courage as we encounter serious challenges in our lives.

---

55. Orson F. Whitney, in *Ninety-Eighth Semi-annual Conference of The Church of Jesus Christ of Latter-day Saints* (Salt Lake City: The Church of Jesus Christ of Latter-day Saints, 1927), 149.

56. Rudger Clawson, in *Ninety-Second Annual Conference of The Church of Jesus Christ of Latter-day Saints* (Salt Lake City: The Church of Jesus Christ of Latter-day Saints, 1922), 47.

57. Dallin H. Oaks, "Spirituality," *Ensign*, November 1985.

58. Alma Sonne, in *One Hundred Thirty-Ninth Annual Conference of The Church of Jesus Christ of Latter-day Saints* (Salt Lake City: The Church of Jesus Christ of Latter-day Saints, 1969), 33.

59. Jean B. Bingham, "That Your Joy Might Be Full," *Ensign*, November 2017.

60. Henry B. Eyring, "Try, Try, Try," *Ensign*, November 2018.

I love these words from Elder Quentin L. Cook: "If the grim realities you are facing at this time seem dark and heavy and almost unbearable, remember that in the soul-wrenching darkness of Gethsemane and the incomprehensible torture and pain of Calvary, the Savior accomplished the Atonement, which resolves the most terrible burdens that can occur in this life. *He did it for you, and He did it for me. He did it because He loves us.*"[61]

He did it for you.

He did it for me.

Why?

Because he loves us.

---

61. Quentin L. Cook, "The Lord Is My Light," *Ensign*, May 2015.

PART III

The Events of Good Friday

Chapter 7

CRUCIFIXION IN THE ROMAN WORLD

I was eating lunch with some colleagues at a small restaurant near the Old City of Jerusalem when it suddenly dawned on me that artwork and movies, rather than historical facts, had shaped my mental representation of how Christ was crucified. I realized that although I had heard about this atoning event my entire life, I had never read a book or taken a class that provided in-depth detail about what happened to Christ on Calvary. I know I'm not the only one who has been influenced more by artwork than historical reality because as I collected questions about crucifixion in preparation for writing this book, several people asked, "Why were the thieves tied to the cross and only Christ was nailed?" Of course, this question is based on the famous Harry Anderson painting, frequently used by Latter-day Saints, and not anything stated in the scriptures.

One reason most of us don't know a lot about the process of crucifixion is that the biblical authors are relatively silent on the subject. For example, all Matthew tells us is, "When [Pilate] had scourged Jesus, he delivered him to be crucified" (Matt. 27:26). He likely assumed readers were already familiar with scourging and crucifixion and, consequently, did not provide any details. But many questions remain for modern readers: When did the practice of crucifixion begin? What do archeological artifacts and ancient historians teach us about the details of crucifixion?

What was the scourging that frequently preceded crucifixion? How were victims affixed to the cross? What was the medical cause of death in crucifixion? Let's explore answers to these and other questions.

Modern scholars have spent tens of thousands of hours writing thousands of pages detailing what is known about crucifixion in the Roman world. In this chapter, I synthesize their insights,[1] acknowledging that not all questions about crucifixion have answers.[2] If you're not interested in the historical details about crucifixion and want to skip this chapter, may I just ask one favor?

Please don't.

An accurate knowledge of ancient crucifixion can help us understand some of the horrors the Savior faced on the cross. It is impossible for us to fully comprehend the spiritual suffering Christ encountered as he atoned for our sins in Gethsemane and on Calvary. However, we can come closer to glimpsing the physical pain he felt from his excruciating experience on the cross. In fact, the word *excruciating* comes from the Latin verb *excruciare* ("to torture"), which the Romans derived from the word for "cross" (*crux*) because they identified torture with crucifixion. How poignant that the English word for extreme agony is based on crucifixion.[3]

---

1. In this chapter I draw primarily on John Granger Cook, *Crucifixion in the Mediterranean World*, 2nd ed. (Tubingen, Germany: Mohr Siebeck, 2019); and David W. Chapman and Eckhard J. Schnabel, *The Trial and Crucifixion of Jesus*, rev. ed. (Peabody, MA: Hendrickson Publishers Marketing, 2019). Scholars continue to debate several details regarding crucifixion in the Roman world. For a brief overview of relevant recent scholarship, see Felicity Harley, "Crucifixion in Roman Antiquity: The State of the Field," *Journal of Early Christian Studies* 27, no. 2 (2019): 303–23.

2. As one of the foremost scholars of crucifixion has noted, "Wisdom requires us to acknowledge from the beginning that there will be questions that remain unanswerable due to limitations in sources and due to the difficulty of developing a composite picture of crucifixion in antiquity with a high degree of certainty." Chapman and Schnabel, *Trial and Crucifixion of Jesus*, 671.

3. The English word *cross* comes from the Latin word *crux*, which can refer to "either the vertical pole or the cross made of two members." Cook, *Crucifixion in the Mediterranean World*, 34. For detailed information on crucifixion vocabulary in Greek and Latin, see Cook, *Crucifixion in the Mediterranean World*, 4–36.

Although most of us will never encounter physical pain akin to crucifixion, each of us have cried out in various forms of agony and anguish in our lives. As a result, we may yearn to connect with a Savior who can sympathize with our sorrows. Learning about the physical aspects of Christ's Crucifixion can help us feel more deeply the reality that *he really understands* the pain we experience. We can unlock spiritual power by learning more about what Christ experienced as he "poured out his soul unto death" (Isa. 53:12).

The details of crucifixion are challenging to explore. It would be easier to not think about the pain Jesus felt. Reading the details of Christ's experience on the cross is like watching a historically accurate movie about a tragic event. A friend of mine was watching such a movie with one of his children and distinctly felt that although watching the film was painful, it was important for his kids to understand the reality of what had happened in history.

Likewise, we should foster a desire to understand what really happened when Jesus Christ was crucified for our sins, even though after reading this chapter, this book, or even a thousand books, we won't completely comprehend the pain of the Crucifixion. But Elder Tad R. Callister taught that the difficulty of understanding what Christ experienced "does not absolve the need (nor should it diminish our desire) to know what is 'knowable.'"[4] Christ understands *our pain*; is it too much for us to learn more about *his pain*?

As I share details about the process of crucifixion with you, I hope that it comes across in the right spirit. My purpose isn't to linger too long on gory details but rather to help us better understand what Christ experienced on the cross. With this context in mind, let's learn a little more about the historical practice of crucifixion.

---

4.   Tad R. Callister, *The Infinite Atonement* (Salt Lake City: Deseret Book, 2000), 19.

WHEN DID THE PRACTICE OF CRUCIFIXION BEGIN?

Although crucifixion is the most famous method of ancient execution, we know very little about its origins. Ancient civilizations such as Babylon, Egypt, and Assyria used bodily suspension as a punishment, though this method took various forms, such as impaling an enemy or tying a person to a tree. The precise "historical origins of cross-shaped execution devices . . . remain murky,"[5] though Persians and Greeks were likely familiar with crucifixion in the fourth century BC. By 200 BC, accounts of crucifixion began to appear in Latin texts.[6] Whatever its origins, the Romans frequently used the torturous practice.[7]

HOW DID ANCIENT HISTORIANS DESCRIBE THE SEVERITY OF CRUCIFIXION?

Ancient authors referred to crucifixion as "the extreme penalty," a "cruel and terrifying penalty," and the "most pitiable of deaths."[8] The first-century Roman philosopher Seneca described the infamous practice as "wasting away in pain, dying limb by limb, or letting out . . . life drop by drop." He asked, "Can any man be found willing to be fastened to the accursed tree, long sickly, already deformed, swelling with ugly tumours on chest and shoulders, and draw the breath of life amid long-drawn-out agony? I think he would have many excuses for dying even before mounting the cross!"[9]

---

5. Chapman and Schnabel, *Trial and Crucifixion of Jesus*, 323.
6. Cook, *Crucifixion in the Mediterranean World*, 51.
7. The Romans were not the only nation to inflict crucifixion. For example, about one hundred years before Christ was born, prior to Roman rule, a Jewish leader in Jerusalem crucified several hundred Jews in front of their wives and children. See Flavius Josephus, *Antiquities of the Jews*, 13:380–81, in *The Works of Josephus: New Updated Edition*, trans. William Whiston (n.p.: Hendrickson Publishers, 1987), 361.
8. Cook, *Crucifixion in the Mediterranean World*, 388, 418–19, citing, respectively, the Roman legal writer Callistratus, the Roman statesman Cicero, and the Jewish historian Josephus.
9. Cook, *Crucifixion in the Mediterranean World*, 102.

WHO WAS CRUCIFIED?

Crucifixion was primarily reserved to punish disobedient slaves, violent thieves, and those who rebelled against the Roman empire. Both men and women were crucified. Given the severity of the punishment, Roman citizens were not crucified except in extremely rare circumstances. In fact, in the first century BC, the Roman statesman Cicero said crucifixion should not even be discussed in polite Roman society, declaring that the word "cross" should "be far removed from not only the person of a Roman citizen but from his thoughts, his eyes, and his ears."[10] In describing the severity of crucifixion, he said, "To bind a Roman citizen is a crime, to flog him is an abomination, to slay him is almost an act of murder: to crucify him is—what? There is no fitting word that can possibly describe so horrible a deed."[11] Crucifixion was such a severe method of execution, it was considered inappropriate for Romans. Instead it was reserved for rebels, outsiders, and those of a lower class.

WHAT IS SCOURGING?

Scourging often took place before crucifixion;[12] a Roman leader (such as Pilate) would assign soldiers to carry out this work. Describing the crucifixion of Jews in approximately AD 70, the Jewish historian Josephus wrote, "They were whipped, their bodies were mutilated, and while still alive and breathing, they were crucified."[13] He also wrote of a Roman leader who scourged a man until "his bones were laid bare."[14] Jesus himself predicted he would be scourged, and the Gospel authors tell us he was subjected to this horrendous punishment (see Matt. 20:19; 27:26; Mark 15:15; John 19:1).

---

10. Cook, *Crucifixion in the Mediterranean World,* 72.
11. Translation from Leonard H. G. Greenwood, as cited by Chapman and Schnabel, *Trial and Crucifixion of Jesus,* 543.
12. See Chapman and Schnabel, *Trial and Crucifixion of Jesus,* 672.
13. Cook, *Crucifixion in the Mediterranean World,* 237.
14. Flavius Josephus, *The Wars of the Jews,* 6:304, in *Works of Josephus,* 742.

A modern medical examiner named Dr. Frederick Zugibe, who has studied crucifixion for decades, wrote, "Although scourging was effected in various ways, the victim was usually stripped naked and shackled by the wrists to a fixed object like a low column, causing him to assume a bent position to make the executioner's task easier. . . . Many people today conceive of the scourging as a mere beating with a whiplike object. In a sense, this is true, but it is like comparing an electric shock to a lightning bolt."[15] The whip often had multiple tails, with sharp objects, such as metal or bones tied to each end, causing multiple lacerations with every stroke.

How did scourging affect the victim? Zugibe wrote, "The victim would writhe and twist in agony, falling to his knees, only to be jerked back on his feet time and time again until he could no longer stand up. The victim's breathing would be severely affected because the severe blows to the chest would cause excruciating rib pain . . . every time he attempted to take a breath."[16]

Though scourging was unimaginably painful on its own, it also added to the crucifixion agony; when the victim was affixed to the cross, the wounds from scourging would be reopened. Moreover, people on crosses constantly shifted their position, and any movement on the coarse beams would aggravate their fresh wounds.[17] Recognizing the realities of this brutal tradition gives new meaning to Isaiah's words: "He *was wounded* for our transgressions, he *was bruised* for our iniquities: the chastisement of our peace was upon him; *and with his stripes we are healed*" (Isa. 53:5).

---

15. Frederick T. Zugibe, *The Crucifixion of Jesus Christ, A Forensic Inquiry*, 2nd ed. (New York: M. Evans, 2005), 20, 19.
16. Zugibe, *Crucifixion of Jesus Christ*, 21.
17. See Kent P. Jackson, "The Crucifixion," in *From the Last Supper through the Resurrection: The Savior's Final Hours*, ed. Richard Neitzel Holzapfel and Thomas A. Wayment (Salt Lake City: Deseret Book, 2003).

WHERE DID CRUCIFIXIONS TAKE PLACE?

Roman leaders took advantage of the stigma and spectacle of crucifixion to discourage unlawful behavior. One author in the first century AD explained, "When we crucify criminals the most frequented roads are chosen, where the greatest number of people can look and be seized by this fear. For every punishment has less to do with the offence than with the example."[18] All aspects of crucifixion, therefore, were specifically designed to inspire fear in onlookers.[19]

WAS THERE A STANDARD PROCEDURE FOR CRUCIFIXION?

Just as biblical writers did not describe the detailed logistics of Christ's execution, ancient Roman commentators largely referred to crucifixion only in passing. While there was likely a standard approach, different forms of crucifixion occurred. Seneca described this variance as follows: "I see crosses there, not just of one kind but made differently by different individuals."[20] Josephus similarly indicated that various methods of crucifixion were used: "The soldiers out of rage and hatred amused themselves by nailing their prisoners in different postures."[21]

Early Christian tradition suggests Peter was crucified upside down,[22] and the Christian historian Eusebius wrote of crucifixions in the early fourth century, stating that people "were crucified, some *as malefactors usually are*, and some, even more brutally, were nailed in the opposite manner, head-downwards, and kept alive until they should perish of hunger."[23] Although no ancient manual detailing a preferred

18. Cook, *Crucifixion in the Mediterranean World*, 109, citing Quintilian.
19. Romans would also crucify wartime captives outside a city to demonstrate what would happen to the city's inhabitants if they did not surrender. See, for example, Josephus, *Wars of the Jews*, 5:450, in *Works of Josephus*, 720.
20. Cook, *Crucifixion in the Mediterranean World*, 34.
21. Cook, *Crucifixion in the Mediterranean World*, 197.
22. This event is recorded in the apocryphal Acts of Peter, written in the second century AD.
23. Cook, *Crucifixion in the Mediterranean World*, 8.

method of crucifixion exists, Eusebius's mention of a usual form of crucifixion and other ancient authors' emphasis on certain variations leads us to "assume a standard crucifixion form existed."[24] Based on ancient artwork and other descriptions, the standard approach appears to have been fastening an individual to a cross that had one horizontal beam and one vertical beam.

WHAT DID THE CROSS LOOK LIKE?

The word for "crucifixion" used by the Romans denotes an execution in which a victim was fastened to one of several possible wooden shapes, as well as sometimes to a tree.[25] The majority of evidence from the ancient world suggests that at the time of Christ, Roman crucifixion typically involved a *patibulum* (horizontal beam) attached to a *stipe* (vertical beam).[26] In many modern depictions of crosses, the horizontal beam is portrayed as being a little lower than the top of the vertical beam.

This shape is known as a Latin cross and is distinguished from crosses shaped like a capital T, in which the horizontal beam is at the very top of the vertical beam. The latter type is called a tau cross (*tau* being the Greek letter *T*). Both crosses are illustrated here.

Latin and tau crosses

24. Chapman and Schnabel, *Trial and Crucifixion of Jesus*, 315.
25. Although some people were literally affixed to trees, any crucifixion could metaphorically be described as hanging somebody on a tree (see Acts 10:39). Thus we sing, "And view thee bleeding on the tree: My Lord, my God, who dies for me." "O Thou, Before the World Began," *Hymns* (Salt Lake City: The Church of Jesus Christ of Latter-day Saints, 1985), no. 189.
26. Crucifixion could take place on a single vertical stake—either the victim's hands were secured to the stake or the victim was impaled. Describing other forms of crucifixion, Seneca recorded, "Some individuals suspended their victims with heads inverted toward the ground; some drove a stake through their excretory organs/genitals; others stretched out their arms on a [horizontal beam]." Cook, *Crucifixion in the Mediterranean World*, 34.

The three earliest images of crucifixion all depict crucifixions on a tau cross. In addition, many early Christians implied that Christ was crucified on a tau cross.[27] Because of the variety of crucifixion methods, it is impossible to state with certainty the shape of Christ's cross, though the best early evidence suggests that Christ was crucified on a tau rather than a Latin cross.

WHAT WERE THE DIMENSIONS OF THE CROSS?

Scholars estimate that crosses most frequently consisted of a six- to eight-foot vertical beam and a five- to six-foot horizontal beam.[28] Thus, contrary to many modern artistic depictions, the victim would have been suspended only one or two feet off the ground. The system of ropes and pulleys portrayed in some movies would likely have been unnecessary. One of the earliest images of crucifixion[29] portrays a vertical beam only about 15 percent taller than the height of the person being crucified.[30] Using this same ratio, and given that the average height of males living in the region of Judea at the time of Christ was five foot, five inches, Christ's cross was probably about six feet tall.[31]

---

27. The Epistle of Barnabas, written between AD 70 and 132, specifically uses the letter tau to describe the shape of the cross, as did Clement of Alexandria and Tertullian, both of whom wrote in the late-second and early-third centuries AD. Similarly, writings likely dating to the second century AD describe a mock trial in which the Greek letter sigma accuses the letter tau of being the source of the shape for crucifixions. See Cook, *Crucifixion in the Mediterranean World*, 5.

28. See Roger W. Byard, "Forensic and Historical Aspects of Crucifixion," *Forensic Science, Medicine, and Pathology* 12, no. 2 (May 2016): 206.

29. This image is the Puteoli graffito (a drawing etched in stone found in Puteoli, Italy, near modern-day Naples, dating to the late-second or early-third century AD). See Felicity Harley-McGowan, "The Passion," in *Routledge Handbook of Early Christian Art*, ed. Robin Jensen and Mark Ellison (London: Routledge, 2018), 290–93.

30. See John Granger Cook, "Crucifixion as Spectacle in Roman Campania," *Novum Testamentum*, 54, no. 1 (2012): 93. It appears that the Romans occasionally crucified some victims higher so that they would be visible from further away; however, this practice does not seem to have been typical. Cook, *Crucifixion in the Mediterranean World*, 427.

31. The proposed height of the cross is based on the average height of males and the dimensions of the Puteoli graffito. For more on the average height of people in the region, see Joan E. Taylor, *What Did Jesus Look Like?* (London: Bloomsbury Publishing, 2018), 158–60.

HOW HEAVY WAS THE CROSS CHRIST CARRIED?

A few ancient accounts of crucifixion (including the Savior's) describe a procession in which the victim carries a cross.[32] Some crucifixion researchers suggest that because of the scarcity of wood in Jerusalem, the vertical beam of the cross was probably a permanent fixture to which a reusable horizontal beam could be affixed.[33] Thus the "cross" victims carried was likely a horizontal beam weighing about eighty pounds.[34] After arriving at the place of crucifixion, the person was probably first attached to the horizontal beam, and then lifted up onto the vertical portion of the cross.

WERE THERE SEATS OR FOOTRESTS ON CROSSES?

Some Roman crosses included a small *sedile* (seat) on which victims could partially rest their weight. The theologian Justin Martyr, writing in approximately AD 150, described a middle piece (a sedile) affixed to the cross: "it projects [outward], and those who are being crucified rest on it."[35] The use of such a seat may have allowed victims to shift some of their body weight to assist with breathing and thus stay alive longer. This was not an act of mercy—it merely prolonged the agonizing crucifixion process.[36]

Although a *suppedaneum*, or board to stand on, appears in many modern depictions of crucifixion, only one of the earliest three artistic depictions of crucifixion includes it. Ancient historians did not describe

---

32. See Chapman and Schnabel, *Trial and Crucifixion of Jesus*, 673.
33. Joseph Zias and Eliezer Sekeles, "BA Report: 'The Crucified Man from Givcat Ha-Mivtar—A Reappraisal,'" *Israel Exploration Journal* 35, no. 1 (1985): 22–27.
34. Estimates of the weight of the crossbeam range between 50 and 125 pounds. Zugibe, *Crucifixion of Jesus Christ*, 46; William D. Edwards, Wesley J. Gabel, and Floyd E. Hosmer, "On the Physical Death of Jesus Christ," *Journal of the American Medical Association* 255, no. 11 (1986): 1459.
35. Cook, *Crucifixion in the Mediterranean World*, 7. The Puteoli graffito also has a sedile. See Cook, *Crucifixion in the Mediterranean World*, 427.
36. See Zugibe, *Crucifixion of Jesus Christ*, 57.

a footrest as part of cross construction, and some modern researchers have determined that "only very rarely, and probably later than the time of Christ, was an additional block (suppedaneum) employed for transfixion of the feet."[37]

DID PEOPLE WEAR CLOTHES WHEN THEY WERE CRUCIFIED?

Images and accounts from the ancient world suggest that people were crucified either naked or wearing only a small loincloth.[38] Only three artistic depictions of crucifixion created prior to AD 300 still exist; in two of the three, the crucifixion victims were naked.[39] While complete nudity was not part of all crucifixions, the general lack of clothing was a physically and emotionally painful aspect of this method of execution.[40] Although difficult to discuss, these details have helped some heal from extremely challenging circumstances, knowing that Christ understands what it means to be a victim of abuse.

WERE VICTIMS TIED OR NAILED TO THE CROSS?

A first-century cure for fevers required the use of "the head of a nail by which someone has been fixed to a cross . . . or a rope from a

---

37. Edwards, Gabel, and Hosmer, "On the Physical Death of Jesus Christ," 1459.

38. One ancient commentator wrote of people being "crucified naked," while another described those to be crucified as being naked but "girded around their private parts," indicating that people described as being "naked" might have worn a loincloth or similar apparel. See Cook, *Crucifixion in the Mediterranean World*, 192–93.

39. Cook, *Crucifixion in the Mediterranean World*, xxviii. Of the three images of crucifixion commonly dated prior to AD 300, one is engraved on a gemstone, and the other two are graffiti—drawings etched on stone. One graffito was found in Puteoli, Italy, and the other was found on Palatine Hill in Rome (see chapter 1). The gemstone and Palatine graffito appear to depict Christ's Crucifixion. The gemstone and Puteoli graffito portray crucifixion victims as naked. Additional pieces of artwork in the region portray individuals awaiting execution (not necessarily by crucifixion) either naked or wearing loincloths. Cook, *Crucifixion in the Mediterranean World*, 192–93. In addition, combinations of Greek letters may be ancient representations of the crucified Christ. See Larry W. Hurtado, *The Earliest Christian Artifacts* (Grand Rapids, MI: William B. Eerdmans Publishing, 2006), 135–54.

40. Lack of clothing, for example, could cause agony by allowing insects to more easily bite wounded parts of the body.

cross."[41] The option of using either ropes or nails in this recipe suggests that both were used in crucifixions. Ancient artwork and descriptions of crucifixion portray both methods for affixing a body to a cross; thus, either tying, nailing, or both could have been used.

WERE VICTIMS NAILED IN THEIR HANDS OR THEIR WRISTS?

Many people are interested in where nails (when used instead of ropes) were placed to fasten victims to a cross. In the New Testament record, the Greek word most commonly translated as "hand" refers to any part of the forearm, leaving the specific nail placement ambiguous.[42] With this textual uncertainty and lack of archeological evidence, scholars have speculated that driving the nails through the wrists or upper forearm would have provided more stability and decreased the chance of the nails tearing through the flesh.[43] Surviving evidence does not confirm or refute the possibility that victims were nailed in both the hands and wrists for increased support.

HOW WERE FEET FASTENED TO THE CROSS?

The remains of only one crucified individual have been identified.[44] Discovered in Jerusalem in 1968, the tomb of a man named Jehohanan included a right heel bone still pierced by a 4.5-inch iron nail, with traces of wood on either side. The placement and length of the nail suggest that Jehohanan was probably crucified with one nail through each

---

41. Cook, *Crucifixion in the Mediterranean World*, 154.
42. Stephen Bordes, Skyler Jenkins, Lexian McBain, Amgad Hanna, Marios Loukas, and R. Shane Tubbs, "The Clinical Anatomy of Crucifixion," *Clinical Anatomy* 33, no. 1 (2019): 12–21.
43. See Roger W. Byard, "Forensic and Historical Aspects of Crucifixion," *Forensic Science, Medicine, and Pathology* 12, no. 2 (May 2016): 207; and Bordes and others, "Clinical Anatomy of Crucifixion."
44. A second possible crucifixion victim was recently identified; for further discussion, see Chapman and Schnabel, *Trial and Crucifixion of Jesus*, viii.

of his ankles, positioned on opposite sides of a vertical wooden stake, as shown here.

This modern illustration of how feet were nailed to the cross is consistent with ancient depictions of Roman crucifixion.[45]

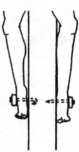

WAS IT COMMON FOR AN ACCUSATION TO BE POSTED ON THE CROSS?

Though posted accusations are not frequently mentioned in crucifixion accounts, a few ancient sources refer to written accusations accompanying those who were crucified or put to death in some other manner.[46] The most famous of these placards is the one Pilate inscribed and put on the Savior's cross, over his head (see Matt. 27:37).[47]

WERE CROWDS USUALLY PRESENT AT CRUCIFIXIONS?

At Christ's Crucifixion, many individuals were present, including both supporters and detractors. Nothing in the historical record indicates this would be abnormal. In fact, "crucifixion was designed to be a public event producing a chastening effect on observers, and so we can be certain there were people around the cross."[48] The exact number of people present likely varied, as did the nature of the crowd—whether most were merely passersby or those who had a specific interest in the person being crucified. Whether or not people would be allowed to be

---

45. Cook, *Crucifixion in the Mediterranean World*, 425.
46. See Chapman and Schnabel, *Trial and Crucifixion of Jesus*, 292–98; and Cook, *Crucifixion in the Mediterranean World*, 110, 180, 427.
47. Because artistic depictions of the Crucifixion often place the placard near the top of the vertical beam and above the horizontal beam on a Latin cross, some assume Christ must have been crucified on a Latin cross. The placard, however, could have just as easily been over Christ's head on the horizontal beam of a tau cross.
48. Raymond E. Brown, *The Death of the Messiah*, vol. 2 (New York: Doubleday, 1994), 1026–27.

close to the cross could also vary depending on the circumstances of the crucifixion.[49]

WHAT WAS A CRUCIFIXION SCENE LIKE, AND WHAT DID THE VICTIM FEEL?

Dr. Frederick Zugibe graphically described a crucifixion scene. He points out that squadrons of four soldiers were likely involved in the process of crucifixion. One soldier would lay across the chest of the victim and another over the legs to hold him still, while a third soldier would nail the person's hands to the horizontal beam.

These iron nails (about 4.5 inches long) would cause brutal pain, "like hot pokers traversing his arms like lightning bolts causing [the person on the cross] to arch his torso and let out piercing screams."[50] The horizontal beam was then lifted up and inserted into the recess of the vertical beam, causing additional pain as the hands pulled on the nails. With the cross now in place, the agonizing process of nailing was repeated with the feet on the vertical beam.

Zugibe wrote, "Even a slight movement would incite the incessant, burning, searing pains. . . . [These] pains would have been unrelenting and brutal, causing severe burning sensations all over his body. [Many factors could] aggravate the condition, including movements of air, the direct sun rays, the heat, the pressure of the nails constantly rubbing against the nerves and the movements of his body on the cross."[51]

These graphic details, so unpleasant to read, can help us feel a new level of appreciation for the sacrifice Jesus Christ willingly made for each of us. While I don't like focusing on the details of Christ's suffering, I'm moved by Jesus's willingness to endure it for you and me.

---

49. Brown, *Death of the Messiah*, 1028–29.
50. Zugibe, *Crucifixion of Jesus Christ*, 66.
51. Zugibe, *Crucifixion of Jesus Christ*, 97, 100.

WHAT WAS THE MEDICAL CAUSE
OF DEATH FOR VICTIMS OF CRUCIFIXION?

Just as the details of crucifixion could differ in each situation, the corresponding causes of death likely varied as well. Methods such as gouging victims with a spear could swiftly bring about death. Another practice known as *crurifragium* entailed breaking the legs of the victim and brought about death more rapidly (see John 19:31), perhaps by making it more difficult to breathe or causing "rapid and severe bleeding from the fractured bone marrows."[52] The most famous example of this method involved the two thieves crucified with Christ. Without such interventions, one could survive on the cross anywhere from a few hours to a few days.[53]

Scholars debate the cause of death in typical instances of crucifixion. One review of forty articles and books authored by physicians identified more than ten "completely different theories" to explain the death of Christ.[54] The three most common hypotheses for the medical cause of death in crucifixion are asphyxiation (suffocation), traumatic shock, and cardiac rupture.

In the case of asphyxiation, the weight of the victim's body would cause it to sag forward, putting it in a position where normal breathing would become increasingly difficult. According to one study, "Over time, breathing required increased effort as muscles became exhausted. . . . The victim would ultimately have been unable

---

52. Erkki Koskenniemi, Kirsi Nisula, and Jorma Toppari, "Wine Mixed with Myrrh (Mark 15.23) and Crurifragium (John 19.31–32): Two Details of the Passion Narratives," *Journal for the Study of the New Testament* 27, no. 4 (2005): 388.

53. Edwards, Gabel, and Hosmer, "On the Physical Death of Jesus Christ." In rare cases, individuals survived crucifixion if they were set free before death. Josephus records seeing three of his former acquaintances on the cross and appealed to the Roman general to set them free, which he did. Two of the freed men died in the care of physicians, and one survived. See Cook, *Crucifixion in the Mediterranean World*, 198.

54. Matthew W. Maslen and Piers D. Mitchell, "Medical Theories on the Cause of Death in Crucifixion," *Journal of the Royal Society of Medicine* 99, no. 4 (2006): 185.

to lift their body enough to breathe sufficiently, leading to death by asphyxiation."[55]

A second hypothesis is that traumatic shock caused death on the cross. This theory suggests that "the cumulative shock involved with beating the victim, driving spikes through the extremities, and denying food and water, would eventually lead to circulatory collapse."[56] Trauma-induced shock could also combine with asphyxiation and become lethal.

Cardiac rupture has also been suggested by some as a potential cause of death.[57] Although this proposal has the least scientific support, it has symbolic beauty and aligns with Elder James E. Talmage's statement in *Jesus the Christ*: "The present writer [Elder Talmage] believes that the Lord Jesus died of a broken heart."[58] This insight has been echoed by other Church leaders, including Elder Jeffrey R. Holland, who stated, "We are to remember in as personal a way as possible that Christ died from a heart broken by shouldering entirely alone the sins and sorrows of the whole human family."[59]

From a strictly medical perspective, the scarcity of available evidence makes it impossible to provide definitive answers as to what caused death in any specific crucifixion victim.[60] The specific reasons for death likely varied among individuals, with multiple factors often leading to death. In the case of Jesus Christ, however, we know that he willingly gave up his life—it was not taken from him (see John 10:15, 18).

---

55. Bordes and others, "Clinical Anatomy of Crucifixion," 19–20.
56. Phillip Bishop and Brian Church, "An Alternative Mechanism for Death by Crucifixion," *The Linacre Quarterly*, 73:3, 283.
57. Bergeron, "Crucifixion of Jesus," 113–16.
58. James E. Talmage, *Jesus the Christ* (Salt Lake City: Deseret Book, 1986), 578.
59. Jeffrey R. Holland, "Behold the Lamb of God," *Ensign*, May 2019.
60. M. W. Maslen, "Medical Theories on the Cause of Death in Crucifixion," *Journal of the Royal Society of Medicine* 99, no. 4 (January 2006): 186.

WHAT HAPPENED TO THE
BODIES AFTER THEY WERE CRUCIFIED?

Historical records do not provide many details on what happened to victims of crucifixion. In some instances, their corpses were likely thrown into paupers' graves; in others, bodies were left on the cross for wild animals to devour. The Jewish historian Philo, writing less than twenty years after the death of Christ, tells of instances in which crucified individuals were restored to their relatives for burial.[61] In at least one location, a legal provision stated that "the corpses of those who were sentenced to die are not to be withheld from their relatives."[62]

WHEN DID THE PRACTICE OF CRUCIFIXION END?

The Roman emperor Constantine the Great abolished the practice of crucifixion in the fourth century. At that time the formal use of crucifixion as a state-sponsored punishment ended; however, rare accounts of crucifixion as a method of torture and execution unfortunately persist to the present day.[63]

HOW CAN ALL THIS HELP ME IN MY LIFE?

Although gruesome details are difficult to read, studying the physical realities of crucifixion can enhance our appreciation for how much the Savior loves us—especially considering that what he physically experienced was only a small part of the overall agony he felt throughout his hours of Atonement as he "descended below" all things (D&C 122:8). Learning about the historical details of Christ's Crucifixion can help us better appreciate passages such as "He loveth the world, even that he layeth down his own life" (2 Ne. 26:24) and "Greater love hath no man than this, that a man lay down his life for his friends" (John

---

61. See Chapman and Schnabel, *Trial and Crucifixion of Jesus*, 666.
62. Cook, *Crucifixion in the Mediterranean World*, 386, citing events taking place in Puteoli, Italy.
63. Zugibe, *Crucifixion of Jesus Christ*, 53–54.

15:13). One woman shared a personal experience about how an awareness of the physical realities of Christ's Crucifixion helped her during a time of devastation:

> Ugly tears coursed down my cheeks. Why? How could this have happened? The betrayal hit me like a gut punch. I wanted to scream it all away, or at the very least tear someone apart with my bare fingernails. But even that wouldn't make it better, wouldn't erase what I was going through. . . . I felt so alone. . . .
>
> Talking to a counselor brought temporary relief but no real solutions. Blocking it out and staying as busy as possible only worked for so long. Then came Jesus. In the darkness, in the depths of my pain, I realized: He knew. . . . He'd experienced the worst pain, the deepest betrayal, the hardest suffering—none of it deserved. . . . And it hurt Him—so very, very badly. But for some reason, I'd never before understood this.
>
> Growing up, I'd been taught Jesus died on the cross, but His suffering seemed abstract. In paintings depicting the crucifixion, the holes from the nails had a bit of blood, and Jesus was frowning beneath His crown of thorns, but it was all rather contained—a PG version of what He'd really been through. Then His suffering was over and, whoosh! Our Savior was dressed in head-to-toe white with a glowing golden halo, smiling like He'd never been gasping for His last breath or sobbing from the pain of being sold for thirty pieces of silver by one of His twelve best friends.
>
> But when I encountered Jesus in my sorrow, it wasn't the Sunday school, family-friendly version kneeling beside me as I collapsed before Him in a darkened room with my prayer of surrender. It was the scarred-up Jesus, the One who remembered the ragged bloodstained holes from where they'd driven the nails in, who didn't wince as they beat Him but cried out in agony, who didn't just quietly and stoically accept that Judas let Him down but ached over the treachery. This Jesus understood. And when I

realized that, and I allowed him to meet me in my suffering, I was no longer alone.[64]

———— ◆◆ ————

As we better comprehend what Christ physically experienced on the cross, we can feel a greater kinship with him in our own agony. Although some of us prefer to focus primarily on the resurrected Redeemer, in our deepest despair, we can also find fortitude in a suffering Savior. One person who drew strength from the Crucifixion was Dietrich Bonhoeffer, a German Christian who actively worked against the Nazi regime. Eventually he was arrested and put in a concentration camp. In a letter written from his prison cell, he said, "Only the suffering God can help."[65] Our awareness of *Christ's sufferings* can help us know that he empathizes with *our sufferings*. He understands our pain and will not leave us to experience it alone.

64. Jessica Brodie, "Finding Jesus in the Center of My Pain," *WhollyLoved* (blog), July 15, 2019, https://whollyloved.com/2019/07/15/finding-jesus-in-the-center-of-my-pain/.
65. Dietrich Bonhoeffer, *Letters and Papers from Prison* (Minneapolis: Fortress Press, 2010), 479.

Chapter 8

FROM GETHSEMANE TO PILATE

There is great value in studying what individual Gospel authors teach about the Crucifixion and learning from the similarities and differences in their accounts. This method of study is discussed in chapter 13; however, in this chapter and the two that follow, we will look at elements from all of the Gospel accounts and harmonize them to present what they collectively teach about the Crucifixion of Jesus Christ. This approach allows us to capture details mentioned in only one Gospel. In these three chapters, the New Revised Standard Version (NRSV) of the Bible is used for Bible quotations, unless otherwise noted. Using this version of the Bible offers a fresh perspective on familiar texts and provides a smoother transition between my modern prose and the scripture verses.

Jesus appeared before Pilate at about 6:00 a.m.[1] on a Friday morning, perhaps on the date that corresponds with our calendar as April 7 in AD 30.[2] The previous twelve hours had been filled with some of the

---

1. The Greek word translated to "early in the morning" in John 18:28 is used elsewhere by John to describe the early morning before sunrise. Compare John 20:1.
2. Determining the date of Christ's birth and death is more complicated than we may think. Most scholars believe Christ was crucified in either AD 30 or 33. For an overview of issues with dating Christ's birth and death, see Lincoln H. Blumell and

most momentous events in history: Christ and his disciples had shared the Last Supper, after which the Savior instructed them as they walked together to Gethsemane. As Jesus entered Gethsemane, he "began to be grieved and agitated" (Matt. 26:37). Elder Neal A. Maxwell described, "Jesus knew cognitively what He must do, but not experientially. He had never personally known the exquisite and exacting process of an atonement before. Thus, when the agony came in its fulness, it was so much, much worse than even He with his unique intellect had ever imagined!"[3]

Separating himself from his disciples, "he threw himself on the ground and prayed that, if it were possible, the hour might pass from him" (Mark 14:35). Later that evening he was "in . . . anguish" as "his sweat became like great drops of blood falling down on the ground" and he suffered for the sins of all humanity (Luke 22:44; see D&C 19:16–19). The Savior's "anguish for the wickedness and the abominations of his people" was exquisite and beyond our comprehension (Mosiah 3:7; see D&C 19:15). He cried, "Abba, Father, for you all things are possible; remove this cup from me; yet, not what I want, but what you want" (Mark 14:36). "An angel from heaven appeared to him and gave him strength" (Luke 22:43).

After trembling "because of pain" and suffering "both body and spirit" (D&C 19:18), the Savior "got up from prayer" and awoke his sleeping disciples (Luke 22:45). At the same moment, Judas arrived with the chief priests to betray the Savior with a kiss (see Matt. 26:47). Peter attempted to fight back, cutting off the ear of one of the servants

---

Thomas A. Wayment, "When Was Jesus Born? A Response to a Recent Proposal," *BYU Studies Quarterly* 51, no. 3 (2012): 53–81. For more context on the date of Jesus Christ's death, see Raymond E. Brown, *The Death of the Messiah*, vol. 2 (New York: Doubleday, 1994), 1373–76.

3. Neal A. Maxwell, "Willing to Submit," *Ensign*, May 1985. Lorenzo Snow connected the experience of Gethsemane and Calvary, saying, "When He knelt there in the garden of Gethsemane, what agony He must have experienced in contemplating His sufferings on the cross!" "Discourse by President Lorenzo Snow [May 8, 1899]," *Millennial Star* 61, no. 34 (August 24, 1899): 531.

of the high priest (see John 18:10). The ever-merciful Savior healed the man's ear and voluntarily surrendered himself to those who hated him, while "all the disciples deserted him and fled," including a young man who "ran off naked" (Luke 22:51; Matt. 26:56; Mark 14:52).

Christ was taken to be tried before the Jewish authorities. Although the Pharisees often opposed Jesus, they are largely absent from the narrative of Christ's capture, trial, and Crucifixion. Rather, the Savior's primary adversaries were "the high priest" (Mark 14:53, 60, 63) and the "chief priests" (Mark 15:1, 3, 10, 11, 31). These individuals had recently met and said regarding Jesus, "What are we to do? This man is performing many signs. If we let him go on like this, everyone will believe in him, and the Romans will come and destroy both our holy place and our nation" (John 11:47–48).

Although it's possible the chief priests were primarily concerned with Christ deceiving the people, disrupting the peace with the Romans, and causing spiritual harm to their nation, they may have also had an ulterior motive. Archeological evidence indicates that the chief priests lived in multistoried homes containing large baths, beautiful tiled floors, and frescoed walls. They owned fine tableware, dressed expensively, and imported delicious delicacies. Keeping these luxuries required they maintain their position with the Roman rulers.[4] Thus, some of these chief priests were likely concerned they could lose their positions because of Jesus, who challenged their authority and was growing in popularity.

At a meeting of Jewish authorities, the high priest Caiaphas said, "It is better for you to have one man die for the people than to have the whole nation destroyed" (John 11:50). Caiaphas was suggesting Christ needed to die in order to maintain the status quo of the chief priests. John found additional meaning in Caiaphas's words, stating

---

4. The idea that there was a financial motive in the Crucifixion of Jesus Christ is corroborated by Jacob, who taught, "Because of priestcrafts . . . , they at Jerusalem will stiffen their necks against him, that he be crucified." 2 Ne. 10:5; see also 2 Ne. 26:29.

that Caiaphas unwittingly prophesied through the Spirit that one man (Jesus) would die—but not to save the power of the chief priests. Jesus would die to save all of God's children (see John 11:51–52).[5]

After that meeting with Caiaphas, the chief priests looked for opportunities to put Christ to death, and now their moment had arrived (see John 11:53). Christ was brought from Gethsemane to "the courtyard of the high priest" (Mark 14:54), where over the next several hours he endured interrogation, false witnesses, and Peter's denial. Christ was mocked, slapped, spat upon, and ultimately condemned to death (see Mark 14:64). The rooster had crowed; it was now "early in the morning" (John 18:28). The chief priests took Jesus from Caiaphas's palace to Pilate's headquarters in Jerusalem.[6] Although the journey was only a ten-minute walk, after the abuse Jesus had endured, every step must have been torturous.

CHRIST'S FIRST APPEARANCE BEFORE PILATE

In approximately AD 26, the Roman emperor Tiberius appointed Pilate to serve as the prefect, or governor, of Judea, making him the principal political authority in Jerusalem. Although he normally resided in Caesarea, a city seventy-five miles to the northwest, on this week he was in Jerusalem—probably to help keep the peace during Passover.

With Jesus standing before Pilate, the Jewish authorities "began to accuse [Christ], saying, 'We found this man perverting our nation, forbidding us to pay taxes to the emperor, and saying that he himself

---

5. For an in-depth examination of Caiaphas's statement, see Frank F. Judd Jr., "Interpreting Caiaphas's 'Prophecy' of the Savior's Death," in *Behold the Lamb of God: An Easter Celebration*, ed. Richard Neitzel Holzapfel, Frank F. Judd Jr., and Thomas A. Wayment (Provo, UT: Religious Studies Center, Brigham Young University, 2008), 87–104.

6. Pilate was most likely stationed in the palace formerly inhabited by Herod the Great. Not only did Pilate apparently set up shields in this location but it was also the best residence in the city and thus the most likely place where the most powerful mortal in Judea would stay while in Jerusalem. See Jerome Murphy-O'Conner, *The Holy Land: An Oxford Archaeological Guide*, 5th ed. (Oxford: Oxford University Press, 2008), 23.

is the Messiah, a king'" (Luke 23:2). When Jesus did not respond to these accusations, Pilate said, "'Do you not hear how many accusations they make against you?' But [Jesus] gave [Pilate] no answer, not even to a single charge, so that the governor was greatly amazed" (Matt. 27:13–14).

Pilate was familiar with the Jewish leaders and knew "it was out of jealousy that the chief priests had handed [Jesus] over" (Matt. 27:18). Although Pilate saw a guiltless man standing before him, the social and political pressure to sentence him to death hung heavy in the air. He told "the chief priests and the crowds, 'I find no basis for an accusation against this man'" (Luke 23:4).

The people present continued to accuse Jesus, saying, "He stirs up the people by teaching throughout all Judea, from Galilee where he began even to this place" (Luke 23:5). Pilate, hearing that Jesus was from Galilee, realized he might have a way out of this sticky situation—he was not the only person in Jerusalem who could try Jesus of Nazareth.

CHRIST'S APPEARANCE BEFORE HEROD ANTIPAS

Luke tells us that at this point, Pilate sent Christ to Herod Antipas to be judged. Herod Antipas was the son of Herod the Great (who ordered the death of young children in Bethlehem shortly after Jesus's birth). Upon his death, Herod the Great's kingdom was divided among his relatives, and Herod Antipas became the designated ruler in the region of Galilee—the area where Christ lived.

The Savior and Herod Antipas were *not* friends. Herod Antipas had murdered Christ's relative John the Baptist, and earlier in the Savior's ministry some Pharisees told Jesus that Herod Antipas wanted to kill him (see Luke 13:31). Although it is doubtful that Christ desired to meet him, Herod "had been wanting to see [Jesus] for a long time, because he had heard about him and was hoping to see him perform some sign" (Luke 23:8). Perhaps Joanna, the wife of Herod's house manager and a believer in Jesus, had told her husband about the

Savior's miracles she had witnessed, and he passed this information on to Herod (see Luke 8:3).

Although Herod was "very glad" to see Jesus and "questioned him at some length," the Savior "gave him no answer" (Luke 23:8–9). This event may have partially fulfilled Isaiah's words: "He was oppressed, and he was afflicted, yet he did not open his mouth; like a lamb that is led to the slaughter . . . he did not open his mouth" (Isa. 53:7).[7] Likely annoyed, Herod and his soldiers treated Christ "with contempt and mocked him; then [Herod] put an elegant robe on him and sent him back to Pilate" (Luke 23:11). The Greek word translated as "elegant" in this passage is elsewhere translated as "bright" or "white"—describing the clothing of an angel (see Acts 10:30, KJV; Rev. 15:6, KJV). Andrew Skinner wrote, "White is a premier symbol of purity and divinity, and though Herod meant its use as a statement of irony, it rightly identified the purest of our Heavenly Father's children."[8]

Although Jesus did not perform any signs for Herod, some see the redemptive power of Christ in the subsequent friendship of Pilate and Herod.[9] Luke informs us that this "same day Herod and Pilate became friends with each other; before this they had been enemies" (Luke 23:12).[10] Maybe the dissolution of their enmity was the result of nothing more than successful political machinations, but perhaps it is a manifestation that Christ can "change frowning foes to smiling friends."[11] Though Herod and Pilate were reconciled through Christ's

---

7. See Brown, *Death of the Messiah*, 772.
8. Andrew C. Skinner, *Golgotha* (Salt Lake City: Deseret Book, 2004), 89.
9. See Brown, *Death of the Messiah*, 778.
10. Although the scriptures do not provide details about this discord, it may have been connected to Pilate's killing of Galileans (see Luke 13:1) or the rift relating to the shields Pilate placed in Herod the Great's palace (described later in this chapter).
11. "Savior, Redeemer of My Soul," *Hymns* (Salt Lake City, The Church of Jesus Christ of Latter-day Saints, 1985), no. 112. If this theory is true, then perhaps the reconciliation of Pilate and Herod Antipas is a personal application of Paul's teaching that "in Christ Jesus you who once were far off have been brought near by the blood of Christ. For he is our peace; in his flesh he has made both groups into one[,] . . . one body through the cross." Eph. 2:13–14, 16.

death, of much more significance was the reconciliation that our Redeemer would bring later that day—the miraculous reconciliation between God and all of humanity.

PILATE'S QUESTIONS FOR CHRIST

Although Matthew, Mark, and Luke indicate Christ made little or no response when the Jewish authorities accused him before Pilate, John recounts the trial differently. In John's record, Pilate initially tells the Jewish authorities to judge Jesus themselves, but they respond by saying, "We are not permitted to put anyone to death" (John 18:31).[12] They desperately wanted Christ to die—anything less was unacceptable. Of course, Jesus had already prophesied that he would be crucified (see John 3:14; 8:28; 12:32; 18:32), and for this to be accomplished, Pilate needed to play a role.

In the Gospel of John, the Jewish authorities do not want to enter Pilate's headquarters because doing so could make them ritually impure for the Passover feast that would take place later that evening.[13] So they remained outside while Pilate questioned Jesus inside the headquarters. He asked the Savior, "'Are you the King of the Jews?' Jesus answered, 'Do you ask this on your own, or did others tell you about me?' Pilate replied, 'I am not a Jew, am I? Your own nation and the chief priests have handed you over to me. What have you done?' Jesus answered, 'My kingdom is not from this world. If my kingdom were from this world, my followers would be fighting to keep me from being handed over to the Jews. But as it is, my kingdom is not from here'" (John 18:33–36).[14]

---

12. It is not clear what the Jewish authorities meant when they said they were not permitted to put people to death. Some interpret this statement to mean that although they could impose capital punishment in some instances, they could not crucify an individual. See Acts 7:54–60; 21:28–31; compare John 18:32.

13. Although the synoptic Gospels present the Last Supper as a Passover meal, in the Gospel of John, the Passover takes place after the Crucifixion. See chapter 10 herein.

14. This statement from Christ highlights the fact that many of the Jews supported the Savior. Only a very small subset of Jews was involved in the death of Christ.

At this point, Pilate may have been puzzled. The Jewish authorities accused Jesus of claiming to be a king—insinuating a revolt against Rome. But Jesus claimed his kingdom was otherworldly. What could this mean? "Pilate asked him, 'So you are a king?' Jesus answered, 'You say that I am a king. For this I was born, and for this I came into the world, to testify to the truth. Everyone who belongs to the truth listens to my voice'" (John 18:37).

In this conversation we see that Jesus was not on trial before Pilate—Pilate was on trial before Jesus. Christ had previously declared, "*I* am the . . . truth" (John 14:6) and told Pilate that if Pilate were on the side of truth, he would listen to the Savior's voice. Pilate failed to acknowledge the capital "T" Truth standing in front of him and instead ironically asked, "What is truth?" (John 18:38). Pilate returned outside to the Jewish authorities and proclaimed, "I find no case against him" (John 18:38).

JESUS THE SON OF GOD OR JESUS BARABBAS?

At this point in the narrative, we learn that a custom allowed Pilate to release a prisoner at the Passover.[15] Pilate offered the people a choice—he would release either Jesus, the Son of God, or Barabbas, a "notorious prisoner," one "who had been put in prison for an insurrection that had taken place in the city, and for murder" (Matt. 27:16; Luke 23:19).[16] In Greek, John refers to Barabbas as a *lestes*, or "robber." Interestingly, the only other place where John uses this word is in chapter 10: "All that ever came before me are thieves and robbers [*lestes*]. . . . I am the good shepherd" (vv. 8, 14; see also v. 1, KJV).

---

15. Outside the Gospels there is no record of this tradition. See Brown, *Death of the Messiah*, 793–95.

16. Josephus, a Jewish historian, provides insight into what Barabbas's crimes might have been. The same Greek word used in the New Testament to describe Barabbas is used by Josephus to depict both a typical robber and Jewish radicals who assassinated Roman and Jewish leaders during religious festivals. See G. J. Goldberg, "New Testament Parallels to the Works of Josephus," accessed August 21, 2020, http://www.josephus.org/ntparallels.htm.

Perhaps John intended this irony; Christ defined himself as the good shepherd, in contrast to a robber, but now the people would choose a robber over the good shepherd.[17]

Some ancient New Testament manuscripts refer to Barabbas as "Jesus Barabbas"; read this way, Pilate asked, "Whom do you want me to release for you, Jesus Barabbas or Jesus who is called the Messiah?" (Matt. 27:17). With this framing, the two prisoners have the same given name—Jesus, a common male name at the time.[18] One possible meaning of the word *Barabbas* is "son of the father."[19] Perhaps Matthew is emphasizing that people had a choice between "Jesus son of the father" and "Jesus son of the *Father*." As Elder Jeffrey R. Holland stated, "One godless 'son of the father' was set free while a truly divine Son of His Heavenly Father moved on to crucifixion."[20]

When Pilate offered a choice between Jesus Christ and Barabbas, "the chief priests and the elders persuaded the crowds to ask for Barabbas and to have Jesus killed" (Matt. 27:20). At least three aspects of Barabbas's role in Christ's Crucifixion provide spiritual insights: (1) Barabbas as a revolutionary, (2) Barabbas as the only person for whom Christ literally carried his cross, and (3) Barabbas as the scapegoat.

Barabbas as a Revolutionary

To you and me, when Pilate says, "Who do you want? Jesus or Barabbas?" the choice is obvious because we are focused on Christ's atoning sacrifice. But many in the crowd were not thinking about spiritual salvation—they were fixated on temporal salvation. For nearly one hundred years Rome had ruled over Jerusalem with an oppressive hand. Taxes were high, and many people desperately wanted to throw

---

17. See Brown, *Death of the Messiah*, 797.
18. In Hebrew, the name is *Yeshua*.
19. Scholars debate the meaning of *Barabbas*, as well as the historical origin and context for the name of *Jesus* before the name *Barabbas*. For more information, see Robert E. Moses, "Jesus Barabbas, a Nominal Messiah? Text and History in Matthew 27.16–17," *New Testament Studies* 58, no. 1 (2012): 43–56.
20. Jeffrey R. Holland, "None Were with Him," *Ensign*, May 2009.

off their Roman overlords. Barabbas had been part of an insurrection in the city, which some may have supported—a rebellion against Rome was what they wanted! Maybe they believed Barabbas was a freedom fighter who could lead a revolt. But Jesus of Nazareth? He had performed miracles, but he hadn't done anything about the yoke of Roman oppression. Because some members of this crowd focused on the wrong problem—*temporal* instead of *spiritual* salvation—they chose the wrong solution.[21]

Metaphorically speaking, we often choose between Jesus and Barabbas—between a spiritual approach (redemption through Christ) and a worldly one (revolution through Barabbas). Pilate says to us, "What do you want? Advice from worldly experts or counsel from prophets? More followers on social media or more time ministering? To buy a luxury item you don't really need or to pay a more generous fast offering? A better body or a better spirit?" Unlike the choice offered by Pilate, our options are not always mutually exclusive; nevertheless, how often do we choose Barabbas over Jesus?

Barabbas and the Cross

Imagine how Barabbas felt when he was released—he was waiting in prison, certain he would die a painful death. And then, one day, to his complete surprise, the guards released him! As one author portrayed the situation:

> Put yourself in his sandals for a minute. You are walking to your death in chains and then all of a sudden, when you least expect it, you are a free man. Then you hear the words begin again: "Crucify him, crucify him." And you see another walking by. Those chants are not for you. The guards are dragging another man to his death—Jesus of Nazareth. He's beaten and flogged and

21. For more insights on this topic, see Leonard Vander Zee, "Jesus Barabbas or Jesus Christ?" *The Banner*, December 31, 2015, https://www.thebanner.org/departments/2015/12/jesus-barabbas-or-jesus-christ.

is forced to carry his cross to his death. It's the very cross you had imagined yourself carrying only moments earlier. You think to yourself, that's my death he's dying.

Barabbas is the one person in history who could say that Jesus literally carried his cross. Jesus took his death, and Barabbas was given the freedom Jesus deserved. Jesus bore the guilt and shame and curse and disgrace and death that Barabbas deserved.[22]

Was Barabbas grateful for what Christ did for him? Or did he just walk away, completely missing the majesty of what had happened? What about you and me? Do we frequently reflect on Christ's choice to continue to Calvary, standing in as our substitute? Or are we passive in our thoughts of the Savior's sacrifice? Considering Barabbas's situation, do we remember that we walk free *today* because Christ didn't *then*?

Barabbas as the Scapegoat

Parallels between Barabbas and the scapegoat in the Day of Atonement provide another spiritual insight. On that day, the high priest would cast lots to select between two goats. One would become the scapegoat and be set free. The other goat was killed as a sin offering (see Lev. 16:8, 15–16, 21).

Elements of this ritual can be seen in the interactions among Pilate, Christ, and Barabbas. Two men, rather than goats, stood before the presiding official. Although no lots were cast, God clearly chose which person would die. The blood of one man was shed as a sin offering, while the other was released. Just as Aaron would "wash his flesh with water" after the sacrifice (Lev. 16:24, KJV), so too did Pilate wash his hands. Barabbas is the scapegoat, and in a sense, each of us is Barabbas—set free because Jesus Christ stood in our place.[23]

---

22. Dave Furman, *Kiss the Wave: Embracing God in Your Trials* (Wheaton: Crossway, 2018), 52–53.
23. What I have suggested here is only one possible interpretation. For a variety of views on Barabbas, Jesus, and their connections to the scapegoat, see Jennifer K. Berenson

In Barabbas we see a powerful personalization of Paul's phrase "While we still were sinners Christ died for us" (Rom. 5:8). Barabbas represents us; we have sinned, fallen short, and are guilty. Christ's Crucifixion allows us to live a new life instead of facing our rightly deserved death. Heavenly Father treated Jesus as Barabbas deserved so that he could treat each of us like Jesus deserves.[24]

PROCULA'S DREAM

Before Pilate sentenced the Savior, Pilate's wife sent him a message: "Have nothing to do with that innocent man, for today I have suffered a great deal because of a dream about him" (Matt. 27:19). A later (noncanonical) text tells us her name was "Procula."[25] Procula's dream is another witness of Jesus Christ, one that goes unheeded by her husband.[26]

PILATE'S EFFORT TO RELEASE CHRIST

A little bit before 9:00 a.m.,[27] Pilate spoke to the people and said, "What do you wish me to do with the man you call the King of the Jews?" (Mark 15:12). In response, the people present "shouted back, 'Crucify him!'" (Mark 15:13).[28] Pilate knew he had to decide. He reaffirmed his previous statement to the Jewish authorities, declaring,

---

Maclean, "Barabbas, the Scapegoat Ritual, and the Development of the Passion Narrative," *The Harvard Theological Review* 100, no. 3 (July 2007): 312–30.

24. Judah Smith, "Jesus Is Loving Barabbas," as recorded in a YouTube video, posted August 3, 2015, https://youtu.be/2E4Pdik0wuY?t=157.

25. This information comes from a fifth-century text known as "The Gospel of Nicodemus."

26. Dreams play a special role in Matthew's Gospel: he is the only Gospel author to write about the dreams Joseph had to wed Mary and flee to Egypt, as well as the dream of the wise men to not return to Herod. See Matt. 1:20; 2:12–13.

27. John presents a different timing than Mark. In Mark, Christ is crucified at about 9:00 a.m., whereas in John, the Crucifixion occurs shortly after noon. See John 19:14.

28. In one of many crucifixion ironies that Mark portrays, he uses the Greek word *krazo* to depict the shouts of the people who want Christ to be killed. Mark used that same word when describing Christ's triumphal entry, describing those who had shouted (*krazo*) "Hosanna! Blessed is the one who comes in the name of the Lord!" Mark 11:9; see Brown, *Death of the Messiah*, 824.

"Take him yourselves and crucify him; I find no case against him" (John 19:6).

Although the Jewish authorities had earlier accused Jesus of being the king of the Jews (see John 18:33), they now said to Pilate, "We have a law, and according to that law he ought to die because he has claimed to be the Son of God" (John 19:7). Upon hearing this new accusation, Pilate was "more afraid than ever." He again returned inside and "asked Jesus, 'Where are you from?' But Jesus gave him no answer." Becoming increasingly frustrated, Pilate said to the Savior, "Do you refuse to speak to me? Do you not know that I have power to release you, and power to crucify you?" Christ responded, "You would have no power over me unless it had been given you from above; therefore the one who handed me over to you is guilty of a greater sin." Convinced of Christ's innocence, "from then on Pilate tried to release him" (John 19:8–12).

PILATE'S PAST

Although Pilate was more powerful than the Jewish authorities, he ultimately caved in to their request. The tide turned when the Jewish authorities said to Pilate, "If you release this man, you are no friend of the emperor. Everyone who claims to be a king sets himself against the emperor" (John 19:12). Why were these words so threatening?

Let's explore Pilate's backstory to understand this crucial moment when Pilate passes judgment on Jesus. Ancient historians, including Josephus (writing in ~AD 90) and Philo (writing in ~AD 40), shared stories that give insight into Pilate's character and provide valuable context for his role in Christ's trial.[29]

On one occasion, Pilate transferred some of his soldiers from Caesarea to Jerusalem and "trampled under foot" Jewish law by attaching images of the emperor to their military standards.[30] Many Jews felt

---

29. For a more extensive commentary on Pilate, see Helen K. Bond, *Pontius Pilate in History and Interpretation* (Cambridge: Cambridge University Press, 1998).

30. Flavius Josephus, *The Jewish War*, vol. 2, Books 3–4, trans. J. Thackeray (Cambridge:

this action violated the commandment against graven images and traveled to Caesarea, asking Pilate to remove the standards from Jerusalem. After six days of continual protest, Pilate summoned the dissenters to an arena. With his army present, Pilate threatened to kill the people if they did not return home. The Jews then prostrated themselves on the ground and said they would rather die than break God's law. Pilate, astonished at the people's commitment to their religious laws, had the standards removed from Jerusalem.

Sometime thereafter, Pilate spent money from the temple treasury to build an aqueduct to bring water to Jerusalem. Apparently, he did so without the approval of the people, for when they heard of it, they "formed a ring round the tribunal of Pilate . . . and besieged him with angry clamour."[31] Pilate refused to listen; instead, he had his soldiers, disguised in Jewish clothing, surround the protestors. The soldiers had orders to beat the rioters with sticks, presumably to injure rather than kill them. However, many Jews were slain by the soldiers' overly aggressive blows, and others were "trodden to death by their companions in the ensuing flight."[32] The protest ended; Pilate had won, but only through violence.

On another occasion, Pilate put gilded shields in Herod's palace (located in Jerusalem) with an inscription honoring Emperor Tiberius.[33] The people, believing Pilate did this "not so much to honour Tiberius as to annoy the multitude," were furious about the shields, believing they violated Jewish customs.[34] The people sent Herod the

---

Harvard University Press, 1976), 389.

31. Josephus, *Jewish War*, 391.

32. See Josephus, *Jewish War*, 393.

33. Given the similarity between this episode and that of the standards, some scholars believe that these are two versions of the same story. While this is a possibility, David W. Chapman and Eckhard J. Schnabel wrote, "It seems more likely that these were two different incidents." *The Trial and Crucifixion of Jesus*, rev. ed. (Peabody, MA: Hendrickson Publishers Marketing, 2019), 170.

34. Philo Judaeus, *The Embassy to Gaius*, trans. F. H. Colson (Cambridge, Harvard University Press, 1962), 151.

Great's four sons, including Herod Antipas, to protest Pilate's actions. These important Jewish leaders shouted at Pilate, saying, "Do not arouse sedition, do not make war, do not destroy the peace; you do not honour the emperor by dishonouring ancient laws. Do not take Tiberius as your pretext for outraging the nation; he does not wish any of our customs to be overthrown."[35]

When Pilate refused to act, the Jewish officials wrote a letter to Tiberius protesting the shields. Tiberius swiftly responded by writing to Pilate "with a host of reproaches and rebukes for his audacious violation of precedent and bade him at once take down the shields."[36] Though the situation was resolved when Pilate removed the shields, the event caused further strain between Pilate and the Jewish people in his jurisdiction.[37]

"YOU ARE NO FRIEND OF THE EMPEROR"

With this background in mind, consider again these words from the Jewish authorities to Pilate: "If you release this man, you are no friend of the emperor" (John 19:12). The Latin phrase translated as "friend of the emperor" is a term for a person who, like Pilate, benefited from an association with the Roman emperor.[38] Pilate was a political appointee who could be removed at will. Thus the statement "You are no friend of the emperor" was not a thoughtless taunt, but rather a carefully crafted threat from the Jewish authorities. Their underlying message seemed to be, "Do you remember the last time we

35. Philo Judaeus, *Embassy to Gaius*, 151.
36. Philo Judaeus, *Embassy to Gaius*, 153.
37. An additional story about Pilate is told by Josephus. In about the year AD 36 (approximately three to six years after Christ's Crucifixion), Pilate violently suppressed an uprising by Samaritans. The emperor then recalled Pilate to account for his actions. What happened to Pilate after he returned to Rome is uncertain. See Flavius Josephus, *Antiquities of the Jews*, 18:85–89, in *The Works of Josephus: New Updated Edition*, trans. William Whiston (n.p.: Hendrickson Publishers, 1987), 482.
38. See Paul Barrett, *Finding the Historical Christ* (Grand Rapids, MI: Wm. B. Eerdmans Publishing, 2009), 143–44.

wrote Tiberius? Do you remember how mad he got? We will write him again and let him know of your support for this Jesus." In the ultimate test of peer pressure, Pilate buckled.

Believing he could "do nothing" and seeing that "a riot was beginning," he "took some water and washed his hands before the crowd, saying, 'I am innocent of this man's blood; see to it your-selves'" (Matt. 27:24). Pilate's handwashing may indicate he was aware of Jewish legal customs:[39] In Deuteronomy 21, the Israelites are instructed that if someone is killed by an unknown person, "the elders of that town . . . shall wash their hands . . . [and] declare: 'Our hands did not shed this blood, nor were we witnesses to it.'" The leaders of the city were then to say, "Do not let the guilt of inno-cent blood remain in the midst of your people" (Deut. 21:6–8). Like the Jewish elders had been instructed to do in Deuteronomy, Pilate washed his hands and declared his innocence.

But in reply, the multitude shouted, "His blood be on us and on our children!" (Matt. 27:25). This horrifying response is the opposite of what Israelite leaders had been instructed to say in the Deuteronomy passage. With Christ, rather than seeking to be absolved of innocent blood, those present that day took responsibility for it. (To be clear, this fact does not justify later generations who blamed their Jewish con-temporaries for what happened to Jesus that Friday morning.)[40]

Probably perplexed and with growing frustration, Pilate "cried out, 'Shall I crucify your King?' The chief priests answered, 'We have no king but the emperor'" (John 19:15). "So Pilate, wishing to satisfy the

---

39. See Brown, *Death of the Messiah*, 834.
40. The statement "his blood be on us and on our children" has been used for centuries to perpetuate anti-Semitism and justify atrocious acts against Jews, including the Ho-locaust. This is, of course, a gross abuse of scripture. As Elder Gerald N. Lund wrote, "We believe that punishment for someone else's sin is unjust. To suggest that Jews of the twentieth century are being punished by God for what their ancestors two millen-nia ago did is unthinkable." *Jesus Christ, Key to the Plan of Salvation* (Salt Lake City: Deseret Book, 1991), 32.

crowd, released Barabbas for them; and . . . handed [Jesus] over to be crucified" (Mark 15:15).

———— ✦ ————

Ultimately there were many individuals present that day who could have intervened in the Savior's behalf. Caiaphas could have dropped the charges. Herod Antipas could have interceded for Christ. Pilate could have listened to Procula. But Christ came into this world to be lifted up upon a cross (see 3 Ne. 27:14). No decision from Pilate or anyone else would change Christ's destiny of dying to bring about our salvation.[41] In a sense, Christ had been traveling the road to Golgotha since the premortal life—now it was time for him to begin the physical journey to Calvary.

---

41. In a prayer uttered shortly after Christ's Resurrection, his disciples said, "For in this city, in fact, both Herod and Pontius Pilate, with the Gentiles and the peoples of Israel, gathered together against your holy servant Jesus, whom you anointed, to do whatever your hand and your plan had predestined to take place" (Acts 4:27–28). This statement clearly indicates the disciples understood that Christ had been foreordained to this mission.

Chapter 9

A CROWN OF THORNS

When Pilate passed his sentence, Barabbas and Christ parted ways—the guilty was set free, and the innocent was sent to be flogged (see Matt. 27:26). Understanding the process of scourging (see chapter 7) allows us to feel more empathy for the Savior as we visualize Roman soldiers viciously lashing him with a whip to which they had attached sharp objects. Unspeakably painful under any circumstance, the torment was compounded by the fact that the Savior likely hadn't slept for more than twenty-four hours.

The merciless treatment continued as the soldiers brought Jesus into Pilate's headquarters and "gathered the whole cohort around him" (Matt. 27:27). Stripping him of his clothing, the soldiers dressed him in a robe (see John 19:2), and "after twisting some thorns into a crown, they put it on his head. They put a reed in his right hand and knelt before him and mocked him, saying, 'Hail, King of the Jews!'" (Matt. 27:29). The parody turned violent as the soldiers spat on Christ and hit him over the head with the reed.

SYMBOLS OF LOVE

The previous scourging and coming crucifixion were incomprehensibly inhumane, but the Roman soldiers had been ordered to take these actions. In contrast, the robe, crown of thorns, pretend scepter, and accompanying abuse seem to have come from the soldiers' own cruel imaginations.[1] This mockery provides us with three significant symbols—a robe, a crown, and a reed. Looking closer at each one can deepen our perspective of the Savior's love for us.

The Robe

Earlier, Herod had given the Savior a white robe; the soldiers now mocked Jesus with a different one. The Greek word John uses to describe Christ's robe can mean any of the colors between blue and red; it is translated into English as "purple" in many Bible translations. Matthew, however, describes the color of the robe with a different Greek word, translated as "scarlet,"[2] the color of the red cloak worn by soldiers.[3] What symbolism might we see in the Savior wearing a red robe?

At the Second Coming, Christ "shall be red in his apparel, and his garments like him that treadeth in the wine-vat. . . . And his voice shall be heard: I have trodden the wine-press *alone* . . . ; and *none were with me*" (D&C 133:48, 50). Twice in his description Jesus emphasizes his solitary state; imagine an enormous vat full of grapes, and Jesus left alone, to step on every single one.

The red robe given to the Savior in derision reminds us that trials can become triumphs. Although Christ was once clothed in red and abandoned, he will again come clothed in red, this time accompanied by angels. Because he wore the red robe, each of us can be "encircl[ed] around in the robe of [his] righteousness" (2 Ne. 4:33).[4]

---

1. See Max Lucado, *He Chose the Nails: What God Did to Win Your Heart* (Nashville: Thomas Nelson, 2017), 16.
2. See Matt. 27:28. The Joseph Smith Translation for this passage uses the word "purple" (JST, Matt. 27:30). A purple robe would increase the irony since the color is a symbol of royalty. Because purple dye was very expensive, it might have been difficult (but not impossible) for the soldiers to procure a purple robe.
3. See Raymond E. Brown, *The Death of the Messiah*, vol. 2 (New York: Doubleday, 1994), 866.
4. See also Lucado, *He Chose the Nails*, 75; and 2 Ne. 9:14.

The Crown

As part of dressing the Savior in royal regalia, the soldiers created a crown of thorns. The Gospel authors do not tell us exactly what type of plant the soldiers used; however, it had to be readily available and pliable in order for the soldiers to turn it into a wreath-shaped crown.[5] In Matthew and Mark, Christ receives the crown just before being led away to be crucified. In John, however, Christ is scourged and given the crown of thorns *before* Pilate passes sentence.[6] In this account, after the scourging, Pilate brings Christ out to the people and says, "'I am bringing him out to you to let you know that I find no case against him.' So Jesus came out, *wearing the crown of thorns*. . . . Pilate said to them, 'Here is the man!'" (John 19:4–5).

The crown of thorns can remind us that soon after Adam and Eve partook of the forbidden fruit in the Garden of Eden, God said, "Cursed is the ground for thy sake; . . . *Thorns* also and thistles shall it bring forth to thee" (Gen. 3:17–18, KJV). As a symbol of the Fall, thorns entered the world, perhaps representing the results of transgression. Many times throughout the Old Testament, the Lord warns the children of Israel that the idolatrous nations they failed to drive out of the promised land would be "*thorns* in their sides," continually tempting them to worship false gods (Num. 33:55; see also Josh. 23:13; Judg. 2:3). In addition, Paul describes one of his afflictions as "a *thorn* . . . in the flesh" (2 Cor. 12:7). Thus thorns could represent not only the results of sin but also the temptations and trials we face.[7]

Given this context, the Savior, wearing the crown of thorns, was figuratively encircled by sin and weakness. Centuries before he was born in mortality, the premortal Christ said to the prophet Ezekiel, "Do not be afraid . . . , though briers and *thorns* surround you"

---

5. The specific plant used cannot be identified. See Brown, *Death of the Messiah*, 866.
6. Luke does not mention the crown of thorns.
7. See Lucado, *He Chose the Nails*, 24–25.

(Ezek. 2:6). Perhaps the Savior was reminded of his own words while his head was literally surrounded by thorns.

When Paul begged the Lord to take away his thorn in the flesh, the Lord said, "My grace is sufficient for you, for [my] power is made perfect in weakness" (2 Cor. 12:9). We can see in the crown of thorns a sign of strength, not a symbol of sorrow. Because Jesus wore the crown of thorns, we do not need to be afraid of our personal thorns in the flesh—our challenges and weaknesses. His grace is enough for each of us.

The Reed

To complete their scornful depiction of Jesus as a king, the soldiers placed a reed in his right hand, representing a royal scepter.[8] In ancient times, a scepter was a symbol of power (see Esth. 4:11). The soldiers meant the gesture as a mockery; they did not know that, with or without the reed, in Christ's "hand is given all power" (D&C 84:28).

After giving Christ the reed, the soldiers physically abused him. They spat on him and mockingly said, "Hail, King of the Jews!" (Mark 15:18).[9] They snatched the reed from him and hit him on the head with it. Reflect on the fact that although Christ had the power to stop the soldiers, *he didn't*. Less than twenty-four hours earlier, when soldiers came to apprehend him, Christ said to his disciples, "Do you think that I cannot appeal to my Father, and he will at once send me more than twelve legions of angels?" (Matt. 26:53). Christ had more than enough power to deliver himself, but still he refrained.

From the reed in the Savior's hand, we learn that although Jesus has all power, he only uses it at the right time. If we occasionally wonder why Christ does not always exercise his power in our behalf, we

---

8. Matthew is the only Gospel author who mentions the reed placed in the Savior's right hand. Mark speaks of the soldiers striking Christ with a reed, but he does not explain that Christ had first been given the reed. John and Luke do not mention the reed at all.
9. Although we sometimes see visual portrayals of the crown of thorns being cruelly pushed into the Savior's head, the Gospels themselves do not mention this detail.

can remember that he did not always exercise it on his *own* behalf. If it seems that Christ is not running to our rescue, perhaps we can be patient. He has said, "All power is given unto me in heaven and in earth" (Matt. 28:18, KJV); he will use that power according to his divine timing.

Triumphs from trials, sources of strength, and reminders of the Savior's power—we see these messages in the robe, the crown of thorns, and the reed. These three items also symbolize Christ's love. Nephi foretold this mockery: "They smite him, and he suffereth it. Yea, they spit upon him, and he suffereth it" (1 Ne. 19:9). An appropriate definition of *suffer* in this instance is "to allow."[10] Why did the Savior allow these things to happen? Nephi continues: "he suffereth [allows] it, because of his loving kindness . . . towards the children of men" (1 Ne. 19:9). All of Christ's restraint was part of his atoning sacrifice. He allowed this mockery because he loves us. Can you feel his love as you visualize the robe, the crown, and the reed?

The soldiers eventually grew tired of taunting the Savior: "They stripped him of the robe and put his own clothes on him. Then they led him away to crucify him" (Matt. 27:31). The robe was removed, but nothing further is mentioned of the crown of thorns. Was Christ wearing it as he walked to Golgotha? Was it upon his head as he hung upon the cross and asked God to forgive those who had mocked him only minutes before?

THE VIA DOLOROSA

With or without the crown, Christ followed the soldiers along the *Via Dolorosa*, which is a Latin phrase meaning "the way of sorrow." This phrase refers to the path Christ walked from Pilate's headquarters to the place of his Crucifixion. Walking the path would have taken

---

10. *American Dictionary of the English Language* (1828), ed. Noah Webster, s.v. "suffer," accessed July 7, 2020, http://webstersdictionary1828.com/Dictionary/suffer.

about ten minutes.[11] The Gospels record two events that took place on the road to Calvary: Simon's carrying the cross and the Savior's words to the lamenting women.

Simon's Carrying the Cross

As Christ continued to Calvary, the physical toll of the past twenty-four hours would have become vividly apparent. Perhaps fearing that Christ would faint or die before reaching Golgotha, the Roman soldiers picked out a "passerby who was coming in from the country" (Mark 15:21). This person likely had no idea of who Christ was or why he was being crucified. The soldiers then "compelled" this man, Simon of Cyrene, to "carry [Christ's] cross" (Matt. 27:32).[12]

The soldiers "laid the cross" (likely just the horizontal beam—see chapter 7), weighing approximately eighty pounds, on Simon's back and "made him carry it behind Jesus" (Luke 23:26). Christ had previously invited those with heavy burdens to come to him for assistance (see Matt. 11:28–29). Simon alone is named in scripture as helping Christ carry a physical burden. What did Simon feel as he bore Christ's cross? Was he willing to help, or did he wish he could escape the situation?

As I picture this scene, I think to myself, "If I had been there, I would have jumped at the chance to carry Christ's cross!" But is that really true? One way we can gauge our willingness to carry Christ's cross *back then* is in our willingness to serve others *right now*. Although we will not physically assist the Savior walking to Golgotha, when we serve "the least of these," we serve Christ (Matt. 25:40); therefore, each

---

11. In modern-day Jerusalem there is a processional route known as the "Via Dolorosa." This specific path is likely not the route Jesus actually walked.

12. The Greek word translated as "compelled" is *aggareuo*; Matthew uses this word only twice in his Gospel. The other instance occurs during the Sermon on the Mount when Christ says, "If anyone forces [*aggareuo*] you to go one mile, go also the second mile" (Matt. 5:41). Perhaps this statement foreshadows the journey Simon was to take with Jesus. See Dale C. Allison, "Anticipating the Passion: The Literary Reach of Matthew 26:47–27:56," *The Catholic Biblical Quarterly* 56, no. 4 (1994): 703–5.

of us can metaphorically carry the cross of Jesus as we help those in need. How could you and I be like Simon today?

Christ's Words to the Women

What was on Christ's mind as he walked alongside Simon? He was now only hours away from completing his atoning sacrifice. According to the Gospel of Luke, Jesus had not said a word since his initial interview with Pilate. However, he now broke his silence to address a group of women who were following him. In fact, more than half the words Luke records Christ saying on the day of his death are addressed to them.

Jesus turned to these women, who were "beating their breasts and wailing for him," and demonstrated his selfless character, telling them to "not weep for [him]" but rather to "weep for yourselves and for your children" (Luke 23:27–28). He prophesied of a coming day of calamity when, rather than rejoicing in posterity, they would say, "Blessed are the barren" (Luke 23:29). Christ was likely referencing the destruction of Jerusalem that took place in AD 70, when according to the historian Josephus, more than one million people were massacred. Josephus described people resorting to eating scraps of leather and, in some instances, their own children.[13] Truly the desolation of Jerusalem was to be so horrific that the people would "begin to say to the mountains, 'Fall on us'; and to the hills, 'Cover us'" (Luke 23:30).[14] Both Jesus and the women awaited unfathomable suffering, yet both were more concerned for the well-being of the other.

Concluding his message to these women, Christ said, "For if they do this when the wood is green, what will happen when it is dry?" (Luke 23:31). Perhaps he was suggesting, "If I who am innocent am

---

13. See Flavius Josephus, *The Wars of the Jews*, 6:193–210, in *The Works of Josephus: New Updated Edition*, trans. William Whiston (n.p.: Hendrickson Publishers, 1987), 737.
14. These words echo Hosea 10:8.

meeting such a fate, what will happen to the guilty in Jerusalem?" Or, "If these evil things are happening while I am present, what will happen in my absence?"[15]

Parallels between the Via Dolorosa and the triumphal entry make Christ's words even more poignant. In his triumphal entry into Jerusalem just a few days earlier, Jesus was accompanied by a "very large crowd," similar to the "great number of the people" who followed him to the cross (Matt. 21:8; Luke 23:27). Although Christ told the daughters of Jerusalem to "not weep" while traveling to the cross, Christ himself "wept over" Jerusalem when he entered the city (Luke 23:28; 19:41).[16]

As Christ both entered and exited Jerusalem, his thoughts and tears centered on others, not himself, manifesting his selfless character. As Elder David A. Bednar taught, "Throughout His mortal ministry, and especially during the events leading up to and including the atoning sacrifice, the Savior of the world turned outward."[17] As we strive to emulate the Savior's example, we can be enabled through Jesus "to reach outward when the natural tendency is for us to turn inward."[18]

---

15. Michael D. Coogan, ed., *The New Oxford Annotated Bible*, 4th ed. (Oxford: Oxford University Press, 2010), 1874. John Taylor used a similar metaphor when, following the deaths of Hyrum and Joseph Smith, he wrote what later became Doctrine and Covenants 135:6: "If the fire can scathe a green tree for the glory of God, how easy it will burn up the dry trees to purify the vineyard of corruption."

16. When Christ both entered and left Jerusalem, he prophesied of its destruction (see Luke 19:42–44). Another parallel exists between the triumphal entry and the Via Dolorosa: the Gospels of John and Matthew reference the "daughter of Zion" as Christ enters Jerusalem (Matt. 21:5; John 12:15), and as the Savior leaves the city, he addresses the daughters of Jerusalem. See Brown, *Death of the Messiah*, 920.

17. David A. Bednar, "The Character of Christ" (address, Brigham Young University–Idaho Religious Symposium, Rexburg, ID, June 25, 2003), https://www2.byui.edu/Presentations/Transcripts/ReligionSymposium/2003_01_25_Bednar.htm.

18. Bednar, "Character of Christ." In this same talk, Elder Bednar shares a powerful example of a woman who emulated the Savior's example of focusing on others amid personal tragedy. The woman, who was both a single mother and Relief Society president, lost her only child in a tragic car accident. Elder Bednar states, "On the day of her daughter's funeral, this Relief Society president . . . received a phone call from an

THE PLACE OF A SKULL

Matthew, Mark, and John all specify that Christ was crucified at a place called *Golgotha*, an Aramaic word[19] translated as "the place of a skull" (Mark 15:22). Perhaps Golgotha was so named because it was a place of execution, or maybe its geographic features resembled a skull.[20] Luke refers to the location as *kranion* in Greek (similar to the English *cranium*), which is translated into English as "Calvary" (Luke 23:33). Although we sometimes use the phrase "Calvary's hill," there is, in fact, no statement in the scriptures about the elevation of Golgotha or Calvary. Scholars continue to debate the exact location of Christ's Crucifixion and Resurrection; the scriptures tell us it was "outside the city gate" but "near the city," likely close to a public road so that people "who passed by" could witness it (Heb. 13:12; John 19:20; Matt. 27:39).

The fact that Christ was crucified outside the walls of the city echoes a provision of the law of Moses that the bodies of some sacrificed animals were taken outside of the camp after being offered to the Lord (see Lev. 4:12, 21). The author of Hebrews highlights this parallel, writing, "For the bodies of those animals whose blood is brought into the sanctuary by the high priest as a sacrifice for sin are burned outside the camp. Therefore Jesus also suffered outside the city gate in order to sanctify the people by his own blood" (Heb. 13:11–12). The author of

---

irritated sister in [her] ward. The complaining sister had a cold and did not feel well, and she basically chewed out the Relief Society president for not being thoughtful or compassionate enough to arrange for meals to be delivered to her home. Just hours before the funeral of her only child, this remarkable Relief Society president prepared and delivered a meal to the murmuring sister. . . . [She] reached outward when most of us would have turned inward."

19. *Golgotha* could possibly be a Hebrew word. See Brown, *Death of the Messiah*, 936.

20. We can also find symbolic meaning in the name "the place of a skull." In the Garden of Eden, God told Lucifer, "I will put enmity between you and the woman, and between your offspring and hers; he will strike your head, and you will strike his heel" (Gen. 3:15). Though Satan was able to "strike [Christ's] heel" with the nails driven through his feet, Jesus crushed the serpent's skull by conquering sin for the entire world.

Hebrews then goes one step further and offers us an invitation: "Let us then go to him *outside the camp* and *bear the abuse he endured*" (Heb. 13:13).

While this phrase certainly should not be interpreted as endorsing any type of violence or encouraging people to remain in abusive situations, it reminds us of the Savior's injunction "Do not resist an evildoer. But if anyone strikes you on the right cheek, turn the other also; and if anyone wants to sue you and take your coat, give your cloak as well" (Matt. 5:39–40). We will likely not be called to mimic Christ's physical punishments, but when we receive evil for doing good, we can recall that Christ also suffered unjustly.

One individual shared the following experience with me: "I was serving in a Church calling and had to make some difficult decisions about how to handle a delicate matter. A member of the ward was extremely angry with me and spent hours berating me both to my face and to others in the ward. Because of confidentiality, I could not explain to this member the full reasons for my actions and my partial explanations proved unsatisfactory. Although it hurt to be falsely accused, I thought of the Savior's example and patiently pressed forward."

What a wonderful example of the injunction to "go to him outside the camp." When we are called to "bear the abuse he endured," we can visualize the moment in the Savior's life when unjust persecutors led him out of the city. Mentally journeying with the Savior "outside the camp" can help us courageously follow his example of meekness in the face of persecution.

THE FIRST OFFERING OF WINE

After arriving at Golgotha but before crucifying Christ, the soldiers "offered him wine to drink, mixed with gall; but when he tasted it, he would not drink it" (Matt. 27:34).[21] Adding gall (a bitter flavor) to sweet wine is a derisive action that one might expect from the soldiers, who had no desire to ease Christ's pain. Perhaps Matthew adds this detail to point us to Psalm 69:21, connecting Christ with this Old Testament passage: "They gave me also gall for my meat" (KJV).

THE CRUCIFIXION

The Gospel authors are extremely brief in their description of the Crucifixion, which has been "more often portrayed in art than any other scene in history."[22] Interestingly, each Gospel writer uses more words to describe the soldiers gambling for Christ's clothes than they do to detail the process of his Crucifixion.

Most of what we can surmise about the specifics of Christ's Crucifixion is detailed in chapter 7. Christ's wrists were likely nailed to the horizontal beam of a T-shaped tau cross, which was then affixed to a vertical beam already in the ground. Next, his feet were nailed to the vertical beam of the cross, with the nails probably entering from the side of each foot. The cross likely stood six to eight feet high.

Average daytime temperatures in Jerusalem at this time of year range from the 40s to the 60s in Fahrenheit. Because it was quite cold during the night when Peter warmed himself by a fire (see John 18:18), it seems probable that "it was cold the day Jesus was crucified." One doctor explains, "Hanging . . . on the cross in cool ambient temperatures, sweaty, and with arms and legs cold due to blood vessel

---

21. In Mark's account, the soldiers "offered [Jesus] wine mixed with myrrh" (Mark 15:23). This would have numbed the pain; presumably Christ did not drink it because "to drink the wine mixed with myrrh given him by his enemies in order to lessen the pain would be to renege on the commitment he had made" to not shrink from the bitter cup. Brown, *Death of the Messiah*, 942.

22. Brown, *Death of the Messiah*, 945.

constriction from the effects of blood loss, make it likely that Jesus was hypothermic."[23] The process of crucifixion was agonizing.[24]

Although both ropes and nails were historically used to affix victims to crosses, Jesus refers to nail marks in his post-Resurrection appearances, testifying that he was crucified with nails (see Luke 24:39; John 20:25; 3 Ne. 11:14). Christ's hands are one of the most moving symbols of his mission and ministry. With his hands, he created "worlds without number" (Moses 1:33; see also Isa. 45:12). With his hands, he healed the sick and made the blind to see (see Matt. 8:3; John 9:6). With his hands, he even raised the dead (see Luke 8:54). The last act of Christ's earthly hands, stretched out upon the cross, was to support the weight of his body while he completed the Atonement. Thinking about these hands can motivate us to be his hands here on earth[25] and to press forward until we are "clasped in the arms of Jesus" (Morm. 5:11).

GAMBLING FOR CLOTHING

After they crucified the Savior, the soldiers "took his clothes and divided them into four parts, one for each soldier."[26] Although we do not

---

23. Joseph W. Bergeron, *The Crucifixion of Jesus: A Medical Doctor Examines the Death and Resurrection of Christ* (n.p.: CrossLink Publishing, 2018), 163.

24. In addition to the historically based description of Christ's Crucifixion, reviewed in chapter 7, in the October 1989 general conference, Elder David B. Haight of the Quorum of the Twelve described a sacred experience that gives insight into Christ's suffering on the cross. While unconscious from a serious illness, Elder Haight was given a "panoramic view" of the life of the Savior. He said, "My soul was taught over and over again the events of the betrayal, the mock trial, the scourging of the flesh of even one of the Godhead. I witnessed . . . His weakened condition carrying the cross and His being stretched upon it as it lay on the ground, that the crude spikes could be driven with a mallet into His hands and wrists and feet to secure His body as it hung on the cross for public display. Crucifixion—the horrible and painful death which He suffered—was chosen from the beginning. By that excruciating death, He descended below all things. . . . I cannot begin to convey to you the deep impact that these scenes have confirmed upon my soul." "The Sacrament—and the Sacrifice," *Ensign*, November 1989.

25. See Dieter F. Uchtdorf, "You Are My Hands," *Ensign*, May 2010.

26. The night before, just prior to washing the Apostles' feet, Jesus left the table and "took off his outer robe" (John 13:4). In this respect, the Last Supper parallels the Crucifixion; in both cases, Jesus's service included the removal of clothing and lowering himself to serve others.

know specifically what these garments were or how they were divided, John tells us that Christ also had a tunic that "was seamless, woven in one piece from the top."[27] How would the soldiers divide this last article of clothing? They said to each other, "Let us not tear it, but cast lots for it to see who will get it."[28] John then explains, "This was to fulfill what the scripture says, 'They divided my clothes among themselves, and for my clothing they cast lots' [Psalm 22:18]. And that is what the soldiers did" (John 19:23–25).[29]

President Dallin H. Oaks reflected on this scene by comparing the soldiers with Esau, who sold his birthright for a mess of pottage: "The Roman soldiers of Pilate provided an unforgettable illustration of the different perspectives of the carnal mind and the spiritual mind. During a tragic afternoon on Calvary, a handful of soldiers waited at the foot of a cross. The most important event in all eternity was taking place on the cross above their heads. Oblivious to that fact, they occupied themselves casting lots to divide the earthly property of the dying Son of God."[30] While it's easy to criticize those soldiers for missing the saving significance of this moment, we can also ask ourselves, "Lord, is it I?" (Matt. 26:22, KJV). Do we ever miss the sacred because we're thinking about trivial things? For example, as the sacrament is being blessed and passed, are our minds riveted on our Redeemer? Or are we like these soldiers, too preoccupied with mundane matters to notice the importance of what is happening right in front of us?

---

27. Historical context does not provide enough information to determine whether there were four pieces of clothing, two articles of clothing that could be divided into four pieces, or some other configuration. Similarly, whether Christ's tunic was a special garment or one worn by typical Galileans cannot be determined. See Brown, *Death of the Messiah*, 952–56.

28. In this passage, "casting lots" refers to some kind of game of chance. Brown notes, "Most scholars think that something like dice would have been thrown. . . . [However, some scholars doubt] that the soldiers would so conveniently have brought a *pyrgos* ("dice box") to the place of crucifixion." Brown, *The Death of the Messiah*, 955.

29. The Greek makes it clear that Christ had *himation* (clothing) that was divided among the soldiers, as well as a *chiton* (tunic/coat).

30. Dallin H. Oaks, "Spirituality," *Ensign*, November 1985.

Psalm 22 and Christ's Crucifixion

The soldiers casting lots for clothing is part of a larger scriptural connection between Psalm 22 and the Savior's death. Multiple phrases in Psalm 22 are related to Christ's Crucifixion; this psalm is quoted or alluded to eleven times in the New Testament.[31] In the King James Version, Psalm 22:7–8 reads, "All they that see me *laugh me to scorn*: they shoot out the lip, they *shake the head*, saying, *He trusted on the Lord that he would deliver him: let him deliver him.*" Verses in Matthew 27 parallel these phrases, stating, "They that passed by *reviled him, wagging their heads*. . . . Likewise also the chief priests mocking him, with the scribes and elders, said, . . . *He trusted in God; let him deliver him now*" (vv. 39, 41, 43).

Psalm 22 also includes the powerful phrase "They pierced my hands and my feet" (v. 16).[32] One scholar has said this passage "may be the clearest prophecy of Christ's crucifixion anywhere in the Old Testament,"[33] suggesting that the original author was speaking on behalf of, or prophesying about, what would happen to Christ. The Psalmist continues: "They part my garments among them, and cast lots upon my vesture" (v. 18), a clear reference to the soldiers' gambling for Christ's clothing (see John 19:23–24; Matt. 27:35).

Perhaps the most striking parallel between Psalm 22 and Christ's Crucifixion is its opening question, "My God, my God, why hast thou forsaken me?" (v. 1). Christ uttered these same words while on the cross (see Matt. 27:46; Mark 15:34).

Recognizing the relationship between Psalm 22 and the Savior's death helps us see that the details of the Crucifixion were known

---

31. See Shon Hopkin, "'My God, My God, Why Hast Thou Forsaken Me?' Psalm 22 and the Mission of Christ," *BYU Studies Quarterly* 52, no.4 (2013): 116–51.

32. The translation of this verse has been contested, but recent evidence favors the King James translation. For more information, see Shon Hopkin, "The Psalm 22:16 Controversy: New Evidence from the Dead Sea Scrolls," *BYU Studies Quarterly* 44, no. 3 (2005): 9.

33. Hopkin, "Psalm 22 and the Mission of Christ," 130.

from the beginning. For me, the final part of Psalm 22 is the most powerful. Although it is not quoted in the Crucifixion accounts, both Jesus and Matthew may have expected their audiences to recall that Psalm 22 ends in triumph: "All the ends of the earth shall remember and turn to the Lord; and all the families of the nations shall worship before him. . . . I shall live for him . . . and proclaim his deliverance to a people yet unborn, saying that *he has done it*" (vv. 27, 29, 31).

CRUCIFIED BETWEEN THIEVES

Mark tells us, "And with him they crucified two bandits, one on his right and one on his left" (Mark 15:27). Latter-day Saint scholar Julie M. Smith wrote that Mark's phrase "one on his right and one on his left" is "not only an odd detail to include but also a very long alternative to having Jesus 'between' two thieves. This language is almost surely used to echo the intemperate request of James and John to be given the seats of honor on Jesus' left and right hand [in his glory] ([Mark] 10:37–40). The alert audience member would thus realize that the crucifixion is, shockingly, the 'glory' of Jesus."

Smith continues, "This connection is strengthened by the fact that, in the exchange with James and John, Jesus referred to his suffering and death as his 'baptism' and 'cup' and asked if they were capable of participating in those with him. Despite James and John's affirmations, it is not them but rather two strangers who are at Jesus' right and left here. Thus, the reference to the thieves is a commentary on the disciples' abandonment of Jesus."[34] In Mark 15:28 we read that the Savior's placement between two criminals also relates with Isaiah 53:12: "And the scripture was fulfilled, which saith, And he was numbered with the transgressors" (KJV).

---

34. Julie M. Smith, *The Gospel According to Mark, Brigham Young University New Testament Commentary* (Provo, UT: BYU Studies, 2019), 79.

THE INSCRIPTION ON THE CROSS

Posted above Christ's cross was an inscription, written by Pilate. It read, "Jesus of Nazareth, the King of the Jews" (John 19:19).[35] The chief priests didn't like this statement and asked Pilate to change it to say, "This man *said*, I am King of the Jews" (John 19:21). Pilate refused; and thus "the representative of the greatest power on earth . . . verified that Jesus is king for every passerby to see."[36]

The inscription was written in three different languages: Hebrew, Latin, and Greek (see John 19:20). Hebrew was the local written language in Jerusalem, Latin was the language of the Romans, and Greek was the international language. Although these languages might not have theological significance, perhaps Pilate's inscription foreshadows the good news of Christ being preached to people "from every tribe and *language* and people and nation" (Rev. 5:9).

———◆◆———

The placard placed over the Savior's head accurately announced Christ's kingship. The truth Pilate proclaimed had been foreshadowed for millennia and would be declared in the generations that followed. Not only is Jesus the "King of the Jews," he is "Lord of lords, and King of kings" (Rev. 17:14). But before exchanging his crown of thorns for an eternal crown of glory, the Savior would be, in his own words, "slain for the sins of the world" (3 Ne. 11:14).

---

35. Traditional crucifixion artwork sometimes shows the initials INRI on the placard. These are the initials of the phrase "Iesus Nazarenus Rex Iudaeorum," which is Latin for "Jesus of Nazareth, King of the Jews."
36. Raymond E. Brown, *A Crucified Christ in Holy Week* (Collegeville, MN: The Liturgical Press, 1986), 64.

Chapter 10

"IT IS FINISHED"

C hrist had arrived at Pilate's headquarters early in the morning, and it was 9:00 a.m. "when they crucified him" (Mark 15:25). Based on this timing, Christ's trials before Herod Antipas and Pilate, his scourging, and the carrying of his cross lasted approximately three hours; he now faced six excruciating hours on the cross.[1]

The Final Hours of Christ's Life: An Approximate Timeline

hrist holds the Last Supper 6 p.m.	Christ is arrested 12 a.m.	Christ is brought before Pilate 6 a.m.	Darkness covers the land 12 p.m.
Thursday	**Friday**		
9 p.m. Christ suffers in Gethsemane	1 a.m. Christ appears before Jewish leaders	9 a.m. Christ is crucified	3 p.m. The death of Jesus Christ

MOCKING AT THE CROSS[2]

As Christ hung from the cross, people walked along the nearby busy road, perhaps purchasing items in preparation for the upcoming

---

1. In John 19:14, Pilate passes judgment on Christ at about noon, shifting the timeline portrayed by the synoptic Gospels. Here, I follow the timing presented by Matthew, Mark, and Luke.
2. Several textual connections and insights throughout this section were gleaned from

Sabbath. "Those who passed by derided him, shaking their heads and saying, 'You who would destroy the temple and build it in three days, save yourself!'" (Matt. 27:39–40). This insult refers to Christ's statement after cleansing the temple: "Destroy this temple, and in three days I will raise it up." In response, Jewish authorities had ridiculed Christ, saying, "This temple has been under construction for forty-six years, and will you raise it up in three days?" They did not realize that Christ "was speaking of the temple of his body" (John 2:19–21). Christian theologian D. A. Carson notes, "The mockers think they are witty and funny as they mock Jesus' pretensions and laugh at his utter weakness after he has claimed he could destroy the temple and raise it in three days. But . . . there is a deeper irony: it is precisely *by staying on the cross in abject powerlessness* that Jesus establishes himself as the temple and comes to the resurrection in fullness of power."[3]

Others walking past the cross mocked, "*If you are the Son of God*, come *down* from the cross" (Matt. 27:40). This phrase echoes Satan's words to Christ when he tempted the Savior to jump from the pinnacle of the temple: "*If you are the Son of God*, throw yourself *down*" (Matt. 4:6). How painful the words "*If* you are the Son of God" must have been on both occasions! But Jesus knew who he was; he ignored the scoffers just as he had refused to heed Satan's temptations.

The jeering continued from the chief priests and scribes, who said, "He saved others; he cannot save himself" (Mark 15:31). The soldiers similarly taunted, "If you are the King of the Jews, save yourself!" (Luke 23:37). They did not realize that by *not* saving himself, he was saving *them*. They were also unaware of Christ's teaching that "those who want to save their life will lose it" (Mark 8:35). He set the ultimate example

---

Raymond E. Brown, *The Death of the Messiah*, vol. 2 (New York: Doubleday, 1994), 982–1000.

3. D. A. Carson, *Scandalous: The Cross and Resurrection of Jesus* (Wheaton, IL: Crossway, 2010), 24.

for all those who would lose their lives in following God and, as a result, find eternal lives in the hereafter (see Matt. 10:39).

Some of the mocking had Old Testament overtones: According to Matthew, one insult hurled at Christ was "He trusts in God; let God deliver him now, if he wants to; for he said, 'I am God's Son'" (Matt. 27:43). Psalm 22:8 says, "*Let [God] deliver*—let him rescue the one in whom he delights," suggesting that the one who truly is favored of God will be delivered.[4] The scoffers thus implied Christ was *not* favored of God or his son.

The soldiers, the Jewish leaders, the random onlookers, and even the thieves crucified with Jesus taunted him (see Matt. 27:44). These people mocked Christ for fulfilling prophecy, challenged his true identity, tempted him to turn from his divine destiny, and used scripture to suggest he was not favored of God. What did the Savior feel when he heard these cruel words? Even in these moments of emotional anguish and physical suffering, we know his heart was full of love; he never retaliated or said an unkind word (see 1 Ne. 19:9).

Contemplating the criticism Christ confronted can help us when we are unjustly treated with contempt—Jesus *knows* what that feels like. Some of us may be mocked for remaining faithful to gospel principles, but even minor aspects of daily life can offer opportunities to reflect on the ridicule Christ received. For example, imagine you're trying to facilitate a wholesome activity for your family or a creative learning opportunity for a Sunday School class and people complain about how stupid it is. Although these scenarios are nothing compared to what Christ endured, criticisms from others can hurt and cause us to wonder why we go through all the effort if no one appreciates it. Jesus can relate (and probably has every right to wonder the same about us at

---

4. In addition, a famous book written shortly before Christ's birth states: "If the righteous man is God's child, he will help him, and will deliver him from the hand of his adversaries" (Wisdom 2:17–20, NRSV). This book is part of the Apocrypha, which is not part of the canon in the Church but would likely have been familiar to Christ and his contemporaries.

times). Though our situations are different, we can look to his reaction as an example for how to respond when we are belittled. Reflecting on his patient perseverance in the face of unjust mocking eliminates our excuses for lashing out in anger when others are unkind to us.[5]

THE WOMEN AT THE CROSS

The crowd at the cross included not only those mocking Christ, but also some of his supporters. Although no male disciples are explicitly named as being present at Christ's Crucifixion,[6] several women are. Mary, the mother of Jesus, as well as two or three other women, stood near the cross.[7] When Christ was an infant, Mary brought him to the temple. While there, Simeon prophesied to her, "This child is destined for the falling and the rising of many in Israel[.] . . . And a sword will pierce your own soul too" (Luke 2:34–35). Although a sword did not literally pierce Mary's body, her heart surely broke as she stood at the cross gazing at her dying son. Do we sufficiently appreciate Mary? As we reflect on Mary, perhaps we can say, "I'm so thankful that she raised [Jesus]. And so thankful that she let him go. Her [child] died so that mine could live."[8]

What would it feel like to have an angel tell you that your child

---

5. Elder Lynn G. Robbins taught, "One reason the Lord illustrates doctrines with the most extreme circumstances is to eliminate excuses." "Tithing—a Commandment Even for the Destitute," *Ensign*, May 2005.

6. The Greek word translated as "acquaintances" in Luke 23:49 is the masculine plural form, suggesting that unnamed male disciples were present. In addition, the unnamed disciple whom Jesus loved was male and may refer to the Apostle John. See Brown, *Death of the Messiah*, 1171; John 19:26.

7. John 19:25 states, "Standing near the cross of Jesus were his mother, and his mother's sister, Mary the wife of Clopas, and Mary Magdalene. Some interpret the phrase "his mother's sister, Mary the wife of Clopas" as one individual, whereas others see two or even three different people listed in this phrase (depending on where commas are placed). John portrays Mary Magdalene as being near the Savior, but Matthew places her at "a distance" from the cross. Matt. 27:55.

8. Debbie McDaniel, "'Mom, Did Jesus Feel Pain?' The Reality of the Cross," *Crosswalk. com* (blog), April 10, 2017, https://www.crosswalk.com/blogs/debbie-mcdaniel/mom -did-jesus-feel-pain.html.

would be "the Son of the Most High" and that God would give your son "the throne of his ancestor David" (Luke 1:32)? How did Mary feel watching Jesus grow older? Did she anticipate this moment when she would watch her son be crucified? A medieval hymn expresses some of what Mary may have experienced:

> *The sorrowing mother stood*
> *Weeping by the cross*
> *While her Son hung there*
> *Her grieving soul*
> *Sad and sorrowing*
> *Was pierced by a sword*
> *What person would not weep*
> *Seeing the mother of Christ*
> *In such torment?*
> *Who would be incapable of sorrowing with her?*
> *For the sins of his people*
> *She sees Jesus in torment*
> *And subjected to scourging.*
> *She sees her sweet child*
> *Dying abandoned*
> *As he gave forth his spirit.*[9]

In addition to Christ's mother, "*Many* women were also there, looking on from a distance;[10] they had followed Jesus from Galilee and had provided for him." These women included "Mary the mother of James and Joseph, and the mother of the sons of Zebedee [that is, James and John]," Mary Magdalene, and others (Matt. 27:55–56). These faithful disciples had traveled a significant distance (about one

---

9. As cited and translated by Richard Viladesau in *The Beauty of the Cross* (Oxford: Oxford University Press, 2006), 133–34.

10. Perhaps in the phrase "looking on from a distance," we see an echo of Psalm 38:11: "My friends and companions stand aloof from my affliction, and my neighbors stand far off." See Brown, *Death of the Messiah*, 1171.

hundred miles) and used their resources to support Christ. Their actions showed an unwavering commitment to and love for Jesus.

As we contemplate the feelings of the women at the cross, we gain a powerful window into our own experiences of watching loved ones suffer. We may have a child who is mistreated, witness a friend who is betrayed, or watch a relative face a terminal disease. In many of these instances, we, like these women at the cross, must stand by helplessly, with no power to change the situation. Do you feel devastated by what is happening to your loved ones? These women can relate.

The women at the cross show us that we can comfort others just by our presence. Sister Elaine L. Jack stated, "At this most dramatic moment of all time, there was the mother, Mary. She couldn't soothe his pain this time, but she could stand by his side."[11] When those we love suffer, we want to take the pain away. But even if their hurts are beyond our help, we can often be with and weep with them. Our empathy might be one of the most powerful of healing balms.

We can find hope in the faith of these women who endured this painful experience—eventually their sorrow was turned to joy. Because of Christ's Atonement, we too can look forward to a time when he "will swallow up death forever . . . [and] wipe away the tears from all faces" (Isa. 25:8).

Seven Statements from the Cross

While on the cross, the Savior said seven statements—each is significant and becomes even more so considering his pain and the extreme effort it would have taken for him to speak. These statements provide important insight into the character of Christ and his experience on the cross. Collectively, they have been referred to or quoted in general conferences more than three hundred times.[12]

11. Elaine L. Jack, "Relief Society: A Balm in Gilead," *Ensign*, November 1995.
12. See John Hilton III, Megan Cutler, and Emily Hyde, "Teachings of Church Leaders

Because each Gospel records different final words of the Savior, we cannot definitively sequence them; they are presented here in the approximate order in which they occurred.[13]

As the soldiers crucified him, the Savior, in an extraordinary act of mercy, said, **"Father, forgive them; for they do not know what they are doing"** (Luke 23:34). The Joseph Smith Translation makes it clear that Christ was referring to the Roman soldiers in this passage.[14] Thus, the Savior generously pleaded for those who were *in the very act of crucifying him*. What a powerful example of his teachings to "forgive your brother or sister from your heart" and to "forgive everyone" (Matt. 18:35; Luke 11:4). Christ was willing to extend forgiveness, even when it was not merited, asked for, or acknowledged.[15]

The Savior also displayed tender compassion in his words to one of the men who was crucified next to him. As Christ hung between two men, one of them "kept deriding him and saying, 'Are you not the Messiah? Save yourself and us!' But the other rebuked him, saying, 'Do you not fear God, since you are under the same sentence of condemnation? And we indeed have been condemned

---

on Christ's Final Seven Statements," *The Religious Educator*, forthcoming, available at http://johnhiltoniii.com/crucifixion.

13. Matthew and Mark each provide one (the same) statement from the Savior on the cross. Luke and John each give three statements from Christ, all of which are unique to their respective Gospels. Because all seven statements are not present in one account, it is difficult to determine their precise order. For additional insights on these seven statements, see Terry B. Ball and Nathan Winn, "Doctrines from Our Savior's Final Words," in *"Behold the Lamb of God": An Easter Celebration*, ed. Richard Neitzel Holzapfel, Frank F. Judd Jr., and Thomas A. Wayment (Provo, UT: Religious Studies Center, Brigham Young University, 2008), 105–24.

14. JST, Luke 23:35 says, "Father, forgive them; for they know not what they do *(Meaning the soldiers who crucified him)*."

15. Referring to the Savior on the cross, President Joseph F. Smith taught, "Go home and dismiss envy and hatred from your hearts; dismiss the feeling of unforgiveness; and cultivate in your souls that spirit of Christ which cried out upon the cross, 'Father, forgive them; for they know not what they do.' This is the spirit that Latter-day Saints ought to possess all the day long." *Seventy-Third Semi-annual Conference of The Church of Jesus Christ of Latter-day Saints* (Salt Lake City: Deseret News, 1902), 87.

justly, for we are getting what we deserve for our deeds, but this man has done nothing wrong'" (Luke 23:39–41).

At this point, the penitent thief pled with Christ, in what would be the final recorded words addressed to the Savior before his death: "Jesus, remember me when you come into your kingdom" (Luke 23:42). The thief's words capture an intimacy and intensity—this is one of the rare times in the Gospels when a person refers to the Savior by his given name of Jesus,[16] and this is the only time anybody asks Christ to remember him or her. Do we similarly feel an urgent need for the grace of Jesus Christ in our lives? Do we cry out, "O Jesus, thou Son of God, have mercy on me" (Alma 36:18)?

Although some might view this crucified criminal as worthless or beyond redemption, "Jesus chose him to show us what he thinks of the human race."[17] In response to the thief, the Savior said, **"Truly I tell you, today you will be with me in Paradise"** (Luke 23:43).[18] Joseph Smith taught that in this statement Christ was saying, "*This day* thou shalt be with *me* in the world of Spirits, then *I* will teach you all about it, and answer your inquiries."[19] Although the Prophet

---

16. See Mark 10:47; see also James Montgomery Boice and Philip Graham Ryken, *The Heart of the Cross* (Wheaton, IL: Crossway Books, 1999), 23.

17. Max Lucado, *On Calvary's Hill* (Nashville: Thomas Nelson, 2013), 66.

18. In the Gospel of Luke, the first words Jesus spoke in his public ministry "proclaimed release to the captives and liberty to those who were oppressed (4:18); it is only fitting that his last words addressed to another human being [in Luke] should fulfill that promise." Brown, *Death of the Messiah*, 1002.

19. "History, 1838–1856, volume D-1 [1 August 1842–1 July 1843]," [1573], The Joseph Smith Papers, accessed August 10, 2020, https://www.josephsmithpapers.org/paper-summary/history-1838-1856-volume-d-1-1-august-1842-1-july-1843/218. President George Q. Cannon echoed the Prophet's sentiment by providing an expanded view of what the Savior was saying to the thief on the cross: "Jesus said to him: 'Today shalt thou be with me in paradise.' 'There I can speak to you,' He might have said, 'more fully than I can now. This is our dying hour, and I am not in a position to preach to you or explain to you the plan of salvation that I have; but wait awhile, before this day ends you will be with me in paradise, and there I can make full explanations to you concerning all that you desire to know.' And this in reality was the case. That day they were in paradise together." In 1903, President Anthon H. Lund offered his perspective on the interaction between Christ and the thief: "Jesus saw that the man was

Joseph makes it clear that the penitent thief will not automatically be exalted, he rephrases the Savior's words to indicate that Christ would personally minister to the thief after they die. Can you imagine the scene when Jesus and this man see each other in the spirit world?

In his words regarding the soldiers and the thief, the Savior demonstrated extreme compassion, even for those who had made serious mistakes. As Emily Freeman has poignantly suggested, Jesus met the thief where he was, and he will also meet us where we are.[20] When we feel beyond the reach of the Savior's love, when we struggle to forgive others amid our own great pain, we can remember these two statements made by Christ on the cross. Jesus is a merciful Savior who reaches out with forgiveness, inspiring us to do the same for others.

When Jesus saw Mary and "the disciple whom [Christ] loved" standing near him, he said to Mary, **"Woman, here is your son."** Then, directing his words to the beloved disciple (often assumed to be John), **"Here is your mother"** (John 19:26–27). In his greatest agony, the Savior focused on the needs of his mother, knowing that his absence would be immensely difficult to bear. As with the women on the Via Dolorosa, the soldiers he forgave, and the thief to whom he offered comfort, Christ lovingly attended to others' needs even in *his* moment of greatest need. He inspires us to look outward, even when we are suffering.

Another possible meaning of Christ's message is Mary's adoption of John as her son, making him Christ's brother. In this

---

penitent, that he had a broken heart and a contrite spirit, and he comforted him with the promise that 'today shalt thou be with me in paradise.' I do not think He held out a fallacious hope to this man when He said that he should be with Him in paradise that day." George Q. Cannon, in *Journal of Discourses*, 26 vols. (Liverpool: F. D. Richards, 1855–86), 26:83 (November 9, 1884); Anthon H. Lund, in *Seventy-Fourth Semi-annual Conference of The Church of Jesus Christ of Latter-day Saints* (Salt Lake City: The Church of Jesus Christ of Latter-day Saints, 1903), 81.

20. See Emily Belle Freeman, *Grace Where You Are* (Salt Lake City: Deseret Book, 2020), 31–32.

interpretation, John might symbolize us—"As John was brought more closely into the family of Christ, . . . so we too are brought into a deeper relationship with our Lord by what happened on the cross."[21]

While Christ hung in agony, he also said, **"I am thirsty"** (John 19:28). Although John points out that Christ said this to fulfill scripture (compare Psalm 69:21), the Savior almost certainly was experiencing unbearable thirst. President Russell M. Nelson elaborated on the depth of suffering behind this phrase: "To a doctor of medicine, this is a very meaningful expression. Doctors know that when a patient goes into shock because of blood loss, invariably that patient—if still conscious—with parched and shriveled lips cries for water. Even though the Father and the Son knew well in advance what was to be experienced, the actuality of it brought indescribable agony."[22] Christ understands intense physical pains and desires. As the time of his death approached, he "cried out with a loud voice, . . . **My God, my God, why hast thou forsaken me?"** (Mark 15:34; see also Psalm 22:1). In his moment of greatest distress, Christ was left to bear the full brunt of the sins of the world without the accompanying help of his Father.

In these two statements we more fully see a Savior who suffers. He is a human Savior, who has felt the feelings of the flesh. In our pain, we can connect with Christ; he has experienced the ultimate anguish and understands feelings of extreme grief and despair.

21. Eric Huntsman, *God So Loved the World: The Final Days of the Savior's Life* (Salt Lake City: Deseret Book, 2011), 83. I also appreciate an insight from Shalissa Lindsay. Describing a time when she was contemplating this moment between Jesus and his mother, she saw in her mind's eye another woman in the distance and heard the Savior say to her, "Behold thy sister." Imagining this woman to be somebody she was assigned to minister to, she wrote, "Will I go to her, as John did, that same hour? Will I consider my responsibility to her as seriously as if she were my own blood sister? Will I wrap my arms around her? What if she tries to rebuff me? . . . Will I keep going back? . . . I hope so." *Answers Will Come: Trusting the Lord in the Meantime* (American Fork, UT: Covenant Communications, 2017), 109.
22. Russell M. Nelson, "The Atonement," *Ensign*, November 1996.

As the end approached, Christ cried, **"Father, into your hands I commend my spirit"** (Luke 23:46).[23] Perhaps the key word in that sentence is *I*—the personal pronoun indicates the Savior's personal agency—he *willingly* gave up his life (see John 10:17–18). In this statement we see Christ giving himself completely to God. Do we do the same? As James Martin, a Jesuit priest, wrote, "[In] the greatest sacrifice the world has ever seen, body and soul he gives himself. Jesus gives himself entirely. This is what we're all called to do: give ourselves totally to God."[24] Note also that the Savior intimately addresses God as "Father." In the Gospel of Luke, Christ's first recorded words concern the importance of doing his "Father's business" (Luke 2:49, KJV)—now he has completed the work his Father sent him to do.[25]

Finally, Jesus said, **"It is finished"** (John 19:30). In spite of earth and hell combining against him, Christ completed the work his Father had sent him to accomplish. In these last two statements we see a divine Savior who, in the face of intense suffering, retains all power and completes his atoning sacrifice. Even when our lives spin *out of control*, we can be confident that Christ is completely *in control*.

Christ is a healing Savior who extends mercy and comfort even in his own agony, a suffering Savior who can relate to our anguish, and an all-powerful Savior, able to help us in every circumstance. Reflecting on these seven statements Jesus said from the cross can invite greater peace in our lives as we think more of Christ and his example.

---

23. In this statement, Jesus echoes the first half of Psalm 31:5: "Into your hand I commit my spirit." Left unsaid by the Savior, though still true, is the second half of this verse: "you have redeemed me, O Lord, faithful God." See Brown, *Death of the Messiah*, 1066–69.

24. James Martin, SJ, *Seven Last Words: An Invitation to a Deeper Friendship with Jesus* (New York: Harper Collins, 2016), 112.

25. See Brown, *Death of the Messiah*, 1068.

THE DEATH OF JESUS CHRIST

At noon, three hours after Christ was nailed to the cross, "darkness came over the whole land until three in the afternoon" (Mark 15:33). Nature itself was testifying of the passing of God's Son. At about 3:00 p.m., Jesus called out, "Eloi, Eloi, lema sabachthani?" which is Aramaic for "My God, my God, why have you forsaken me?" (Mark 15:34). Some of those who were present appear to have misinterpreted Christ's cry as a call for help to Elijah.[26]

After hearing these words from the Savior, "someone ran, filled a sponge with sour wine, put it on a stick, and gave it to him to drink, saying, 'Wait, let us see whether Elijah will come to take him down'" (Mark 15:36). Previously, Christ had been offered sweet wine mixed with a bitter gall. Now he was offered sour (vinegary) wine in fulfillment of Psalm 69:21: "For my thirst they gave me vinegar to drink."[27] Elijah did not come; instead, "Jesus gave a loud cry and breathed his last" (Mark 15:37; compare Matt. 27:50).[28]

At the moment of Christ's passing, "The earth shook, and the rocks were split,"[29] and "the curtain of the temple was torn in two, from top to bottom" (Matt. 27:51). This curtain, or veil, marked the entrance to the Holy of Holies, which was such a sacred part of the temple; it

---

26. "Eloi," sounds like the Aramaic word for Elijah. For further analysis, see Michael Flowers, "The Bystanders at the Cross and Their Expectations about Elijah," *The Catholic Biblical Quarterly* 80, no. 3 (2018): 448–69.

27. Matthew and Mark do not state whether Christ drinks the sour wine offered to him; in John 19:30 Christ receives it, perhaps in fulfillment of his statement, "Am I not to drink the cup that the Father has given me?" John 18:11.

28. Luke portrays the final moment of Christ's life by stating, "Then Jesus, crying with a loud voice, said, 'Father, into your hands I commend my spirit.' Having said this, he breathed his last" (Luke 27:46), whereas John records, "Jesus . . . said, 'It is finished.' Then he bowed his head and gave up his spirit" (John 19:30). The Joseph Smith Translation of Matthew's account states, "Jesus, when he had cried again with a loud voice, saying, Father it is finished, thy will is done, yielded up the ghost" (JST, Matt. 27:54).

29. Matthew also records that after the Savior's Resurrection, "The tombs also were opened, and many bodies of the saints who had fallen asleep were raised. After his resurrection they came out of the tombs and entered the holy city and appeared to many." Matt. 27:52–53; compare Ezek. 37:11–14.

could only be entered once each year, and, even then, only by the high priest.[30] The Holy of Holies represented the place where God dwelled and was completely inaccessible to the people. But with the veil now torn open, everybody could symbolically enter into the presence of God (see Heb. 10:19–20).[31]

As if to emphasize that *all* can now enter into the presence of God, Mark tells us that the military leader in charge of the Crucifixion said, "Truly this man was God's Son!" (Mark 15:39; see also 15:44). This Roman centurion is the only person in Mark's Gospel to verbally recognize Jesus as the Son of God. As Christian author Timothy Keller points out, "Every Roman coin of the time was inscribed 'Tiberius Caesar, son of the divine Augustus.' The only person a loyal Roman would ever call 'Son of God' was Caesar—but this man gave the title to Jesus."[32] If even

---

30. In the temple two curtains were used to signal increasingly holy places. One curtain separated the outer courtyard from the holy place, and the second curtain separated the holy place from the holiest place—the Holy of Holies. I assume that Matthew's statement refers to this second curtain, although it could refer to the first curtain.

31. In the Gospel of Mark, the Greek word *schizo* is used to describe the tearing of the temple veil (Mark 15:38). This word is used only one other time in Mark: In Mark 1, at the baptism of Jesus Christ, "just as [Jesus] was coming up out of the water, he saw the heavens torn apart [*schizo*] and the Spirit descending like a dove on him. And a voice from heaven said, "You are my Son, the Beloved" (Mark 1:10–11). The declaration "You are my Son" accompanies the rending of the heavens. Perhaps similarly, a divine declaration to all that Christ is God's Son can be seen in the tearing of the temple curtain. See Daniel M. Gurtner, "The Veil Was Torn in Two: What Happened on Good Friday?" Desiring God, April 19, 2019, https://www.desiringgod.org/articles/the-veil-was-torn-in-two.

32. Timothy Keller, *Jesus the King* (New York: Penguin Books, 2016) 227. Julie M. Smith notes, "Two thousand years of Christian tradition have probably made it impossible to appreciate how odd it was for a soldier to look at the corpse of a criminal and announce that the dead man was God's Son. The parallel with the baptism, where the voice from heaven pronounces Jesus to be God's Son, makes the centurion's exclamation all the more profound because he is occupying the narrative role of God when he is the voice that attests to Jesus' identity. Just as the rending of the heavens comes immediately before the divine announcement that Jesus is God's son at the baptism, the rending of the temple veil comes immediately before the centurion's announcement that Jesus is God's son. In other words, Mark's narrative teaches that the death of Jesus makes it possible for a centurion to do what God does. Even a hated pagan soldier can be elevated to a godlike status and possess a godlike knowledge because of the death of Jesus." *Gospel According to Mark*, 81.

a Roman centurion can recognize Jesus as God's Son, we certainly cannot prejudge who will see and believe.

BROKEN BONES AND A SPEAR IN THE SIDE

After the centurion's declaration, the crowds returned home, leaving the women, who lingered "at a distance, watching these things" (Luke 23:49). Because the following day was the Sabbath, "the Jews did not want the bodies left on the cross. . . . So they asked Pilate to have the legs of the crucified men broken," knowing that broken legs would lead to swift death (John 19:31). Granting their request, the soldiers broke the legs of the two thieves, but seeing that Christ was already dead, the soldiers did not break his legs (see John 19:32–33).

Christ as the Passover Lamb

Our minds instinctively link the phrase "Lamb of God" to Jesus Christ. Surprisingly, in the Gospels, only John uses this phrase (see John 1:29; 1:36). John specifically portrays Jesus as the Passover Lamb—an allusion to the time when a firstborn lamb was killed to protect the Israelites from the final plague that came upon the Egyptians. This death of the firstborn could only be prevented by killing a lamb and then using the blood to mark the home so that the destroying angel would "pass over," not killing the firstborn inside (Ex. 12:13). In the centuries that followed, the ancient Israelites offered up a sacrificial lamb at Passover.

Although Matthew, Mark, and Luke portray the Last Supper as a Passover meal, in John, the Passover takes place *after* Christ's Crucifixion. In John's account, when the Jewish authorities bring Christ to Pilate, they had not yet eaten the Passover meal and were planning to do so that evening (see John 18:28). Thus, Christ was on trial while the Passover feast was being prepared (see John 19:14). In the Gospel of John, Christ dies at the exact time Passover lambs were being slain in the temple.[33] The Passover lamb was thus sacrificed simultaneously with the person whom it represented— Jesus, the Lamb of God.

A second connection between Christ and the Passover lamb is that while Christ was hanging on the cross, "a jar full of sour wine was standing there. So they put a sponge full of the wine on a branch of *hyssop* and held it to his mouth" (John 19:29). Hyssop is the plant that the Israelites in Egypt had used to paint their doorways with the lamb's blood so that the destroying angel would pass them by (see Ex. 12:22). The same plant used to provide deliverance to the firstborn of the Israelites delivered drink to the Firstborn of God.

Finally, during the original Passover, the Lord commanded that the sacrificed lambs have no broken bones (see Ex. 12:46). John specifically notes that although the legs of the two thieves were broken, when the soldiers "saw that [Jesus Christ] was already dead, they did not break his legs[.] . . . These things occurred so that the scripture might be fulfilled, 'None of his bones shall be broken'" (John 19:33, 36).[34] The relationship between the Passover and Christ's Crucifixion reminds us that "our paschal lamb, Christ, has been sacrificed" for each of us (1 Cor. 5:7).

To ensure the Savior was truly dead, "one of the soldiers pierced his side with a spear, and at once blood and water came out" (John 19:34). John connects this event with Zechariah 12:10, writing, "These things

---

33. Christ died at approximately 3:00 p.m. (see Mark 15:34; Matt. 27:46; Luke 23:44). Josephus tells us that the "high-priests, upon the coming of that feast which is called the Passover . . . slay their sacrifices, from the ninth hour [3:00 p.m.] till the eleventh [5:00 p.m.]." *The Wars of the Jews*, 6:423, in *The Works of Josephus: New Updated Edition*, trans. William Whiston (n.p.: Hendrickson Publishers, 1987), 749.

34. Christ's unbroken bones also fulfills Psalm 34:19–20: "Many are the afflictions of the righteous, but the Lord rescues them from them all. He keeps all their bones; not one of them will be broken."

occurred so that the scripture might be fulfilled. . . ,'They will look on the one whom they have pierced'" (John 19:36–37).

Christ's wounded side offers us the hope of becoming a new creation in Jesus Christ. The Greek word used for Jesus's "side" is also used to refer to Adam's rib in the Greek translation of the Old Testament. Just as Adam's side was a key symbolic part of Creation, the wound in Jesus's side is a symbolic token of our rebirth in him: "While God is the father of the spirits of all humankind, and as our earthly parents gave us biological life, through his Atonement Jesus becomes yet another Father for his Saints, giving them eternal life."[35] We find additional theological significance in Christ's side being pierced in the Savior's declaration "If any man thirst, let him come unto me, and drink. He that believeth on me, as the scripture hath said, out of his belly shall flow rivers of living water" (John 7:37–38, KJV). The blood and water pouring from Christ's side on the cross provide everlasting life to all who come unto him.

THE BURIAL

As the crowds dispersed, a question remained—what would happen to the Savior's body? Joseph of Arimathea,[36] described as a "rich man"[37] and "a good and righteous man," was "a disciple of Jesus, though a secret one because of his fear of the Jews" (Matt. 27:57; Luke 23:50; John 19:38). Although a member of the Jewish council, he "had not agreed" with the action taken by the Jewish authorities in condemning Christ (Luke 23:51). Now, Joseph "went *boldly* to Pilate and asked for the body of Jesus" (Mark 15:43).

Think of the bravery it took for Joseph to show loyalty to Jesus at his death, especially when his colleagues had condemned Christ

---

35. Huntsman, *God So Loved the World,* 91; see also Mosiah 5:7.

36. Where Arimathea was located is unknown.

37. Perhaps there is a connection between Joseph of Arimathea's wealth and Isaiah 53:8–9: "He was cut off from the land of the living. . . . They made . . . his tomb with the rich."

to this fate (see Mark 14:64). With Christ gone, it would have been easy for Joseph to retreat from following him—but he didn't. In addition to being fearless, Joseph worked quickly and effectively. With the sun setting soon, running to Pilate's residence, gathering necessary supplies, returning to and removing Christ's body from the cross, and burying the Savior would have taken a significant amount of time and coordination.

Pilate, surprised Christ had died so soon, received verification of his death from the supervising centurion and then granted Joseph's request to take custody of Christ's body. Joseph proceeded to take down the lifeless body of Christ from the cross and carefully wrapped it in a linen cloth (see Mark 15:46). Although little is recorded about Joseph removing Christ's body from the cross, it must have been a very tender moment. What would you or I have seen had we been present? What would we have felt?

Joining Joseph was Nicodemus, a Pharisee and a "leader of the Jews" (John 3:1), who had once approached Jesus by night and later defended the Savior in front of the chief priests (see John 3:1–13; 7:45–52). Nicodemus now "came, bringing a mixture of myrrh and aloes, weighing about a hundred pounds" (John 19:39). The price of these ointments was enormous; previously, when Mary anointed Jesus with *one* pound of oil, Judas Iscariot had been indignant about the exorbitant cost. Nicodemus now brings one-hundred times that amount—truly burial preparations fit for a king.[38] Perhaps in Nicodemus's coming at this moment, we see a fulfillment of the Savior's earlier phrase "I, when I am lifted up from the earth, will draw all people to myself" (John 12:32). Christ, having been lifted up on the cross, was already bringing people to him.[39]

---

38. Due to differences in measurements, the amount reported as one hundred pounds in John 19:39 is approximately seventy-five pounds by today's standards. For more information about the specific ointments used, see Brown, *Death of the Messiah*, 1260–66.
39. Raymond E. Brown, *A Crucified Christ in Holy Week* (Collegeville, MN: The Liturgical Press, 1986), 67.

Joseph owned "a rock-hewn tomb where no one had ever been laid" in a garden located "in the place where [Christ] was crucified" (Luke 23:53; John 19:41). Together, Joseph and Nicodemus "took the body of Jesus and wrapped it with the spices in linen cloths, according to the burial custom of the Jews" and then placed him in the tomb and "rolled a stone against the door of the tomb" to seal it shut (John 19:40; Mark 15:46).

Of course, Joseph and Nicodemus were not alone. "The women who had come with [Jesus] from Galilee," including "Mary Magdalene and Mary the mother of Joses," "followed, and they saw the tomb and how his body was laid" (Luke 23:55; Mark 15:47). Despite what appeared to be the complete collapse of all their hopes, *Jesus's followers stayed near the tomb.* They could have left town, but even though they did not understand what had or would happen, they remained close to where Jesus was. Consider what you do when you're in the position of those early disciples. Max Lucado asks believers, "When it's Saturday in your life, how do you react? When you are somewhere between yesterday's tragedy and tomorrow's triumph, what do you do? Do you leave God—or do you linger near him?"[40] In this critical moment, many of the Savior's followers stayed—setting a powerful example for each of us.

Elder Joseph B. Wirthlin testified:

> Each of us will have our own Fridays—those days when the universe itself seems shattered and the shards of our world lie littered about us in pieces. We all will experience those broken times when it seems we can never be put together again. We will all have our Fridays.
>
> But I testify to you in the name of the One who conquered

---

40. Max Lucado, *He Chose the Nails: What God Did to Win Your Heart* (Nashville: Thomas Nelson, 2017), 206.

death—Sunday will come. In the darkness of our sorrow, Sunday will come.

No matter our desperation, no matter our grief, Sunday will come. In this life or the next, Sunday will come.[41]

———————————◆◆————————————

Although all seemed lost, Sunday was coming soon. The women who stayed nearby, then steeped in sorrow, would return to the tomb on Easter morning and become the first witnesses of the resurrected Savior (see Matt. 28:9). Crucifixion was not the end for Jesus; he was already in the spirit world, "declaring liberty to the captives who had been faithful" (D&C 138:18). He would soon break the bands of death, bringing to pass the saying "Death has been swallowed up in victory" (1 Cor. 15:54; compare Isa. 25:8).

———————————

41. Joseph B. Wirthlin, "Sunday Will Come," *Ensign*, November 2006.

PART IV

Deepening Your Personal Connection to Christ's Atonement

Chapter 11

THE POWER OF THE RESURRECTION

Because my name is John Hilton III, people often ask me about the first "John Hilton." He was my grandfather, an incredible man who served the Lord and loved his family. After retiring as a nuclear physicist, he moved to Provo, Utah, where he became an adjunct faculty member at Brigham Young University. His research focused on using statistical analyses to demonstrate the authenticity of the Book of Mormon; he always shared with me interesting details about what he was learning. As a BYU student, I spent lots of time with him and my grandmother. They met my then girlfriend (now wife), Lani, before my parents did, and Lani always says she fell in love with my grandfather before she fell in love with me.

One month before Lani and I were to be sealed, I received a phone call from my uncle, who told me that my grandfather had unexpectedly passed away. It was my responsibility to call my parents and notify them. I sobbed as I shared the news.

I often think about my grandfather John, as well as my grandfather Jack, who passed away several years later. As I write this chapter, my paternal grandmother, Jan, is ninety-one years old and still exercises daily! My maternal grandmother, Rose, also ninety-one, has terminal cancer and is on hospice care. All too soon, each of my grandparents—so influential in my life—will be on the other side of the veil. Even though I miss my deceased grandparents, I have a firm hope that I will see them in the future. Not only will we reunite in the spirit world, but we will each be resurrected and able to physically hug each other once again. We'll be able to do this because of the Savior, who made it so "the grave hath no victory, and the sting of death is swallowed up in Christ" (Mosiah 16:8).

On one occasion President Gordon B. Hinckley wrote, "There would be no Christmas if there had not been Easter."[1] To this we could add that without Christ's Crucifixion, there would be no Easter and therefore no Christmas! Scriptures and modern Church leaders consistently teach that Resurrection is made possible only through the *death* of Jesus Christ. Lehi said Christ "*layeth down his life* . . . that he may bring to pass the *resurrection* of the dead" (2 Ne. 2:8). Samuel the Lamanite taught that Christ's "*death* bringeth to pass the *resurrection*" (Hel. 14:16), and Moroni echoed, "The *death of Christ* bringeth to pass the *resurrection*" (Morm. 9:13).

The doctrine of the Resurrection offers us peace as we face challenges with mortal bodies—including sickness and death itself. This chapter explores four themes: messages from the empty tomb, the hope offered by the Resurrection, how Jesus broke the bands of death, and the intimate nature of the Savior's scars. As we learn more about Christ's Resurrection, we will be able to say with increasing power, "This is the testimony . . . which we give of him: *That he lives!*" (D&C 76:22).

MESSAGES FROM THE EMPTY TOMB

I had a choice opportunity to reflect on Christ's Resurrection when I lived in Jerusalem. Elder Dale G. Renlund came to speak at our district conference, and through a fortuitous set of circumstances, I was

---

1. Gordon B. Hinckley, "The Wondrous and True Story of Christmas," *Ensign*, December 2000.

invited to go with him and a few other people to the Garden Tomb and ponder the events of Easter morning.

As we sat together, Elder Renlund invited us to read Mark 16, Matthew 28, Luke 24, and John 20, looking for similarities and differences in the Gospel accounts. Being in that special place, with a special witness of Christ, was a powerful spiritual experience. While we can't all be at the Garden Tomb together, I'd like to recreate that moment with you by looking at what Gospel authors shared about what initially happened at the empty tomb. Let's begin with Mark, which many scholars suggest was the first Gospel to be written.

Mark 16:1–8

In the Gospel of Mark, we learn that on the first day of the week, "very early in the morning," Mary Magdalene, Mary the mother of James, and Salome came to the sepulcher at sunrise to anoint Christ's body with sweet spices. As they traveled to the tomb, they said to each other, "Who shall roll us away the stone from the door of the sepulchre?" However, they didn't need to worry because when they arrived, "they saw that the stone was rolled away" (Mark 16:2–4).[2]

As they entered the tomb, they saw "a young man . . . clothed in a long white garment; and they were affrighted." The man told them not to be afraid and then proclaimed, "Ye seek Jesus of Nazareth, which was crucified: he is risen; he is not here: behold the place where they laid him." The man then gave the women at the tomb a specific invitation: "Go your way, tell his disciples and *Peter* that he goeth before you into Galilee" (Mark 16:5–7).

The mention of Peter stands out to me. The last time we heard about Peter in the Gospel of Mark was when he denied the Savior three times. If we were reading this account for the first time, we might assume, "It's too late for Peter. When things looked bad, he denied the Savior—there is no coming back now." But with the specific inclusion

---

2. This is a great life lesson: we often worry about things that the Lord will take care of.

of Peter by the young man at the tomb, we learn that *it is not too late*. In effect Jesus is saying, "Peter, you're still on my team!" It wasn't over for Peter, and it's not over for us. Christ beckons us to join him, even when we stumble.[3]

As recorded by Mark, the women's response to the invitation to spread the good news of the Savior's Resurrection is surprising. Rather than going to tell the disciples, the women "fled from the sepulchre; for they trembled and were amazed: neither said they any thing to any man; for they were afraid" (Mark 16:8). In the earliest extant manuscripts of Mark, this is the ending point of the Gospel—a rather abrupt conclusion.[4]

If we assume Mark's account originally ended here, with the remaining verses added later, perhaps the concluding words are a rhetorical device designed to leave readers wondering what will happen next. As New Testament scholar Mary Ann Tolbert wrote, "If the women do not carry the message, is there anyone else who can? Is there anyone

---

3. See Julie M. Smith, *The Gospel According to Mark*, Brigham Young University New Testament Commentary (Provo, UT: BYU Studies, 2019), 834–35. Smith also notes the strong similarity between the "young man" at the tomb and the "young man" at Gethsemane (Mark 16:5; 14:51). Smith wrote, "The young man in Gethsemane was dressed in a linen cloth (using the same Greek word as is used to describe Jesus' burial shroud . . .), and he runs away—sans clothing—when the authorities attempt to arrest him. . . . The young man is presented as a close follower—at least before he flees. That is a picture of shame: the cloth suggests that he showed up with the intent of dying with Jesus but, under pressure, preferred the humiliation of running away naked to the pain of death. Jesus is crucified without clothing, just as the young man runs away without clothing, implying that Jesus is symbolically taking the young man's shame upon himself. When the young man reappears at the tomb, he is now wearing clothing associated with honor and glory—clothing described as being like Jesus' clothing at the Transfiguration. . . . In other words, he has not only been restored from shame but is now assuming an even more honorable position. In effect, Jesus has swapped roles with this young man and thus made the young man's restoration and glorification possible. The subtle but clear implication is that Jesus' death and Resurrection have made this change possible for the young man." *Gospel According to Mark*, 827–28.

4. It's possible that the phrase "neither said they any thing to any man" means they didn't stop to speak to anyone as they ran to tell the disciples; however, I have interpreted Mark's portrayal to mean they did not say anything to anybody—including the disciples—at least, not initially. See Smith, *Gospel According to Mark*, 828–35.

else who has heard Jesus' preaching, seen his healings, watched his crucifixion and burial, and listened to the wondrous announcement of his resurrection? . . . The audience of the Gospel of Mark . . . [is] challenged to become themselves faithful disciples, carrying the message to the world."[5] In effect, we see Mark inviting readers: "Now you know about Christ's Resurrection. Will you go and tell others, or will you keep it a secret?" This conclusion may be related to a pattern in Mark in which those who are asked to not say anything about Jesus's power often instead tell everybody about it (see Mark 1:45; 7:36). At the end of his Gospel, Mark reverses that pattern with the women at the Garden Tomb—they are asked to tell others about Jesus but instead keep silent. The question then for readers is, "What will you do?"[6]

Matthew 28:1–8

Matthew tells us that when Mary Magdalene and another woman named Mary came to the sepulcher, "there was a great earthquake" and an "angel of the Lord descended from heaven, and came and rolled back the stone from the door, and sat upon it." The angel's "countenance was like lightning, and his raiment white as snow." His appearance caused the guards to "shake," and they "became as dead men" (Matt. 28:2–4).

To the women, the angel said, "Fear not ye: for I know that ye seek Jesus, which was crucified. He is not here: for he is risen, as he said. Come, see the place where the Lord lay." The angel also instructed them to go and tell Christ's disciples of his Resurrection. The women

---

5. Mary Ann Tolbert, "Mark," in *The Women's Bible Commentary*, ed. Carol A. Newsom and Sharon H. Ringe (London: SPCK; Louisville: Westminster/John Knox Press, 1992), 274.

6. Julie M. Smith points out another powerful lesson from the early ending of Mark's Gospel: "The Gospel ends with Mark's audience still in the tomb, left to contemplate, facing the reality that Jesus is no longer there. They are left with the invitation to leave the tomb and proceed to Galilee to continue following Jesus. . . . Mark's audience members are invited to seek their own resurrection appearance by choosing to follow Jesus." *Gospel According to Mark*, 834.

"departed quickly from the sepulchre with fear and great joy; and *did run* to bring his disciples word" (Matt. 28:5–6, 8).

I love the phrase "they . . . *did run.*" What's the longest and fastest you have ever run? Could you have run longer and faster if you had this type of news to share? Can you imagine the feelings of those women on that Resurrection morning? Can you feel their excitement, the adrenaline pumping through their bodies, at this pivotal time in the world's history? They must have had friends and family who were mourning, and they knew the peace and joy their message would bring! Can you feel their driving desire to share the good news that Jesus Christ lives? Perhaps imagining the joy of this moment will motivate us to also be quick to open our mouths and share the gospel of Christ.

Luke 24:1–10

Again, we read of the faithful women who came to the tomb early on the first day of the week to anoint the body of the Savior. In Luke, this group includes "Mary Magdalene, and Joanna, and Mary the mother of James, and other women" (Luke 24:10). They were surprised to discover the "stone rolled away" and Christ's body missing. The women were then greeted by two angels who asked, "Why seek ye the living among the dead? He is not here, but is risen: remember how he spake unto you when he was yet in Galilee." The women "remembered his words," returned, and "told all these things unto the eleven, and to all the rest" (Luke 24:2–6, 8–9).

While living in Jerusalem, I frequently visited the place traditionally believed to be the location of Christ's burial and Resurrection. When I went there for the last time before returning to the United States, I was feeling sad about leaving Jerusalem, a place I loved so much. I wondered how I could continue to deepen my connection with Christ as I had done for the past twelve months. While pondering this thought, the words from the angel came to my mind: "Why seek ye the living among the dead? *He is not here, but is risen*" (Luke

24:5–6). I realized I didn't need to walk where Christ had walked in the past to be close to him; I just need to walk toward him now. And I could walk toward him no matter where I lived. Like the women on Easter morning, I left the tomb with joy, ready to share the message of the resurrected Jesus (see Luke 24:6–10).

John 20:1–18

John's description of the first Easter morning provides the most insight into the experience of Mary Magdalene, who is mentioned by name in every Gospel account as being at the tomb that morning. Mary Magdalene came early on "the first day of the week . . . , when it was yet dark, unto the sepulchre and seeth the stone taken away." She ran to Peter and John to tell them the devastating news: "They have taken away the Lord out of the sepulchre, and we know not where they have laid him" (John 20:1–2).[7]

Note Mary's assumption: the only explanation for Christ not being in the tomb is that somebody had taken him away. I don't blame her. Without a knowledge of the Resurrection, it would have been the only thing that made sense to me as well. Both disciples ran to the tomb; all they saw were "the linen clothes" and the "napkin, that was about his head, not lying with the linen clothes, but wrapped together in a place by itself" (John 20:6–7).

Peter and John returned home, but Mary stayed at the empty tomb, weeping. Upon looking into the sepulcher again, she saw "two angels in white sitting, the one at the head, and the other at the feet, where the body of Jesus had lain." When they asked her why she was weeping, she responded, "Because they have taken away my Lord, and I know not where they have laid him" (John 20:12–13).

The angels did not reply. Mary turned around and saw a man she assumed was the gardener. He spoke to her, saying, "Woman, why

---

7. Mary's word "we" indicates that others were with her (as in the other Gospel accounts); however, other women at the tomb are not named in John's account.

weepest thou? whom seekest thou?" (John 20:15). As New Testament scholar Gail R. O'Day notes, "These questions are the first words spoken by the risen Jesus. His question, 'Whom are you looking for?' mirrors the first words he spoke in his ministry. When the followers of John the Baptist approached Jesus, he asked them, 'What are you looking for?' ([John]1:38). This question is an invitation that introduces one of the marks of discipleship . . . : to look for Jesus."[8] Who are *we* looking for?

Mary pleaded with the man to tell her where Christ's body had been laid. Then he spoke one word that changed everything: "Mary" (John 20:16). She realized she was speaking with her Savior. Stop for a moment and ask yourself, *What would this experience have felt like for Mary? For Jesus?* The love and devotion between Savior and disciple made this reunion a truly joyous one. In this interaction we see a fulfillment of Christ's words: he is the good shepherd who "calleth his own sheep by name." And Mary? She is one of the sheep who "know his voice" (John 10:3–4).

Mary may have tried to embrace the Savior, who said to her, "Hold me not; for I am not yet ascended to my Father: but go to my brethren, and say unto them, I ascend unto my Father, and your Father; and to my God, and your God" (JST, John 20:17). Although the Savior's words to Mary may sound harsh, O'Day suggests a possible interpretation that resonates with me:

> Jesus' command, "Do not hold on to me," is the first postresurrection teaching. When he speaks these words, Jesus teaches Mary that he cannot and will not be held and controlled. One cannot hold Jesus to preconceived standards and expectations of who he should be, because to do so is to interfere with Jesus' work and thereby limit what Jesus has to offer. . . . Jesus' prohibition to

---

8. Gail R. O'Day, "John," in *Women's Bible Commentary*, 301. O'Day also points out that "the repetition of that question in chapter 20 establishes continuity between Mary and the first disciples of Jesus" (301).

Mary thus actually contains the good news of Easter: Do not hold on to me, but let me be free so that I can give you the fullness of what I have to offer.[9]

I love the idea that we "cannot hold Jesus to preconceived standards and expectations." We will often have unmet expectations—we might hope to be healed but remain sick. We might expect to have a loyal spouse but instead live alone. We may assume our children will receive temple ordinances, but they choose not to do so. All of us will have times when we want to hold onto what we think Christ should do for us, but he has a different plan. We can let go of our preconceived expectations and instead trust in him.

Because the Savior invited Mary Magdalene to tell the Apostles of his Resurrection, she is sometimes called an apostle to the Apostles. Perhaps we don't reflect often enough on the fact that Jesus did not appear first to Peter or John—but to Mary. Earlier in her life, she had been possessed by seven devils (see Luke 8:2). We cannot know for sure what that means, but it was *not* good. Mary went from an extremely low state to becoming the first witness of the resurrected Lord! One lesson we learn from Mary's life is that even those of us struggling today may soon have momentous spiritual experiences.

Although there are small differences among the four Gospel accounts, the core messages are the same—the tomb was empty, women were the first witnesses of the Resurrection, and the good news of the Savior should be shared. The similarities, as well as the differences in these accounts, are in some respects proof that the Gospel authors were not creating a fictional event.[10]

---

9. O'Day, "John," 301–2.
10. After all, don't people tend to recall the same event with different details? Even the same person may remember an event differently across time. A modern example of this phenomenon is the different First Vision accounts given by the Prophet Joseph Smith. Although some detractors argue that an account (of the Resurrection or First Vision) can't be true because there are discrepancies in the details, if the stories were identical, critics would likely argue that this indicated a fictionalized, rehearsed story.

Moreover, if the Gospel authors had invented the Resurrection story, they likely would not have made their principal witnesses women; at that time a woman's testimony was not considered as valid as a man's in a court of law.[11] Even the Apostles thought the words of the women were "idle tales" and "believed them not" (Luke 24:11). Why would Luke add this detail, portraying the Apostles in a negative light, if he were making up the story? But Luke and the other Gospel authors were not making up a story—Jesus Christ had in fact been raised from the dead, and those who knew about his Resurrection were commissioned to share it with others.

THE HOPE OFFERED BY THE RESURRECTION[12]

We have inherited nearly two thousand years of teachings regarding the Resurrection, and thus it can be challenging to deeply empathize with how the Savior's followers felt in the hours after the Crucifixion. Clearly, they didn't know Jesus Christ would be resurrected. Even at the empty tomb, they still "did not understand the scripture that [Jesus] must rise from the dead" (John 20:9, NRSV). From their perspective, they had experienced months of miracles with their master and teacher, and suddenly it was over. They had seen him raise others from the dead, and now, he was gone! You and I know there is a happy ending— but they did not. What sorrow, shock, and grief they must have felt!

On Resurrection Sunday, two followers of Jesus, were walking on the road to Emmaus, discussing the Savior's death. They likely were unsure of what to do next or where to go. In one day, their entire lives had been turned upside down. As they walked and talked together, a stranger approached them and asked, "What are you discussing with each other while you walk along?" They didn't answer but instead

---

11. See Ilan Fuchs, "Women's Testimony in Jewish Law: A Historical Survey," *Hebrew Union College Annual* 82 (2012): 119–59.

12. This section draws on material from John Hilton III, *The Founder of Our Peace* (Salt Lake City: Deseret Book, 2020), 173–74.

"stood still, looking sad" (Luke 24:17, NRSV). This is one of the greatest understatements in the scriptures—they weren't just sad; they were devastated! One of the men said to the newcomer, "Are you the only stranger in Jerusalem who does not know the things that have taken place there in these days?" The stranger, who was in fact Jesus Christ, asked, "What things?" (Luke 24:18–19, NRSV).

They replied, "The things about Jesus of Nazareth, who was a prophet mighty in deed and word before God and all the people, and how our chief priests and leaders handed him over to be condemned to death and crucified him. But we *had hoped* that he was the one to redeem Israel" (Luke 24:19–21, NRSV). Can you hear the sorrow in their words? And did you notice another point of grief in the last sentence? "Hoped." Past tense. "We *had hoped*—but I guess we were wrong."

Actually they were not wrong; they just didn't understand that the redemption they had been promised was different than the one they imagined. In the very moment they were giving up hope, Jesus was walking with them. Some days we will be like these disciples—despairing even as Christ is with us, just not in the way we expect him to be.

The ancient apostle Peter wrote, "Blessed be the God and Father of our Lord Jesus Christ, which according to his abundant mercy hath begotten us again unto *a lively hope* by the resurrection of Jesus Christ from the dead" (1 Pet. 1:3). *Lively* here means "fresh," "strong," or "powerful."[13] We don't have to say we "had hoped" because our hope is not in the past; it is present—a lively hope! This fresh, strong, powerful hope is ours because Christ broke the bands of death.

BREAKING THE BANDS OF DEATH

During his mortal ministry Christ brought three different people back to life: the daughter of Jairus, the son of the widow of Nain, and

---

13. Blue Letter Bible Lexicon, s.v. "*zao*," accessed August 17, 2020, https://www.blueletterbible.org/lang/lexicon/lexicon.cfm?Strongs=G2198&t=KJV.

his friend Lazarus (see Mark 5, Luke 7, John 11). Though these individuals were raised from the dead, their revival was only temporary. They still had to face the common fate of all: one day, our mortal bodies will fail us, and we will die.

But Christ's Crucifixion and subsequent Resurrection sealed his victory over death for all humankind. Ancient and modern prophets have described his triumphant Resurrection as the breaking of the "bands of death," an expression that originates in scripture with Abinadi. Abinadi used this phrase to teach that Christ's Crucifixion leads to the destruction of death itself. He taught: "Yea, even so he shall be led, *crucified, and slain.* . . . Thus God *breaketh the bands of death,* having gained the victory over death; giving the Son power to make intercession for the children of men" (Mosiah 15:7–8).

Echoing Abinadi, Amulek taught, "*The death of Christ shall loose the bands of this temporal death,* that all shall be raised from this temporal death. The spirit and the body shall be reunited again in its perfect form" (Alma 11:42–43). Alma also emphasized that Christ would "*take upon him death,* that he may *loose the bands of death* which bind his people" (Alma 7:12). As we rightly focus on the beauty of the Resurrection, Book of Mormon prophets repeatedly teach that *the death of Christ* makes *our resurrection* possible—*we cannot separate the two events* (see 2 Ne. 2:8; Hel. 14:15; Morm. 9:13). What happened at Golgotha and the Garden Tomb were integral, intertwined parts of the Savior's Atonement.

THE SAVIOR'S SCARS

The Savior frequently emphasized the physical reality of his Crucifixion and Resurrection by calling attention to the scars on his hands, feet, and side. In his first appearance to his Apostles, he said, "Behold *my hands and my feet,* that it is I myself: handle me, and see; for a spirit hath not flesh and bones, as ye see me have. And when he had thus spoken, *he shewed them his hands and his feet*" (Luke 24:39–40).

The Apostle Thomas wasn't present when the Savior first appeared to the other remaining Apostles. Upon hearing their account of the Savior's Resurrection, Thomas replied, "Except I shall see in his hands the print of the nails, and put my finger into the print of the nails, and thrust my hand into his side, I will not believe." A week later, the Lord appeared to his Apostles again, and he specifically invited Thomas to "reach hither thy finger, and behold my hands; and reach hither thy hand, and thrust it into my side: and be not faithless, but believing" (John 20:25, 27).

The presentation of the prints in his hands and feet was crucial to the Apostles' recognizing the reality of the Resurrection. The same is true for Christ's disciples in the New World (see 3 Ne. 11:14–15). In modern times the Savior taught that when he returns, he will reveal his true identity by the marks he received on the cross: "Then shall they know that I am the Lord; for I will say unto them: These *wounds* are the *wounds* with which I was *wounded* in the house of my friends. I am he who was *lifted up*. I am Jesus that was *crucified*" (D&C 45:52). Notice how the Savior uses his Crucifixion five times to identify himself in this verse!

Why does the Savior retain Crucifixion scars on his resurrected body?[14] Not only do these scars clearly identify who he is, but they also serve as reminders for both him and us. Speaking through the prophet Isaiah, the Lord said, "Can a woman forget her sucking child, that she should not have compassion on the son of her womb? yea, they may forget, yet will I not forget thee. Behold, I have graven *thee* upon the palms of my hands; thy walls are continually before me"

---

14. Elder Jeffrey R. Holland stated, "As a reminder of those days, Jesus has chosen, even in a resurrected, otherwise perfected body, to retain for the benefit of His disciples the wounds in His hands and in His feet and in His side." "Teaching, Preaching, Healing," *Ensign*, January 2003.

(Isa. 49:15–16).[15] Notice that the word "thee" is a singular pronoun—it's personal. It's "you," not "you all." Also note that the Lord doesn't say, "I have graven *your name*," but rather, "I have graven *you*—your circumstances, your hopes, your fears, every part of you—on the palms of my hands."[16]

The Savior's scars remind us of his love. Young Women General President Bonnie H. Cordon taught, "The Savior knows you and loves you. If you wonder if that is true, you need only contemplate that He has 'graven [you] upon the palms of [His] hands' [1 Ne. 21:16]."[17] In addition, Latter-day Saint scholar Jennifer Lane wrote, "His wounds and nail marks are his witness to us that he has succeeded. They are his witness that, through him, we have succeeded if we trust and follow him."[18]

Jesus doesn't want us to look at his scars and feel guilty or sorrowful. He wants us to see in them his commitment and love. He received his wounds willingly and keeps the scars purposefully because he loves us—wholly and infinitely. When I see depictions of his scars, I see me.

---

15. Although this verse can be interpreted to refer to an "ancient custom of tattooing sacred images or symbols on one's palms as a constant reminder of that to which one was devoted," we can also see in this verse a reference to the Crucifixion marks in the Savior's hands. Commenting on this passage, Elder Jeffrey R. Holland explained, "Although a mother may forget her sucking child (as unlikely as any parent might think that could be), Christ will not forget the children he has redeemed or the covenant he has made with them. . . . The painful reminders of that watch care and covenant are the marks of the Roman nails graven upon the palms of his hands, a sign to his disciples in the Old World, his Nephite congregation in the New World, and *to us in latter-day Zion* that he is the Savior of the world." On another occasion, Elder Holland taught, "Jesus still stands triumphant over death, although He stands on wounded feet. . . . He still extends unending grace, although He extends it with pierced palms and scarred wrists." Hoyt W. Brewster, *Isaiah Plain and Simple: The Message of Isaiah in the Book of Mormon* (Salt Lake City: Deseret Book, 1995), 199; Jeffrey R. Holland, *Christ and the New Covenant* (Salt Lake City: Deseret Book, 1997), 84; Jeffrey R. Holland, "Where Justice, Love, and Mercy Meet," *Ensign*, May 2015.
16. See Alistair Begg, "I Have Engraved You," Devotionals, Truth for Life, November 7, 2019, https://www.truthforlife.org/resources/daily-devotionals/11/7/1/.
17. Bonnie H. Cordon, "Becoming a Shepherd," *Ensign*, November 2018.
18. Jennifer C. Lane, *Finding Christ in the Covenant Path: Ancient Insights for Modern Life* (Provo, UT: Religious Studies Center, Brigham Young University, 2020), 152.

I see you. I see us, there, a part of him forever. I also see an invitation to let him be a part of us forever. His scars do not taint his perfect body—they are part of his perfection.

———— ⬥ ————

Because of the Savior's atoning sacrifice and subsequent Resurrection, we can receive freedom, life, and salvation instead of captivity, death, and hell. We don't need to fear the certainty of death or the uncertainty of what follows because he has ensured that we will be resurrected, even as he is.

The empty tomb on Easter morning renews our hope in Christ. He has broken the bands of death, and because he has, those who we love, and indeed all people, will be resurrected. The scars in his resurrected body remind us he will not forget us. They are a perfect, physical manifestation of his perfect, permanent love. These truths offer us peace and comfort in the darkest of times and heighten our joys in the best of times.

Chapter 12

SYMBOLS OF THE ATONEMENT IN GOSPEL ORDINANCES

A man once asked President Spencer W. Kimball, "What do you do when you find yourself in a boring sacrament meeting?" After a moment of thought, President Kimball responded, "I don't know. I've never been in one."

Some who read this may think, "That's because he's never been to my ward!"

Elder Gene R. Cook, who related this story, said, "That's interesting, isn't it? That tells me that the real meeting was between President Kimball and the Lord. . . . If you enter a meeting with your heart prepared to be written upon by the Lord, then that will happen."[1]

If you have ever left a Church meeting or the temple wishing for a more spiritually enriching experience, you're not alone. But I love Elder Cook's idea that we can prepare our hearts to be written upon by the Lord. One way we can prepare our hearts is to deepen our understanding of the relationship between gospel ordinances and Christ's Atonement—including his Crucifixion.

We participate in ordinances at key stages in our lives, and we typically experience at least one each week. Let's discover how the ordinances of baptism and the sacrament and, most significantly, the ordinances of

---

1. Gerry Avant, "Learning Gospel Is Lifetime Pursuit," *Church News*, March 24, 1990, 10.

the temple connect to the Savior's Crucifixion. This knowledge can increase the spiritual power we feel at Church and the temple as well as our commitment to, and appreciation for, our covenants.

BAPTISM

In 1830, the Lord counseled Emma Smith to make a collection of sacred hymns. The earliest church hymnbook[2] included the following lyrics to describe the Savior's baptism: "Jesus descends beneath the wave, / The emblem of his future grave" and "As an emblem of thy passion, / And thy vict'ry o'er the grave, / We, who know the great salvation, / Are baptized beneath the wave."[3]

This hymn is based on Paul's teachings that we are "baptized into *[Christ's] death*," "*buried with him* by baptism *into death*," and "*crucified* with him." By so doing, we are raised into a "newness of life" (Rom. 6:3–4, 6). Baptism, the first of the saving ordinances, is symbolized by being buried in the water, or "planted together in the likeness of his death," and subsequently being raised up out of the water again "in the likeness of his resurrection" (Rom. 6:5). This new life means that we must consider ourselves "dead indeed unto sin, but alive unto God through Jesus Christ," for "as many of [us] as have been baptized into Christ have put on Christ" (Rom. 6:11; Gal. 3:27). With new life, we keep God's commandments with transformed faith.

When Alma introduced baptism to the people of King Noah, he said that part of being baptized was being willing "to stand as witnesses of God at all times and in all things, and in all places that ye may be in, *even until death*" (Mosiah 18:9). This verse has been incorporated

---

2. For additional details regarding the coming forth of the first hymnbook, see the historical introduction to "Collection of Sacred Hymns, 1835," The Joseph Smith Papers, accessed August 16, 2020, https://www.josephsmithpapers.org/paper-summary/collection-of-sacred-hymns-1835/73#historical-intro.

3. "Hymn 55" and "Hymn 54," in *A Collection of Sacred Hymns for the Church of the Latter Day Saints* (Kirtland, OH: F. G. Williams & Co., 1835), 71, available at https://www.josephsmithpapers.org/paper-summary/collection-of-sacred-hymns-1835/73.

into the Young Women theme.[4] The final phrase, however, is not included—I sometimes joke with my BYU students that it might seem strange for newcomers to hear young women recite "even until death."

But for Alma and his people, this phrase was no laughing matter. The prophet Abinadi had recently stood as a witness of God, literally *even until death* (see Mosiah 17:20). Even though our baptism probably won't lead to physical death, it could mean the death of other meaningful things, like a lost opportunity, friendship, or life we had envisioned. When we face such challenging circumstances, we can remember that our baptism symbolizes Christ's Crucifixion and Resurrection. This knowledge can help us carry the burden of things we've lost as we realize what we have gained—access to eternal life. Whether we were baptized recently or a long time ago, we can choose to uphold our complete commitment to Christ. Thankfully, we have another ordinance that allows us to formally recommit ourselves to Christ nearly every Sunday.

THE SACRAMENT

Another hymn from Emma's hymnbook poetically portrays Christ's Last Supper and beautifully explains the relationship between the Crucifixion and the sacrament:

> *He took the bread, and bles'd, and brake—*
> *What wondrous words of grace he spake!*
> *"This is my body broke for sin;*
> *"Receive and eat the living food."*
> *Then took the cup, and bless'd the wine,*
> *"'Tis the new cov'nant in my blood."*
> *For us his flesh with nails was torn,*
> *He bore the scourge, he felt the thorn;*
> *When for our sins, he suff'ring dies*
> *And gave his life a sacrifice.*

---

4.   See "Young Women Theme," The Church of Jesus Christ of Latter-day Saints, https://www.churchofjesuschrist.org/study/manual/young-women-theme/young-women-theme.

> *"Do this", he cried, "till time shall end,*
> *"In mem'ry of your dying friend;*
> *"Meet at my table, and record*
> *The love of your departed Lord."*[5]

At the Last Supper, Christ gave his disciples a cup and said, "Drink ye all of it; For this is *my blood* of the new testament [covenant],[6] which is shed for many for the remission of sins" (Matt. 26:27–28).[7] Elder David B. Haight explained, "The cup [is] symbolic of *His blood* that was shed on the cross."[8]

The Apostle Paul specifically connected the sacrament with the death of Christ, saying, "For as often as ye eat this bread, and drink this cup, *ye do shew the Lord's death till he come*" (1 Cor. 11:26). What does it mean to "shew the Lord's death"? The Greek word translated as "shew" in this verse is most frequently translated as "preach" in the King James Version.[9] If we substitute the word "preach" for "shew," we more clearly see that partaking of the sacrament is a way we testify

---

5. "Hymn 58," in *Collection of Sacred Hymns*, 77.

6. The Greek word translated as "testament" in the King James Version of this verse means "covenant." See Blue Letter Bible Lexicon, s.v. *"diatheke,"* accessed August 17, 2020, https://www.blueletterbible.org/lang/lexicon/lexicon.cfm?Strongs=G1242&t=KJV.

7. As a precursor to what Christ would do, Moses initiated a covenant with blood. After receiving the Ten Commandments, Moses sacrificed oxen and put some of the blood from the sacrificed animals into a basin. The people promised to obey God, and Moses sealed their covenant by throwing blood onto the people, saying, "Behold the blood of the covenant" (Ex. 24:8; see also Heb. 9:19–22). Note the similarity between the phrase, "the blood of the covenant" (Ex. 24:8) and the "the blood of the new [covenant]" (Matt. 26:28). Jeremiah alluded to both these events when he foretold that a new covenant would be made (see Jer. 31:31; Heb. 8:7–13; 9:13–21).

8. David B. Haight, "The Sacrament," *Ensign*, May 1983. Similarly, Elder Mark E. Petersen taught, "Did he not give us that great ordinance [the sacrament] emblematic of the suffering on the cross? Of course he did." Elder D. Todd Christofferson also taught, "As we drink the water, we think of the blood He shed in Gethsemane and on the cross and its sanctifying power." Mark E. Petersen, "The Covenant People of God" (devotional, Brigham Young University, Provo, UT, September 28, 1980); D. Todd Christofferson, "The Living Bread Which Came Down from Heaven," *Ensign*, November 2017.

9. See Blue Letter Bible Lexicon, s.v. *"katangello,"* accessed August 17, 2020, https://www.blueletterbible.org/lang/lexicon/lexicon.cfm?Strongs=G2605&t=KJV.

of the atoning death of Jesus Christ. Alternate Bible translations of this verse state, "As often as you eat this bread and drink the cup, you *proclaim* the Lord's death" (NRSV), and "Every time you eat this bread and drink this cup, you are *announcing* the Lord's death" (NLT). When I learned we testify of Christ's death as we partake of the sacrament, the ordinance became even more meaningful for me—partaking of the bread and water was almost the same as standing up on a fast Sunday to bear my testimony. Remembering this principle helps me feel the Holy Ghost more abundantly during the sacrament.

We can further intensify our feelings for the sacrament by visualizing Christ ministering to the Nephites and introducing this ordinance to them. Imagine you were there: Jesus stands directly in front of you. You're looking at him, face-to-face. You see his eyes, his clothing, his glory. He is real. Then, he invites you to feel "the prints of the nails in his hands and in his feet" (3 Ne. 11:15). Awestruck, you touch his scars with your own hands. What would you feel as you handled the remnants of these sacred wounds? Would you ever forget that moment?

Just a few hours after you personally touched him, the Savior calls for bread and wine. As he now introduces the sacrament, he describes the bread to be broken "in remembrance of my body, which *I have shown unto you*" (3 Ne. 18:7). When Christ showed you his body, he focused on the marks of his Crucifixion; he now asks you to remember *that* body as you take the sacrament.

Next, the Savior invites you to drink wine "in remembrance of my blood, which I have shed for you" (3 Ne. 18:11). The color of the wine, much closer to blood than the water we use today, would provide a visual reminder of the Savior's atoning sacrifice. How would you feel if you had been given this gift of the sacrament to remember and relive the intimate experience you had with the Savior?

Although we were not present for that scene with the Nephites, the Savior has given similar directions to his disciples in this dispensation. In a revelation given to Joseph Smith, Jesus taught that when we take the sacrament, we should "[remember] unto the Father my body *which was laid down for you,* and my blood *which was shed for the remission of sins*" (D&C 27:2).

As we look at the white cloth draped over the sacrament trays, we can recall Joseph of Arimathea taking Christ's body down from the cross and wrapping "it in a clean linen cloth" (Matt. 27:59). We can remind ourselves that we publicly testify of Christ's death as we take the sacrament. And we can follow Christ's counsel to remember his body and blood. By deeply connecting the sacrament with the event it represents, we can feel closer to Christ and more motivated to keep the commitments we make at the sacrament table—to be willing to take upon us the name of Christ, always remember him, and keep his commandments (see Moro. 4:3).

TEMPLE ORDINANCES

Like baptism and the sacrament, temple ordinances closely connect to Christ's Crucifixion. In a sense, all vicarious temple work is emblematic of the Savior's Atonement as we do work for others that they cannot do for themselves. Sister Elaine S. Dalton taught, "As you do this [temple] work, you will become *saviors* on Mount Zion."[10]

Many of the connections between temple ordinances and Christ's Crucifixion are symbolic. Elder John A. Widtsoe explained the importance of identifying these symbols: "No man or woman can come out of the temple endowed as he should be, unless he has seen, beyond the symbol, the mighty realities for which the symbols stand."[11] Though I will not explicitly mention all of these symbols, I hope to provide enough insight to assist those who have participated or will participate in these ordinances to see Crucifixion imagery in the temple.

---

10. Elaine S. Dalton, "Now Is the Time to Arise and Shine," *Ensign,* May 2012.
11. John A. Widtsoe, "Temple Worship," *The Utah Genealogical and Historical Magazine* 12 (1921): 62.

Baptism for the Dead

Some of the Crucifixion symbols found in baptisms for the dead are identical to those of regular baptisms described earlier (see D&C 128:12). An additional symbol found in many temples is the location of the baptismal font. Joseph Smith taught, "The baptismal font was instituted *as a similitude of the grave*, and was commanded to be in a place *underneath where the living are wont to assemble*, to show forth the living and the dead" (D&C 128:13). The very location of the temple baptismal font, typically below ground level, is symbolic of the grave that Christ overcame.

Initiatory

The Lord instructed Moses, "Thou shalt bring Aaron and his sons unto the door of the tabernacle of the congregation, and wash them with water. And thou shalt put upon Aaron the holy garments, and anoint him, and sanctify him; that he may minister unto me in the priest's office" (Ex. 40:12–13). Although endowed Latter-day Saints are familiar with these phrases, we may not be aware that similar instructions were given in Exodus 29:4–9. After the Lord teaches Moses about washing, anointing, and wearing sacred clothing, he adds that animals should be sacrificed "for atonement" (Ex. 29:36).

Although we don't sacrifice animals in temples today, in ancient times, washing, anointing, and dressing in sacred garments was connected to killing animals to atone for sin—a foreshadowing of the death of Christ. In our day, after the initiatory ordinances are completed, we enter the endowment room(s), where we covenant to live the law of sacrifice.[12] Thus, sacrifice follows the washing, anointing, and clothing ceremonies today, just as it did in the days of Moses and Aaron.

Adam and Eve initially tried to cover their nakedness by making

---

12. See "About the Temple Endowment," Temples, The Church of Jesus Christ of Latter-day Saints, accessed August 17, 2020, https://www.churchofjesuschrist.org/temples/what-is-temple-endowment.

fig-leaf aprons, symbolic of their efforts to hide their sins from God. In place of these aprons, the Lord made coats of skins for Adam and Eve (see Gen. 3:21). These coats of skins, represented by the temple garment, can be seen "as a symbol of the true 'covering over' of guilt which Christ's atonement provides when we repent; the animal which God presumably killed in order to make the coats of skin could be read as a symbol of Christ."[13] Thus, the garment itself is a constant reminder of Jesus Christ. This "coat of skin," symbolic of his sacrifice, not only covers our physical nakedness but also reminds us that our sins will be completely covered and atoned for as we are faithful to our covenants. In addition, the parallels between the temple veil (a symbol of Christ's sacrificed body, discussed in the next section) and the temple garment (with its "several simple marks"[14]) help us see the garment as a powerful symbol of the Savior's body, sacrificed for us.[15]

Endowment

Several aspects of the temple endowment relate to Christ's Crucifixion. In the endowment ceremony, we learn that after Adam and Eve were cast out of the Garden of Eden, God commanded them to "offer the firstlings of their flocks" (Moses 5:5). They were later told that killing these firstborn animals was "a similitude of the sacrifice of the Only Begotten of the Father" (Moses 5:7).

As part of the endowment ceremony, "men and women dressed in temple clothing, surround an altar in a circle formation to participate unitedly in prayer."[16] Note that the altar is at the center of this special

---

13. John D. Charles, *Endowed from on High* (Bountiful, UT: Horizon Publishers and Distributors, 1997), 59.
14. Carlos Asay, "The Temple Garment, an Outward Expression of an Inward Commitment," *Ensign*, August 1997.
15. This perspective perhaps adds a symbolic meaning to Paul's phrases "always bearing about in the body the dying of the Lord Jesus" and "I bear in my body the marks of the Lord Jesus" (2 Cor. 4:10; Gal. 6:17).
16. George S. Tate, "Prayer Circle," in *Encyclopedia of Mormonism*, ed. Daniel H. Ludlow (New York: Macmillan, 1992), 1120.

temple prayer. For millennia, altars have pointed to the death of Jesus Christ. For example, Abraham "built an altar . . . and bound Isaac his son, and laid him on the altar" (Gen. 22:9), which was "a similitude of God and his Only Begotten Son" (Jacob 4:5).[17] This symbolism suggests that as Latter-day Saints today surround an altar to pray, Christ's death is central to the prayer. Those participating in this ceremony can easily identify additional Crucifixion imagery that is part of "the true order of prayer."[18]

Some of the most important Crucifixion symbolism takes place at the veil of the temple. In the ancient temple, the Holy of Holies, representing God's dwelling place, was separated from other parts of the temple by a veil. At Christ's Crucifixion, the veil of the temple was torn in two (see Matt. 27:51). According to the author of the book of Hebrews, the torn veil means that now all humanity can enter into God's presence through "the blood of Jesus, by a new and living way . . . through *the veil, that is to say, his flesh*" (Heb. 10:19–20). In other words, the temple veil represents Christ's sacrificed body.

In modern temples, "a veil symbolically divides the terrestrial room from the celestial room," which represents "the highest degree of heaven."[19] Terryl and Fiona Givens wrote, "The rituals of the temple . . . crescendo with *palpable crucifixion imagery at the veil,* that symbolic, porous membrane joining heaven and earth. It is through . . . *the severed flesh of Christ . . .* that all find full incorporation into the Heavenly Family."[20] This "palpable crucifixion imagery at the veil"

---

17. Moses similarly alluded to the altar as a symbol of Christ's death when he instructed Aaron to "go unto the altar, and offer thy sin offering . . . and make an atonement for thyself, and for the people" (Lev. 9:7). Generations later, priests slaughtered animals and "made reconciliation with their blood upon the altar, to make an atonement for all Israel" (2 Chron. 29:24).

18. Bruce R. McConkie, as quoted in Russell M. Nelson, "Sweet Power of Prayer," *Ensign,* May 2003.

19. Immo Luschin, "Temples," in *Encyclopedia of Mormonism,* 1447.

20. Fiona and Terryl Givens, *The Christ Who Heals: How God Restored the Truth That Saves Us* (Salt Lake City: Deseret Book, 2017), 61–62.

allows "participants [to] symbolically return to the Lord's presence as they enter the celestial room."[21] In the endowment ceremony, Christ's Crucifixion is the symbolic key to entering the place where God lives.

Sealing of Husband and Wife

In sealing rooms, the altar (a symbol of Christ's death) is often placed in the center of the room. Elder Bruce C. Hafen described a time when he sealed a couple in the temple: "I invited them to the altar, and as the groom took the bride by the hand, I realized that they were about to place upon that altar of sacrifice their own broken hearts and contrite spirits—an offering of themselves to each other and to God *in emulation of Christ's sacrifice for them*."[22]

Picture the scene described by Elder Hafen: the husband and wife are on opposite sides of the altar. The bride and groom take each other by the hand, ready to sacrifice themselves to each other as Christ sacrificed himself for each of them. *Whether one thinks of the altar, or the hands clasped together on the altar, the Crucifixion of Jesus Christ is literally at the center of the sealing ordinance.* When a husband and wife are sealed together in the temple, their marriage is no longer just about a man and a woman—the Savior is a central third party.

This teaching helps us better understand Ephesians 5:25, which also connects marriage to Christ's death: "Husbands, love your wives, even as Christ also loved the church, and gave himself for it." Regardless of our mood on any given day, we can choose to love our spouse as Christ loved the Church and gave himself for it. Authors Timothy and Kathy Keller beautifully expressed this concept as follows: "When Jesus looked down from the cross, he didn't think, 'I am giving myself to you because you are so attractive to me.' No, he was in agony, and he looked down at us—denying him, abandoning him, and betraying

21. "About the Temple Endowment," The Church of Jesus Christ of Latter-day Saints, https://www.churchofjesuschrist.org/temples/what-is-temple-endowment.
22. Bruce C. and Marie K. Hafen, *The Contrite Spirit: How the Temple Helps Us Apply Christ's Atonement* (Salt Lake City: Deseret Book, 2015), 132.

him—and in the greatest act of love in history, he *stayed*. . . . He loved us, not because we were lovely to him, but to make us lovely."[23]

I have personally felt spiritual power by contemplating how Christ's Crucifixion is an essential component of, and a model for, my own marriage. His selfless act motivates me to give more to my spouse. Considering the Crucifixion symbolism in a temple sealing eliminates the justifications for trivial arguments. The Savior can help us bite our tongues when tempted to criticize a spouse and help us handle the frustrated expectations that inevitably come with marriage; he "suffered for us, leaving us an example, that [we] should follow his steps" (1 Pet. 2:21).[24] Husbands and wives can experience a completely new kind of love because Christ demonstrated that love on the cross. This love is symbolically at the center of a temple sealing and can be at the heart of married life.[25]

Sealing of Parents to Children

When I was in college, a professor said, "Our largest challenges in life often come through our spouses or our children." I bristled at this statement, thinking I wanted my family to be my prime source of joy, not trials. But as I'm raising six children and have observed numerous other families, I now believe this professor's statement is true. For many of us, both our greatest happiness and our greatest heartache come from immediate family members.

Some of these sorrows come when children choose not to follow

---

23. Timothy and Kathy Keller, *The Meaning of Marriage* (New York: Penguin Books, 2016), 116–17, emphasis in original.

24. In stating that we should follow Christ's example in suffering, I'm referring to the typical conflicts that arise in marriage and not suggesting that abuse should be excused or tolerated.

25. Timothy and Kathy Keller wrote, "Only if I love Jesus more than my wife will I be able to serve her needs ahead of my own. Only if my emotional tank is filled with love from God will I be able to be patient, faithful, tender, and open with my wife when things are not going well in life or in the relationship. And the more joy I get from my relationship with Christ, the more I can share that joy with my wife and family." *Meaning of Marriage*, 135.

Christ. It's comforting to know that President Lorenzo Snow told parents that there is hope for each of their children:

> Mourn not because all your sons and daughters do not follow in the path that you have marked out to them, or give heed to your counsels. Inasmuch as we succeed in securing eternal glory, and stand as saviors, and as kings and priests to our God, we will save our posterity. *When Jesus went through that terrible torture on the cross, He saw what would be accomplished by it.* . . . *I believe that every man and woman who comes into this life and passes through it, that life will be a success in the end.*[26]

In the temple, parents are sealed to children at the altar of the sealing room as participants clasp hands. In a sense, we can see children supported on the foundation of Christ's cross. This symbolism can help both parents and children understand the significance of their family relationships. Just as recognizing Christ as part of their marriage covenant encourages spouses to hang on when things get hard, knowing Christ's involvement in parent-child sealings can help parents and children to not give up on each other—ever.

We began this chapter with a story about an individual who wondered about being bored during sacrament meeting. Although we will probably all experience meetings that are less spiritually enriching than we might hope, focusing on the death of Christ can prepare our hearts to feel the Holy Spirit during gospel ordinances. Seeing how his sacrifice connects to baptism, the sacrament, and temple ordinances can also strengthen our resolve to keep our covenants. As we participate in, witness, and reflect on these ordinances through the lens of the atoning power of his death, we will more fully appreciate our Redeemer.

---

26. "Discourse by Lorenzo Snow" (October 6, 1893), in *Millennial Star* 56 (January 22, 1894): 52. See also David A. Bednar, "Faithful Parents and Wayward Children," *Ensign*, March 2014.

Chapter 13

"LOOK UNTO ME IN EVERY THOUGHT"

As a religion professor at Brigham Young University, one of my least favorite days of the semester is the last day of class. By this point I know my students' names and feel close to them. I deeply hope they will continue to grow their testimonies, and so on that final day of class, I spend time focusing on what they can do throughout their lives to increase their understanding of the things we have studied throughout the semester.

As our time together in this book nears an end, I similarly want to provide suggestions to help each of us continue our journey in learning more about the Savior's Crucifixion. Even more important than *knowing* about his sacrifice on Calvary is *feeling* of its deep significance in our hearts. For me, five approaches have been particularly powerful in increasing my personal connection with Christ's Crucifixion: doing a synopsis study of the Crucifixion accounts, reading additional books, engaging with the Crucifixion in film and music, celebrating Good Friday, and contemplating the Savior's atoning death. These are not the only ways to deepen our feelings about the Savior's sacrifice on Calvary, but each can help us feel God's love and more appreciation for Jesus Christ.

A SYNOPSIS STUDY

One powerful way to come to know Jesus Christ is through a synopsis study. This entails a side-by-side reading of Matthew, Mark, Luke, and John, looking for similarities and differences in their accounts.[1] Specifically, doing a careful synopsis study of Christ's Crucifixion can help us recognize and appreciate details that we might otherwise miss.[2] For example, in chapter 10, we identified John as the only Gospel author to refer to Jesus as "the Lamb of God." His account of the Crucifixion contains small details that only John includes, like "hyssop" being used as the plant to give Jesus a drink and the fact Christ's bones weren't broken. By carefully reading John's account and noticing its unique aspects, we clearly see the Savior as the Passover Lamb. By way of illustration, let's consider two additional insights gained by identifying similarities and differences among the Gospel accounts.

Example #1: Simon and the Cross

Consider what Matthew, Mark, Luke, and John recorded about the Savior's carrying his cross to Golgotha:

Matthew 27:32	Mark 15:21	Luke 23:26	John 19:16–17
And as they came out, they found *a man of Cyrene, Simon by name*: him they *compelled* to bear *his* cross.	And they *compel* one *Simon a Cyrenian,* who passed by, coming out of the country, *the father of Alexander and Rufus,* to bear *his* cross.	And as they led him away, they laid hold upon one *Simon, a Cyrenian,* coming out of the country, and on him they laid the cross, that he might bear it *after Jesus.*	They took Jesus, and led him away. And *he bearing his cross* went forth into a place called the place of a skull.

1. A more intricate form of synopsis study seeks to identify *why* there are differences in the Gospel accounts and whether the differences are related to themes emphasized by individual Gospel authors. See the example of John's account of Christ carrying his cross in this chapter.
2. This principle is also true of other parts of Christ's life. For example, in the first section of chapter 11, we did a partial synopsis study of the Resurrection accounts.

Matthew, Mark, and Luke all mention a man named Simon, from Cyrene,[3] who assisted the Savior in carrying his cross to Golgotha. Matthew and Mark emphasize the fact that Simon was bearing *his* (Christ's) cross. Do we pause to consider the significance that the Son of God himself was served? Sometimes, perhaps to protect our privacy or pride, we do not allow others to help us. Christ is indeed the ultimate example, not only of serving others but also of accepting service since he "allowed a man he created to help him carry the cross."[4]

Matthew and Mark both use the word *compel* to describe the fact that Simon was forced into service. Simon didn't choose to carry the Savior's cross. Likewise, we rarely get to pick the burdens we bear, but we can choose whether we become resentful or allow our crosses to draw us closer to Christ.

Only Mark informs us that Simon is the father of Alexander and Rufus; mentioning Simon's children by name suggests they were known in Mark's Christian community.[5] Perhaps Simon's carrying the Savior's cross influenced him and his children to become faithful Christians. How will our reactions to the unchosen crosses placed upon our shoulders affect us and those we love?

Luke alone records that Simon carried the cross "after," or in other words, "while following," Jesus. Perhaps Luke wanted to remind readers of the Savior's statement "If any man will come after me, let him deny himself, and take up his cross daily, *and follow me*" (Luke 9:23).[6] In

---

3. Cyrene is a city in northern Africa (modern-day Libya). A large number of Jewish people lived in Cyrene, many of whom likely made pilgrimages to Jerusalem. See Acts 2:10.

4. Chris Nye, "Simon of Cyrene: The Man Who Carried Jesus' Cross," *Medium* (blog), April 18, 2019, https://medium.com/@chrisnye/simon-of-cyrene-the-man-who-carried-jesus-cross-303d86ed2ac8.

5. Mark's specificity is a testament to the historical nature of this account—Alexander and Rufus, and perhaps Simon as well, would have been alive at the time Mark's Gospel was first circulated. Surely some readers of Mark asked Alexander or Rufus to verify Mark's account, illustrating that this is a detail that Mark would not have made up. See Nye, "Simon of Cyrene."

6. See Raymond E. Brown, *The Death of the Messiah*, vol. 2 (New York: Doubleday, 1994), 914.

this respect, Simon sets an example for each of us. He did not simply suffer with a trial, doing the best he could on his own; he carried his cross *while following Jesus*. We can do likewise. When we struggle under burdens of circumstances and sin, we can continue to move forward, step by step, following Christ, for it is in him we will find power and peace.

Of course, the largest difference among the Gospels is in John's account, in which Simon is not mentioned at all—Christ carries his own cross. This fits within a broader theme in the Gospel of John in which the Savior does not need help, knows all things, and is completely in control (see John 10:18; 18:4). John portrays a Jesus who needs no assistance from mortals.

This type of synopsis study may not dramatically impact how we view Christ's Crucifixion, but it can add a rich layer of context as we learn from both Simon and Christ. Will we allow others to serve *us*? Can we remember that we and those we love might be blessed when we do good—even when we are *compelled*? Will we pick up our own crosses in the attitude of *following* Jesus? And on a day when it seems like we can't go on, will we remember a Savior who carried his own cross and know that *he can help us carry ours*?

Example #2: The Burial Clothes

Matthew 27:59	Mark 15:46	Luke 23:53	John 19:40
When Joseph had taken the body, he wrapped it in *a clean linen cloth*.	[Joseph] bought fine linen, and took him down, and wrapped him in *the linen*.	[Joseph] took it [Christ's body] down, and wrapped it in *linen*.	Then took they [Joseph and Nicodemus] the body of Jesus, and wound it in linen *clothes* with the spices.

Matthew, Mark, and Luke all contain the same basic idea—Christ was wrapped in a piece of cloth—something that might have looked like a modern bedsheet. This piece of cloth was draped over or around Christ's body; we see a similar image on the sacrament table each week.

But note how John's description is different: John portrays Joseph wrapping Christ's body with multiple pieces of cloth.[7] John also emphasizes the grave clothes in his account of the Resurrection; he notes that Peter and the other disciple (often assumed to be John) "saw the linen clothes lying . . . and the napkin, that was about his head, not lying with the linen clothes, but wrapped together in a place by itself" (John 20:5, 7; compare Luke 24:12).

John specifically records that seeing the clothes, along with the empty tomb, led this disciple to believe (see John 20:8). The grave clothes proved Christ truly was resurrected; if somebody had stolen the body of Jesus, wouldn't they have taken the material to cover Christ while carting him away? And even if they left the clothes behind, would they have taken the time to fold them neatly?[8] Even tiny details, such as burial clothing, testify of the reality of Christ's Atonement.

As modern readers, we don't need to be unduly concerned about the differences among the Gospel accounts; instead we can appreciate how each Gospel author seeks to reveal truths about Jesus Christ. The unique details in the Gospel accounts illuminate distinct aspects of the Savior. As Raymond Brown, a late twentieth-century theologian, wrote, "When these different passion narratives are read side-by-side, one should not be upset by the contrast or ask which view of Jesus is more correct: the Marcan Jesus who plumbs the depths of abandonment only to be vindicated; the Lucan Jesus who worries about others and gently dispenses forgiveness; or the Johannine Jesus who reigns

---

7. Scholars are unsure about what significance (if any) multiple cloths might have in the burial process. See Brown, *Death of the Messiah*, 1264–65.

8. See Max Lucado, *He Chose the Nails: What God Did to Win Your Heart* (Nashville: Thomas Nelson, 2017), 123–24.

victoriously from the cross in control of all that happens. All three are given to us by the inspiring Spirit, and no one of them exhausts the meaning of Jesus."[9]

For me, doing a synopsis study of the Savior's Crucifixion has been an exhilarating opportunity to come closer to Christ. Digging deeply into these scriptural passages increases our understanding of and feelings for Christ's death on the cross. To assist you in your own study, I've created a document of the four Gospel accounts of the Crucifixion, arranged side-by-side. You can access this and the other online resources mentioned later in this chapter at http://johnhiltoniii.com/crucifixion. Many insights await you in your synopsis studies of the Gospels.

ADDITIONAL READINGS

I love reading books; since you're reading this one, I assume you do too. We can learn more about Christ's Crucifixion by reading books by people who have carefully studied it, including those of other faiths. Here are a few books I recommend to further your study.

A Crucified Christ in Holy Week, by Raymond E. Brown. Brown, a consummate scholar and devout Catholic, packed this short book (seventy-one pages) with spiritual insights on the final twenty-four hours of the Savior's life. Brown published *A Crucified Christ in Holy Week* while writing his much more extensive and scholarly book, *The Death of the Messiah*. This latter work, comprising two volumes and more than 1,600 pages, remains the definitive academic work on the Crucifixion of Jesus Christ. It examines every verse from Christ's suffering in Gethsemane to his burial—often analyzing each word of the text. In it, Brown synthesizes the work of countless scholars who have researched aspects of Christ's Crucifixion. If you want the short version, read *A Crucified Christ in Holy Week*. If you love that book or you don't want to miss a single detail, check out *The Death of the Messiah*.

---

9. Raymond E. Brown, *A Crucified Christ in Holy Week* (Collegeville, MN: The Liturgical Press, 1986), 70.

He Chose the Nails, by Max Lucado. Many people are familiar with Max Lucado's book for children, *You Are Special*, about Wemmicks who stick dots on people. Lucado is a pastor in Texas who has written more than seventy books, most of them for adults. In *He Chose the Nails*, Lucado shares personal stories, gives poignant parables, and shows how elements of the Crucifixion apply personally to our lives. For example, in one chapter, he shows how the physical construction of a cross represents the extent of our Father's love. In another, he highlights several instances in which Christ fulfilled prophecy through his death and shows how those instances testify that we can trust in both the Savior and scripture. Packed with stories and practical applications, *He Chose the Nails* is a quick, easy read that left a lasting impression on me.

Golgotha, by Andrew C. Skinner. In this book, Skinner, a former dean of religion at BYU, points out dozens of spiritual lessons we can learn from the Christ on Calvary. Beginning with the Savior's betrayal in Gethsemane, he walks readers through the final fifteen hours of the Savior's life. Along the way, he shares several personal experiences, insights from Church leaders, and valuable scriptural nuggets. *Golgotha* is available as an ebook and is included in the three-in-one compilation, *The Savior's Final Week*, also by Skinner.[10]

In addition to the above books, people have written numerous inspirational and informative articles about Christ's Crucifixion. I have collected links to several essays, along with other additional resources such as videos and podcasts (all free) at the website mentioned earlier.

FILM AND MUSIC

If you're thinking to yourself, "Doing a synopsis study and reading more books sounds hard. Couldn't I just watch a movie instead?" The answer is yes!

---

10. Andrew C. Skinner, *The Savior's Final Week* (Salt Lake City: Deseret Book, 2013). Full citations for the other books mentioned here can be found throughout the footnotes of this book.

My first memory of watching a movie about Jesus is as a nineteen-year-old in the Missionary Training Center. A large group of missionaries gathered to watch *The Lamb of God*.[11] As I saw the Savior nailed to the cross, the Spirit washed over me and testified to me that what I was viewing really happened. Others have had similar experiences when seeing movies about Jesus.

One woman told me about her feelings when she saw the movie *The Testaments*:[12] "Watching Christ be crucified filled me with such an agony in my soul that I just sobbed. I knew that I had caused some of the pain he felt, but I also knew that Christ didn't hold it against me. I felt he loved me and did it willingly—for me. I was of worth to him! I'll never forget the Spirit I felt as I saw that powerful scene."

In recent years, I've deeply enjoyed watching what filmmakers both inside and outside the Church have portrayed about the Savior's life. Among many other excellent choices, here are two movies that can enhance your appreciation for Jesus Christ in general, and specifically for his Crucifixion.[13]

The Gospel of John.[14] Except for an introductory preface, all text in this movie comes from the Gospel of John; every verse is present (using the Good News Translation), and no extra scenes are added. This film is extremely engaging, portraying several events from the Savior's life that are not often shown in film. For instance, John records the Savior's serious conflicts with the chief priests leading up to the Crucifixion; watching these encounters helps us understand why some people

11. *The Lamb of God*, directed by Russell Holt (The Church of Jesus Christ of Latter-day Saints, 1993).

12. *The Testaments of One Fold and One Shepherd*, directed by Kieth Merrill (The Church of Jesus Christ of Latter-day Saints, 2000).

13. In addition to the movies described in this chapter, I recommend the following: *The Jesus Film*, directed by Peter Sykes and John Krish (Warner Brothers, 1979); *The Nativity Story*, directed by Catherine Hardwicke (New Line Cinema, 2006); *Risen*, directed by Kevin Reynolds (Columbia Pictures, 2016); and *The Visual Bible: Gospel of Matthew*, directed by Regardt van den Bergh (Visual Bible International, 1993). These movies can be viewed (some of them for free) on various video-streaming websites.

14. *The Gospel of John*, directed by Philip Saville (Visual Bible International, 2003).

perceived Jesus to be a societal threat. The depiction of Christ on the cross, including his conversation with his mother, is especially poignant.

The Son of God.[15] Unlike *The Gospel of John*, this movie harmonizes the Gospel accounts and adds extra scenes not included in the biblical record, some of which are historical. For example, one scene portrays the Jews protesting the aqueduct Pilate built, adding relevant background information to the Savior's trial. Pilate appears in several scenes throughout the movie, some of which are at least partially scriptural, such as his dialogue with his wife as she pleads with Pilate to leave Jesus alone. You can sense Pilate's consternation as he wants to follow his wife's counsel but also feels compelled to avoid further arguments with the Jewish authorities. The movie also powerfully portrays both Mary Magdalene and Mary the mother of Jesus at the trial and Crucifixion, helping us see what they may have felt as they watched their Savior suffer. Seeing this representation gave me deeper feelings of appreciation for both Jesus Christ and the women who loved him.

Some Latter-day Saints intentionally avoid cinematic depictions of the Crucifixion. However, the scriptural statements about viewing the death of Christ, described later in this chapter, can encourage us to at least be open to viewing such scenes. I'm not suggesting that all Crucifixion scenes are appropriate for all ages; however, I do think that for some of us, as well as those we love, viewing visual representations of the Crucifixion could be deeply impactful.

Like movies, music also has the power to stir our souls. We love to sing "Joy to the World" at Christmastime and "He Is Risen" on Easter morning. Our hymnbooks are also replete with hymns centered on the Crucifixion of Jesus Christ. Emma Smith's 1835 hymnbook includes the following lyrics from the hymn "Arise, My Soul Arise," which portrays Christ's wounds on the cross as praying for us and pleading for our forgiveness.

---

15. *The Son of God*, directed by Christopher Spencer (20th Century Fox, 2014).

My name is written on his hands. . . .
Five bleeding wounds he bears,
Receiv'd on Calvary;
They pour effectual prayers,
They strongly speak for me;
Forgive him, O forgive, they cry,
Nor let that ransom'd sinner die![16]

Our current hymnbook also includes many moving lyrics related to Christ's Crucifixion. Richard Alldridge penned the beautiful words of "We'll Sing All Hail to Jesus' Name," in which we sing, "Praise and honor give, / To him who bled on Calvary's hill, / And died that we might live."[17] Eliza R. Snow wrote the following lyrics: "Behold the great Redeemer die, / A broken law to satisfy. / He dies a sacrifice for sin, / That man may live and glory win."[18]

Singing or listening to these hymns can turn our thoughts to Christ's Crucifixion. Beyond the hymns, other music can also bring us closer to our Savior's sacrifice on Calvary. Those who prefer classical choral music might enjoy listening to excerpts from Handel's *Messiah* or Bach's *Passion According to St. John*. In addition, contemporary Christian musicians, including Latter-day Saints, provide powerful music focused on the Savior's Crucifixion. I've created a playlist of my favorites that can be accessed at http://johnhiltoniii.com/crucifixion, and I would love to learn of songs you love that I have missed!

CELEBRATE GOOD FRIDAY

Think of two of the most celebrated events in the life of Christ—his birth and Resurrection. We commemorate these with Christmas

---

16. "Hymn 59," in *A Collection of Sacred Hymns for the Church of the Latter Day Saints* (Kirtland, OH: F. G. Williams & Co., 1835), 79, available at https://www.josephsmithpapers.org/paper-summary/collection-of-sacred-hymns-1835/81.

17. "We'll Sing All Hail to Jesus' Name," *Hymns* (Salt Lake City: The Church of Jesus Christ of Latter-day Saints, 1985), no. 182.

18. "Behold the Great Redeemer Die," *Hymns*, no. 191.

Day and Easter Sunday and feel love and gratitude for Jesus as we do so. The buildup and excitement surrounding these sacred holidays add to our appreciation for the Savior. We have a similar opportunity to increase our connection with Christ by remembering another important event in his life—Good Friday.

Since at least the third century, Christians have been celebrating Good Friday as a time to commemorate the death of Jesus Christ. Although some have suggested that the "Good" in "Good Friday" (an English phrase coined more than six hundred years ago) is related to the word "God" or to the fact that what happened on that day was "good" for humanity, these explanations are likely historically incorrect.

The "Good" in "Good Friday" comes from an archaic meaning of the word "Good": "Holy." In Spanish, "Good Friday" is called "El Viernes Santo," and in French, "Le Vendredi saint," both of which translate into English as "Holy Friday." Thus when we think of Good Friday, we can think of "Holy Friday," or, as Elder Jeffrey R. Holland phrased it, "atoning Friday with its cross."[19]

Elder Marion D. Hanks, speaking on a Good Friday, said, "I . . . thank God for this Good Friday, tragic as are the events which it commemorates, and for what it means to me and to all men, . . . for *this day had to happen in order that Easter and its glorious events could come.*"[20] Without Good Friday there would be no Easter.

Whether we call it Holy Friday, Atoning Friday, or Good Friday, this day is a spiritual opportunity to reflect on the love of the Father and the Son, manifested on the cross. In some areas of the world, including parts of the United States, Good Friday is recognized by the community as an important event. Dr. Gaye Strathearn, now a professor of ancient scripture at BYU, grew up in Australia, where Good

---

19. Jeffrey R. Holland, "None Were with Him," *Ensign,* May 2009.
20. Marion D. Hanks, in *One Hundred Thirty-Ninth Annual Conference of The Church of Jesus Christ of Latter-day Saints* (Salt Lake City: The Church of Jesus Christ of Latter-day Saints, 1969), 25. At that time, general conference sessions were held on Fridays, Saturdays, and Sundays. This conference was held on both Good Friday and Easter.

Friday is a national holiday. She wrote of her experience as a new student at BYU: "It was a huge culture shock for me when Easter came and I realized that Good Friday was a nonevent at BYU. Honestly, I was quite surprised that it was business as usual with classes being held on what I considered to be one of the holiest days in the Christian calendar."[21]

Although Good Friday has not traditionally been observed in our Church community, individuals and families can certainly celebrate it through a variety of approaches. Here are a few ideas you could consider implementing in your observance of Good Friday.

- *Make time for the special day.* Most of us do not work on Christmas or Easter; perhaps some of us could find a way to take all or part of Good Friday as a holiday. If not, we could wake up a little earlier or block out time in the evening to celebrate this sacred day individually or as a family.

- *Reflect on the events of Good Friday.* President Anthon H. Lund of the First Presidency taught that we should reflect on the Savior on Good Friday: "Today, Good Friday, the day on which He suffered so much for us, let us not forget to let our thoughts go to Him in thankfulness."[22] This reflection can be done in a focused pondering session or by marking specific events that happened to the Savior on that day. For example, at dawn we can remember the Savior coming before Pilate; soon after we can reflect on the trial, the scourging, and the crown of thorns. At 9:00 a.m. we can remember Christ being placed on the cross. We can imagine the sky turning dark at noon and finally remember his death at 3:00 p.m. and his burial shortly thereafter.

- *Do a synopsis study of the Crucifixion.* Good Friday provides an

21. Gaye Strathearn, "Christ's Crucifixion: Reclamation of the Cross," in *With Healing in His Wings*, ed. Camille Fronk Olson and Thomas A. Wayment (Provo, UT: Religious Studies Center; Salt Lake City: Deseret Book, 2013).

22. Anthon H. Lund, in *Eighty-Second Annual Conference of The Church of Jesus Christ of Latter-day Saints* (Salt Lake City: Deseret News, 1912), 12.

excellent occasion to reread what each Gospel author wrote about the events that happened on this day, as we discussed at the beginning of the chapter.

- *Attend worship services.* Although most Latter-day Saint congregations do not have special services on Good Friday, many other Christian denominations do. For me, gathering with fellow Christians to worship together on this sacred day invites the Holy Ghost into my life. Either in addition to or instead of attending Good Friday services, others may enjoy attending the temple, with a special focus on what it teaches about the Crucifixion of Jesus Christ.

- *Seek and extend forgiveness.* It is always good to repent and to forgive others. Good Friday provides us with a valuable opportunity to let go of an unrepented sin or a long-standing grudge.

- *Engage with Crucifixion film, music, or art.* Good Friday is the perfect time to watch a movie about Jesus Christ or listen to music that honors his death and Resurrection. Watching the movies listed earlier (or just the sections of those movies that focus on the Crucifixion) or viewing Crucifixion artwork can be beneficial.

- *Make time to bear a simple testimony.* When a centurion saw the signs accompanying Christ's Crucifixion, he exclaimed, "Truly this [is] the Son of God" (Matt. 27:54). On Good Friday, consider testifying of Christ to family members or others.

- *Eat special foods.* Special foods on significant days can help make them even more memorable. Without going overboard and thus missing the mark, designated Good Friday foods can turn our focus to the Savior. For example, Eric Huntsman and his family eat at the same restaurant each Good Friday and make hot cross buns at home.[23] Christians in many faith traditions fast on Good

---

23. Personal communication to John Hilton III, May 28, 2020. In many locations, hot cross buns are a traditional Good Friday food. Legend has it that a twelfth-century monk initiated this tradition by marking the top of a lightly sweetened bun with a

Friday; perhaps a fast is an appropriate way for some of us to commemorate this special day as well.

- *Use the senses.* Seeing, touching, or tasting objects related to the Crucifixion can be helpful, especially for children, in remembering the events of Good Friday. For example, making or holding a crown of thorns, carrying a heavy beam, handling a long nail, or tasting vinegar could connect participants with the events of Good Friday.[24] Displaying some of these objects as part of our home décor at this time of year might help focus our minds on the Savior's sacrifice for us.

CONTEMPLATE CHRIST ON CALVARY

Many Church members have told me something like this: "I don't like thinking about Jesus on the cross because it makes me sad."[25] Does that statement resonate with you? Although some Latter-day Saints avoid thinking about Christ's death, ancient prophets and the Savior himself have commanded us to contemplate it. Mormon wrote to his son Moroni, "May Christ lift thee up, and *may his* sufferings and *death . . . rest in your mind forever*" (Moro. 9:25). Similarly, Jacob wrote, "We would to God that we could persuade all men [to] . . . believe in Christ, and *view his death*, and suffer his cross" (Jacob 1:8).

These words from Book of Mormon prophets become even more

---

cross. If you're interested in making them, an online search for "hot cross buns" will help you identify recipes.

24. For additional ideas on helping younger children engage with Good Friday, see Joe and Janet Hales, *A Christ-Centered Easter* (Salt Lake City: Deseret Book, 2002).

25. Patrick Mason has observed this phenomenon: "In my church we don't like to think very much about the crucified Jesus. We focus instead on the resurrected Christ. We like the glow, the glory, the happily ever after story. We don't much like the mangled, tortured, bloody body hanging limply on the cross. But Jesus doesn't want us to look away. When Jesus revealed himself after his resurrection, he showed the people the scars in his hands and feet and side. When you look at me, Jesus insists, don't forget my murdered body on the cross. . . . The resurrected, glorified Christ points us to the crucified Jesus [see D&C 6:37; 45:32]" "George Floyd and Jesus: A Eulogy," *Medium* (blog), June 5, 2020, https://medium.com/@pqmason/george-floyd-and-jesus-a -eulogy-b36c475d4694.

impactful when we consider what Jesus Christ has directly revealed in our day. Many of us are familiar with Doctrine and Covenants 6:36, in which the Savior personally says, "Look unto me in every thought; doubt not, fear not." But do we notice the very next verse? Immediately after telling us to look unto him, Jesus says, "Behold [meaning "fix your eyes upon"[26]] the wounds which pierced my side, and also the prints of the nails in my hands and feet" (D&C 6:37). In our day, the living Christ has personally invited us to fix our eyes on the wounds in his side, hands, and feet.

This does not mean we need to constantly stare at pictures of Christ's Crucifixion, but some of us could benefit from spending more focused time pondering the death of Christ. Such a meditation might entail picturing the Savior before Pilate, envisioning a crown of thorns placed on his head, or visualizing him on the cross. We might imagine how we would have felt if we were Mary Magdalene, Mary the mother of Jesus, or a Roman soldier present that afternoon.

Yes, the image of his death may evoke feelings of sorrow for those who love Jesus and prefer not to dwell on his Crucifixion; however, it can also evoke feelings of joy and hope as we remember Christ's statement "Greater love hath no man than this, that a man lay down his life for his friends" (John 15:13). As we "view his death," we view his love (Jacob 1:8). Contemplating what Christ experienced on Calvary provides us comfort in crisis, causing our hearts to stir with sentiments like those shared by Elder Jeffrey R. Holland:

> However dim our days may seem, they have been a lot darker for the Savior of the world. As a reminder of those days, Jesus has chosen, even in a resurrected, otherwise perfected body, to retain for the benefit of His disciples the wounds in His hands and in His feet and in His side—signs, if you will, that painful things

---

26. *American Dictionary of the English Language* (1828), ed. Noah Webster, s.v. "behold," accessed July 6, 2020, http://webstersdictionary1828.com/Dictionary/behold.

happen even to the pure and the perfect; signs, if you will, that pain in this world is not evidence that God doesn't love you; signs, if you will, that problems pass and happiness can be ours. . . .

It is the wounded Christ who is the Captain of our souls, He who yet bears the scars of our forgiveness, the lesions of His love and humility, the torn flesh of obedience and sacrifice. These wounds are the principal way we are to recognize Him when He comes.[27]

One young adult shared her experience with pondering Christ's Crucifixion: "I used to not like seeing pictures of the Savior on the cross; however, after learning more about what the scriptures teach, I tried to focus on Christ's Crucifixion during the sacrament. This gave me something to focus on and really helped me feel my Savior's love. Thinking about the Crucifixion has helped me feel closer to Jesus Christ."

The powerful practice of pondering the Savior's Crucifixion can help us keep our sacramental promise to always remember him. As we picture Jesus on the cross, we can remember the loving Christ, the triumphant Christ, and a Savior who understands the pain we experience. Above all, we can remember that Christ was crucified to "draw all [people] unto [him]" (John 12:32). Reflecting on our Redeemer's sacrifice connects us with him.

———————

In concluding this chapter, I'm reminded of my most recent experience with a Good Friday. I had planned to lead a tour in Jerusalem and looked forward to reflecting on the final day of the Savior's mortal life while standing on the steps that led up to Pilate's headquarters. We were to walk the Via Dolorosa and meditate at the traditional place of Christ's death and burial. However, with a worldwide pandemic, all those plans evaporated, and I found myself at home in quarantine for Good Friday.

———————

27. Jeffrey R. Holland, "Teaching, Preaching, Healing," *Ensign*, January 2003.

Although my special plans—and even normal traditions, such as attending the temple—were disrupted, applying the suggestions we've discussed made it a sacred day. I did a focused synopsis study, watched a movie about Jesus Christ, and spent time pondering the events of the day nearly two thousand years ago. Would it have been nice to have been in Jerusalem for Good Friday? Of course! But we don't have to travel anywhere, and we don't even need to wait for a special day, to spend more time remembering the Savior's sacrifice on Calvary. As we put into practice the simple principles discussed in this chapter, along with other actions we feel inspired to take, we will come closer to Jesus Christ.

THREE PILLARS OF CHRIST'S ATONEMENT

Elder Bruce R. McConkie taught, "The three pillars of eternity, the three events, preeminent and transcendent above all others, are the creation, the fall, and the atonement."[1] We have focused on the third of these three pillars—the "perfect atonement" wrought by Jesus (D&C 76:69). Christ's Atonement is vast, reaching beyond our comprehension. It began in the premortal life and continues into the eternities (see Moses 7:47; Abr. 3:27).

Just as there are three key aspects—pillars, if you will—of eternity, there are three pillars of the Savior's Atonement. Sister Wendy W. Nelson referred to them as "three principal events: *First*, . . . his incomprehensible suffering in the Garden of Gethsemane. . . . *Second*, . . . his Crucifixion—during which time all the incomprehensible mental anguish, the immeasurable emotional grief, and the unimaginable physical pain of Gethsemane *returned* to Him. . . . *Third*, his literal and glorious Resurrection from the garden tomb."[2]

Although we have focused on Christ's Crucifixion, each aspect of the Savior's Atonement is vital. Indeed, every part of our Redeemer's

---

1. Bruce R. McConkie, "The Three Pillars of Eternity" (devotional, Brigham Young University, Provo, UT, February 17, 1981), https://speeches.byu.edu/talks/bruce-r -mcconkie/three-pillars-eternity/.
2. Wendy W. Nelson, *The Heavens Are Open* (Salt Lake City: Deseret Book, 2019), 105–7, emphasis in original.

ministry is important for us to study. My hope is that this book motivates each of us to more carefully learn all we can about every aspect of Christ's life and teachings. As we conclude our time together, let's briefly review the three principal events of the Savior's Atonement, beginning with Gethsemane, then moving ahead to the Garden Tomb, and ending with the focus of this book—Golgotha.

GETHSEMANE

In Doctrine and Covenants 19:16–19, we hear the Savior's firsthand account of what he suffered in the Garden of Gethsemane. He said, "I, God, have suffered these things for all, that they might not suffer if they would repent; But if they would not repent they must suffer even as I; Which suffering caused myself, even God, the greatest of all, to tremble because of pain, and to bleed at every pore, and to suffer both body and spirit—and would that I might not drink the bitter cup, and shrink—Nevertheless, glory be to the Father, and I partook and finished my preparations unto the children of men." Christ shared this experience with us to urge us to repent rather than suffer as he did.

When I lived just a short walk away from Gethsemane, I frequently spent time at this special site pondering the verses that recount what took place there. One memorable experience occurred on the Thursday before Easter, the night in holy week when Christ suffered in Gethsemane. That evening, I attended an interfaith service held at the Catholic church building in Gethsemane. The service was spiritually moving, and at the end, those present walked to Caiaphas's palace, following the steps Christ would have walked after the chief priests captured him. On that dark March night, when we exited the chapel, it was pouring rain. Within seconds we were soaked and freezing; nevertheless, we proceeded with the mile-long walk, shivering the whole way.

I'm not claiming it was raining the night Christ suffered in Gethsemane—but during that season it could have been; I had never previously considered this possibility. We do know it was a cold night because Peter "warmed himself at the fire" while Christ was on trial (Mark 14:54). Reflecting on little details, like a dark, cold (and perhaps rainy) night have helped Gethsemane feel more tangible to me, as do two tidbits of archeology.

First, on the site known today as Gethsemane, archeologists found a first-century olive press, tucked inside a small cave. I'm not sure whether this cave has anything to do with Christ's suffering, although it's interesting to contemplate if Christ left his disciples in the cave (maybe that's why they fell asleep). But cave or no cave, consider the significance of an olive press being discovered in Gethsemane. President Russell M. Nelson explained, "The word *Gethsemane* comes from two Hebrew roots: *gath*, meaning 'press,' and *shemen*, meaning 'oil,' especially that of the olive. There olives had been pressed under the weight of great stone wheels to squeeze precious oil from the olives. So the Christ in the Garden of Gethsemane was literally pressed under the weight of the sins of the world. He sweated great drops of blood—his life's 'oil'—which issued from every pore."[3]

A second archeological feature is an ancient road, just steps away from Gethsemane, that led to another city. We sometimes view Christ's Atonement with a sense of inevitability—of course it was going to happen. But the Savior didn't have to suffer for us that night; a nearby road literally led straight out of town. It was the perfect escape from the anguish he would face. However, even though the Savior wanted to shrink from this bitter cup, he "finished [his] preparations" for each of us individually (D&C 19:19). As we reflect on Gethsemane, let's remember and feel his love and devotion to us; he didn't walk away from us then, and he is not walking away from us now.

THE GARDEN TOMB

Although the events of Gethsemane and Calvary are of supreme importance, they would be meaningless without the Resurrection.

---

3. Russell M. Nelson, "Why This Holy Land?" *Ensign*, December 1989.

Multiple witnesses testified of the risen Lord, including Mary Magdalene, disciples on the road to Emmaus, Peter and the other Apostles, plus more than three thousand additional witnesses in the Old and New Worlds (see 1 Cor. 15:6; 3 Ne. 17:25; 19:3–5). In modern times, Joseph Smith and Sidney Rigdon declared, "This is the testimony, last of all, which we give of him: That he lives! For we saw him, even on the right hand of God" (D&C 76:22–23).

Whether we see the resurrected Christ in this life or the next, we can obtain a sure witness of his Resurrection now. Speaking in general conference less than two weeks prior to his passing, Elder Bruce R. McConkie declared, "I am one of his witnesses, and in a coming day I shall feel the nail marks in his hands and in his feet and shall wet his feet with my tears. But I shall not know any better then than I know now that he is God's Almighty Son, that he is our Savior and Redeemer."[4]

Some might wonder, Is such a strong testimony available only to Apostles? The answer is a resounding no! Elder Dale G. Renlund described a powerful spiritual witness of Christ that his elderly father had received and then said, "My dad [who did not hold prominent Church callings] . . . lived his life in accordance with the light and knowledge he had received. He did all that he was ever asked to do. He became one who *qualified for that gift of the Spirit to know that Jesus is the Christ and was crucified for the sins of the world, and for his sins. Qualifying for this gift is not gender-dependent and it is not priesthood office–dependent. It is dependent upon qualifying for that gift by choosing faith, by choosing the covenant path.*"[5] We do not need to be called as General Authorities or General Officers of the Church to have a powerful witness of our resurrected Lord. This spiritual gift is available to each of us and can be

---

4. Bruce R. McConkie, "The Purifying Power of Gethsemane," *Ensign*, May 1985.

5. Dale G. Renlund, "Doubt Not, but Be Believing" (Seminaries and Institutes of Religion annual training broadcast, June 12, 2018), https://www.churchofjesuschrist.org/study/broadcasts/miscellaneous-events/2018/06/doubt-not-but-be-believing.

ours as we continue to diligently seek the Savior and the guidance of the Holy Ghost.

We will of course feel sorrow at the passing of loved ones and may even fear the end of our own lives. However, we can replace our sorrow and fear with the sure knowledge that because of Christ, each of us will "rise from the dead and shall not die after" (D&C 63:49). We can be confident that those who die in Christ "shall not taste of death, for it shall be sweet unto them" (D&C 42:46). Our knowledge of the Savior's Resurrection can become certain and bring us deep peace.

GOLGOTHA

In between Gethsemane and the Resurrection stands the Savior's sacrifice on the cross. Although my understanding is far from complete, learning more about what transpired on Calvary has furthered my quest to "attain to a perfect knowledge of [Christ]" and come closer to him (Jacob 4:12). I hope you've had a similar experience.

Throughout this book we've discussed several life-changing lessons from Calvary. We've seen how hundreds of scriptures and prophetic statements teach that the Savior's Crucifixion is an important part of our redemption from sin. We've learned more fully how Christ's experiences help him empathize with our anguish. We've seen the Savior's example of turning outward in personal crisis and recognized how gospel ordinances can become even more meaningful when we see their connection to Calvary.

We've covered a lot of ground together, and at this point, I believe the question for each of us is this: *Now that I have a deeper understanding of the Crucifixion of Jesus Christ, what will I do?*

Less than twenty-four hours before the death of Christ, he shared the Last Supper with his disciples: "As they did eat, Jesus took bread, and blessed, and brake it, and gave to them, and said, *Take*, eat: this is my body" (Mark 14:22). Notice that the disciples, while participating in this symbolic act that would later be done in remembrance of

Christ's sacrifice, *took* the bread—action was required on their part, as it is on ours.

As you and I metaphorically stand beside the Savior, viewing him on the cross (see Jacob 1:8), what action do we feel inspired to take? Paul tells us, "Those who belong to Christ Jesus have crucified the flesh with its passions and desires" (Gal. 5:24, NRSV). Is there a sin we need to nail to his cross today? How will we more fully accept and act on his sacrifice?

What will we *stop* doing?

What will we *keep* doing?

What will we *start* doing?

Our lives will change as we act on divinely given answers to these questions.

As you reach the end of this book, I hope you've not only learned something, but that something has changed inside of you. I hope you more fully feel the joy that comes with knowing you are engraved on the Savior's hands, never to be forgotten by him. I hope you kneel more often to pray and bend more willingly to carry your cross as you follow him.

I hope your love for Jesus has grown. Most of all, I hope you better understand the Savior's perfect love for you. I hope you really *feel* it. Jesus bore your burdens so he can lighten your load. He experienced pain so he can offer you peace. And he suffered for your sins so you can be free to follow him.

Jesus is the living Christ and the loving Christ. His Crucifixion is a sign of his love. He implores, "Take up the cross, and follow me" (Mark 10:21). If we replace "the cross" with what it symbolizes—his love—we hear Jesus Christ offering a plea I hope each of us will accept: "Take up my love, and follow me."

Image Credits

p. 17, 1852 European edition of the Doctrine and Covenants: courtesy Megan Cutler, used with permission; edition found in L. Tom Perry Special Collections, Harold B. Lee Library, Brigham Young University, Provo, UT.

p. 18, Amelia Young: used by permission, Utah State Historical Society.

p. 18, Nabby Young: used by permission, Utah State Historical Society.

p. 19, tombstone of B. H. Roberts: courtesy John Gibby, used with permission.

p. 115, image of crucified feet: originally published in Joseph Zias and Eliezer Sekeles, "The Crucified Man from Givcat Ha-Mivtar—A Reappraisal," *Israel Exploration Journal* 35, no. 1 (1985): 27; used with permission.

Index